The Clinical Benefits of Coffee/Caffeine

A Latte to Review

Mark W DelBello MD

Published by Mark W DelBello, MD

ISBN: 9798842074518

Printed in the United States of America.

Table of Contents

Preface

The book is divided into three sections. The first section is "Highlight Reel" and uses bullet points to grasp the key points. The second segment "The Narrative" describes many of the ideas supported by research. The third section consists of clinical studies/research providing evidence to support or refute a claim. The studies in the book do not come to the same conclusion.

The focus of the book is to educate more than entertain and provide fair balance. The gist of the book is that coffee has gone from a luxury stimulant drink to a health promoting beverage that can improve athletic performance and lower morbidity and mortality. I have also included chapters on exercise and longevity since my literary style is "stream of consciousness".

As medical knowledge accumulates over time, newer studies may be of higher quality and accuracy than older studies. Newer studies do a better job at looking at confounding factors. Confounding factors are variables that can significantly interfere with results such as tobacco smoking or obesity. Clarifications of some phrases or concepts are added at the end of the back to help understanding. It is important to realize that women and minorities need to be included more to provide a complete and accurate clinical picture. A medical background is helpful for reading this book but not necessary. As I was gathering information for this book, I came across an article that inspired me and I wanted to share it. I hope you enjoy it.

The Knowledge Disease

By GRAHAM HILLS

Former principal and vice chancellor of the University of Strathclyde, Glasgow. Hills, a physical chemist, was knighted in 1988 for his services to education.

Knowledge is luggage; it is best to travel light.

We live in times dominated by knowledge. Knowledge is heaped on each of us from the cradle to the grave. Every day at school, every examination, and every qualification is a test of the retention of knowledge. To be knowledgeable is considered important; to be called knowledgeable is a compliment. Erudition, scholarship, and intellect are supplementary words to savor. Ignorance may be bliss for some, but not if we want to get on in life. And yet, as knowledge piles up by the hour, do we really benefit from carrying as much as we can in our heads? After all, so much knowledge exists on a myriad of topics. As each topic grows and multiplies there is no end to it. It is evident, at least to the discerning, that the "knowledge base" is exploding in front of us. What good fortune then that, in the nick of time, the computer memory has arrived to save us the bother of remembering all that knowledge. Why not dump most of the knowledge in the memory bank, to be recalled at the touch of a button or mouse? A totally comprehensive, continuously updated encyclopedia: what could be better? We could then turn our attention to other valuable activities that cannot be computerized, such as doing things. There is another reason for skepticism about the value of retained knowledge. Firstly, it decays. Almost all knowledge has a shortening shelf life. For computer science it is a matter of years; for molecular biology it is even shorter. The old knowledge is then not just rusty but obsolete. Secondly, as we cannot yet rinse out the human memory the old knowledge remains firmly in place, often barring the entry of the new. This common frame of mind is often referred to as NIH-not invented here. It is the normal obstacle to progress. Filling up the head with more and more about less and less is undoubtedly the way to academic success, but it carries the danger of obstructing the process of making connections. So many specialists fall into the habit of looking where the light is-that is, offering solutions only in territory familiar to them. Those trees that obscure the wood are actually trees of knowledge, and wonderful examples exist of otherwise excellent researchers who are unable and unwilling to recognize evidence contrary to their beliefs. This is the land of prejudice, and such a state of mind can be dangerous, even fatal, when those beliefs are religious or political. The burden of the past has always been a problem. The metaphor of the human race marching backwards into the future does not upset traditionalists, who see virtue only in the past. But it is a great weight to carry if the world itself is changing fast and the price of prosperity is the willingness to ride the crest of that wave of change. Not for nothing were Dickens's books on the wisdom of the ages just empty covers. Not for nothing was the advice given to shoot every officer over the rank of captain if the next war was not to be fought on the principles of the last. Too much knowledge can therefore be a handicap. Our preoccupation with knowledge has led to a serious neglect of other forms of learning. Skills are often only for blue collar workers. And yet skills, especially intellectual skills, are the very stuff of life, of jobs, and certainly of wealth creation. Skills are acquired by practice under the eyes of others. Their acquisition is a rewarding process that adds to the human persona in a way that knowledge does not. Doctors and lawyers have always known that, and the curious position of medicine and law in universities reflects the distance between them and the more knowledge-based disciplines. Good citizens are sorely in need of skills, be they computational, language, financial, management, or, of course, social skills. Skills are rooted in reality; knowledge is not. Knowledge quite quickly engenders hypotheses and theories, which take on an unrealistic life of their own. Reverence for theories is even greater than for knowledge. As the professor of economics said, "That's all very well in practice but will it ever work in theory?" Anyone pedaling abstract ideas (or paintings) is bound to make a good living because people are gulled by their assumed ignorance. If these theories touch life, as with politics and economics, only tragedy can be expected. The person who first said that a little knowledge is a dangerous thing could have gone on to say that more of the knowledge might be even more dangerous. Knowledge is fine in small doses. But generally speaking, knowledge is luggage, and it would be best to travel light.

Highlight Reel

The most important ideas and concepts of the book have been highlighted below.
"It's like déjà vu all over again" Yogi Berra.

- More than 85% of adults in the U.S. regularly consume caffeine.
- Caffeine is the most widely consumed psychoactive drug in the world.
- Trends in caffeine consumption have been stable among adults and children aged 2-19 years old for the past two decades.
- Cigarette smoking doubles the rate of caffeine clearance by increasing liver enzyme activity, which may explain the higher rate of caffeine consumption among smokers. Smokers have to drink more coffee to potentially obtain the benefits of coffee compared to non-smokers.
- The typical dose of caffeine is roughly 70 to 100 mg per drink. The average caffeine consumption in the United States is 76 mg/person/day. In Canada, it is 210–238 mg/person/day and in Sweden and Finland, it exceeds 400 mg/day. The average daily dose of caffeine in adults is about two cups of coffee.

- According to the U.S. Food and Drug Administration, 400 mg a day, about four or five cups of coffee, is the amount of caffeine "not generally associated with dangerous, negative effects" for healthy adults.
- The American College of Obstetricians and Gynecologists consider 200 mg of caffeine per day to be safe during pregnancy.
- The European Commission's Scientific Committee of Food Safety Authority and Health Canada both recommend that women consume no more than 300 mg of caffeine a day during pregnancy.
- On June 15, 2016, The International Agency for Research on Cancer and several large prospective trials concluded that caffeine is not carcinogenic.
- Caffeine is a constituent of many over-the-counter pain relievers and prescription drugs because the vasoconstricting and anti-inflammatory effects of caffeine act as a complement to analgesics, in some cases, increasing the effectiveness of pain relievers by up to 40%.
- Caffeine has a diuretic effect that is not likely to have adverse consequences for healthy adults. It may aggravate people prone to urinary incontinence (leakage).
- Concerns regarding unwanted fluid loss and dehydration with caffeine consumption are unwarranted particularly when ingestion precedes exercise.
- Caffeine as an ingredient in food has been regulated by the US Food and Drug Administration since 1958. It is listed as a substance that is "generally recognized as safe" by experts.
- In 1980, the FDA "… found no evidence to show that the use of caffeine in carbonated beverages would render these beverages injurious to health."
- High versus low coffee consumption was associated with a lower risk of prostate cancer, endometrial cancer,

melanoma, oral cancer, leukemia, non-melanoma skin cancer, and liver cancer.

- In addition to beneficial associations with liver cancer, all categories of coffee exposure were associated with lower risk for a range of liver outcomes. Any versus no coffee consumption was associated with a 29% lower risk of non-alcoholic fatty liver disease, a 27% lower risk for liver fibrosis, and a 39% lower risk for liver cirrhosis. The advantageous associations between coffee consumption and liver conditions stand out as consistently having the highest magnitude compared with other outcomes.
- An extra two cups of coffee per day was associated with a 35% reduction in the risk of hepatocellular cancer.
- Increased consumption of caffeinated coffee and, to a lesser extent, decaffeinated coffee is associated with reduced risk of hepatocellular cancer, including pre-existing liver disease.
- Coffee consumption has not been reported to generate any deleterious effects on the various organs of the digestive tract.
- There was no significant relationship between coffee consumption and the four major acid-related upper gastrointestinal disorders (gastric ulcer (GU), duodenal ulcer (DU), reflux esophagitis (RE), and non-erosive reflux disease (NERD). Coffee consumption was defined as one or more cups of coffee per day and non-drinkers were less than a cup of coffee per day.
- The key to accepting the research is the major role confounders like smoking and Helicobacter infection play.
- Coffee consumption has favorable associations with metabolic conditions including type 2 diabetes, metabolic syndrome, gallstones, gout, renal stones, and liver conditions.

- A systematic review supports the conclusion that habitual coffee consumption is associated with a 28-35% lower risk of type 2 diabetes.
- Long-term preservation of liver and beta cell function may account for the association of habitual coffee drinking with a lower risk of type 2 diabetes, rather than an acute improvement in lowering glucose levels.
- To stress how instrumental decreasing diabetes risk is, the estimated lifetime risk of developing diabetes for babies born in 2000 is 32.8% for males and 38.5% for females, with Hispanics having the highest estimated lifetime risk (males, 45.4% and females, 52.5%) among ethnic groups.
- Type 2 diabetes is estimated to cost men 11.6 life-years and women 14.3 life-years.
- A 30% lower risk of type 2 diabetes for high versus low coffee consumption and 6% lower risk was found for one extra cup a day. The diabetes risk was lower for each dose between one and six cups.
- Coffee consumption was inversely associated with the risk of type 2 diabetes in a dose-response manner. Both caffeinated and decaffeinated coffee were associated with reduced diabetes risk.
- Coffee consumption was consistently associated with a lower risk of Parkinson's disease across all categories of exposure.
- There is no consistent evidence of harmful associations between coffee consumption and health outcomes, except for those related to pregnancy and for risk of fracture in women. A review and meta-analysis in 2014 showed that daily consumption of coffee is associated with an increased risk of fractures in women and a decreased risk in men.
- Coffee inhibits vitamin D receptors which is important in the absorption of calcium in building bone; this results in an increased risk for osteoporosis.

Highlight Reel

- Coffee consumption was consistently associated with a 19% lower risk of mortality from all causes of cardiovascular disease, 16% lower risk of coronary heart disease, and 30% lower risk of stroke with summary estimates indicating largest reduction at three cups a day.
- Remember, about half of all adults today in the United States have some form of cardiovascular disease. Other estimates indicate that the largest relative risk reduction is associated with intakes of three to four cups a day. Importantly, increased consumption beyond this intake does not seem to be associated with increased risk of harm, rather the magnitude of the benefit is reduced.
- In people who have already suffered a cardiovascular event, habitual coffee consumption does not increase the risk of a recurrent cardiovascular event or death, but may lower the risk of cardiovascular disease and ischemic heart disease mortality.
- Caffeine enhances performance in trained athletes in low-to-moderate dosages (~3-6 mg/kg) (two to four cups) and does not enhance further performance at higher dosages (>/= 9 mg/kg). General guidelines recommend the consumption of 3–6 mg/kg of caffeine, typically 60 minutes before the start of exercise or competition.
- Caffeine has consistently been shown to improve endurance by 2% to 4% across dozens of studies in doses of 3–6 mg/kg.
- Caffeine has been shown to be of benefit in several endurance-type sports, including cycling, running, cross-country skiing, and swimming.
- Although reviews of the literature show that caffeine ingestion is, on average, helpful for a wide range of sport-specific tasks, its use might not be appropriate for every athlete. Athletes should gauge their physical response to caffeine during practice and competition in addition to

monitoring mood state and potentially disrupted sleep patterns.

- The literature is equivocal on strength-power performance with caffeine supplementation.
- Study findings from 2021 indicate that acute caffeine supplementation has positive effects on several mood and psychological responses, along with performance. Caffeine supplementation increases beneficial tension, vigor, and subjective perception of vitality, while it reduces the rating of perceived exertion. These responses favor an optimal psychological state.
- The International Olympic Committee and World Anti-Doping Agency (WADA) removed the classification of caffeine as a controlled substance in 2004. However, caffeine is still monitored by WADA, and athletes are encouraged to maintain a urine caffeine concentration below the limit of 12 μg/ml, which corresponds to 10 mg/kg body mass. This is more than triple the intake reported to enhance performance.
- Caffeine is categorized as a banned substance by the National Collegiate Athletic Association (NCAA) if urinary caffeine concentration exceeds 15 μg/ml.
- In an evaluation of 20,686 urine samples of elite athletes, 73.8% of the samples contained caffeine with endurance-sport athletes showing the highest urine caffeine concentrations after competition. Whether this is just a reflection of increasing social use of coffee or to improve performance or both is not clear.
- Several meta-analyses examining caffeine effects on a broad array of exercise tests showed performance enhancements from 16% to 51%. Performance improvements of this magnitude usually involve non-elite athletes.
- Caffeine exerts acute cognitive benefits, especially in sleep-deprived subjects. This has been explored in military personnel, athletes, and the general public with caffeine

improving cognitive and physical performance, both during overnight operations and following sleep restriction.

- Caffeine is an effective countermeasure to total sleep deprivation.
- Caffeine is more effective than placebo but does not replace sleep.
- Caffeine is so close in structure to adenosine that it is able to bind to the receptors that are specific to adenosine. Caffeine acts as a nonselective adenosine receptor antagonist. As a consequence, caffeine, does the opposite of adenosine. The major known effect of adenosine is decreasing the concentration of many central nervous system neurotransmitters, including serotonin, dopamine, acetylcholine, norepinephrine and glutamate.
- Caffeine exerts its effect on the central nervous system by increasing neurotransmitter release, motor unit firing rates, and pain suppression. This results in positive effects on mood, vigilance, focus, and alertness in most, but not all, individuals.
- There are four distinct adenosine receptors, A1, A2A, A2B and A3. A1 and A2A, which are highly concentrated in the brain, appear to be the main targets of caffeine.
- The attenuation of pain during exercise from caffeine supplementation may result in a decrease in the rating of perceived exertion. Acute caffeine ingestion has been shown to alter this rating. A person's effort may be greater under caffeinated conditions, while not being perceived as such.
- CYP1A2 and ADORA2A are two of the genes which are thought to have the largest impact on the effects of caffeine. CYP1A2 is responsible for the majority of the metabolism of caffeine, and ADORA2A has been linked to caffeine-induced anxiety.
- More than 95% of caffeine is metabolized by the CYP1A2 enzyme, which has been used to categorize individuals as

"fast", "slow", or normal metabolizers of caffeine. One study indicated that the intake of coffee was associated with an increased risk of nonfatal myocardial infarction only among individuals with slow caffeine metabolism, suggesting that caffeine plays a role in this association.

- Caffeine ingestion in slow caffeine metabolizers is more likely to have an increased blood pressure response. This seems to be reasonable since caffeine will stick around longer in slow metabolizers.
- The ADORA2A gene is a genetic modifier of the effects of caffeine. The ADORA2A gene encodes for the adenosine A2A receptor and different versions of the gene will categorize individuals as having a 'high' or 'low' sensitivity to caffeine.
- An athlete or person with the ADORA2A gene with "high" sensitivity may experience greater increases in feelings of anxiety after caffeine intake.
- There does not appear to be a consistent difference in the performance effects of acute caffeine ingestion between habitual and non-habitual caffeine users when looking at the conclusions of the majority of studies. Some studies are equivocal and some will disagree with that conclusion.
- High acute doses of caffeine (9 to 11 mg/kg) did not improve muscle strength nor muscle endurance in athletes who were habitual caffeine users (~411 mg/day).
- A 3 mg/kg dose of caffeine significantly improves exercise performance regardless of whether a four-day withdrawal period is imposed on habitual caffeine users.
- People with chronic low-dose caffeine use develop tolerance. Therefore, individuals with low habitual intake should refrain from caffeine supplementation temporarily to maximize performance benefits from acute caffeine ingestion.
- A 2011 systematic review and meta-analysis of 21 investigations concluded the co-ingestion of carbohydrate

and caffeine significantly improved endurance performance when compared to carbohydrate alone.

- Several studies show the effects of caffeine to be similar in both sexes.
- A review by Shabir et al. reported a placebo effect of caffeine on performance in 13 out of 17 studies. The placebo effect has been associated with opioid, endocannabinoid, serotonin, and dopamine systems, while the most common view is that various neurotransmitter systems are in fact turned-on at the same time in the placebo effect. This especially applies to the placebo effect of caffeine, as the main effect of this substance on the brain is to block adenosine receptors, resulting in higher concentrations of serotonin, dopamine, and norepinephrine. In this regard, the endogenous opioids and endocannabinoid system are implicated in pain mechanisms and analgesia, the serotonin system is associated with anxiety while dopamine has been investigated in the context of motivation.
- Athletes or anyone facing an important event always worry whether he or she will perform well; caffeine may help with focus or drive to allow the person to better achieve the goal.
- The ability of caffeine to improve the "rating of perceived exertion" allows one to train harder, feel better about training and increase the chance of success. It's like being "on your game" or "in your zone," and that is very productive
- Significantly faster performance times of about 5% were similar for both caffeine and coffee, compared to decaf and placebo. This provides evidence that the caffeine and not the other components in coffee improve performance.
- Acute caffeine ingestion positively enhances functional performance, manual dexterity and readiness to exert effort in healthy older adults (61-79 years old).

- Higher coffee consumption was independently associated with better physical performance in men with mean age 87 years.
- Habitual coffee consumption was associated with a lower risk of falling in older adults in a 2019 study from Spain and the United Kingdom.
- Exercising after ingestion of caffeine (3 mg/kg) resulted in significantly greater calorie burning than exercise alone and also led to exercise being perceived as less difficult and more enjoyable.
- Caffeine can promote weight loss by increasing the number of calories burned with exercise.
- A low to moderate dose (1.9 ± 0.3 mg/kg) (about two cups) of caffeine consumed before and during a round of golf improves golf-specific measures of performance and reduces fatigue in skilled golfers.
- Compared with the lowest level of consumption, <u>coffee</u> consumption decreased risk for depression by 24%; <u>caffeine</u> consumption decreased risk by 28%. The association between caffeine consumption and depression became significant when the caffeine consumption was between 68 and 509 mg/day.
- Both coffee and caffeine consumption were significantly associated with decreased risk of depression. Essentially, a cup of coffee daily decreases the risk of depression.
- Freedman et al. considered seven specific causes of death and observed inverse associations between coffee consumption and mortality from heart disease, respiratory disease, stroke, injuries and accidents, diabetes, and infections.
- Decaffeinated coffee consumption was associated with a small reduction in all-cause and cardiovascular disease mortality.

Higher consumption of green tea and coffee was associated with reduced all-cause mortality. Their combined effect appeared to be additive in patients with type 2 diabetes. This makes me think that 2 fruits or vegetables (polyphenols) are better than one at promoting health.

- Regular consumption of a green/roasted coffee blend may be recommended to healthy and hypercholesterolemic people to prevent metabolic syndrome as it produces positive effects on blood pressure, glucose and triglyceride levels.
- Regular tea consumption is associated with decreased prevalence and progression of coronary artery calcium, and with a decreased incidence of cardiovascular events. Regular tea consumption has been recommended by the American Heart Association for several years.
- Pooled results from a 2020 study revealed that green coffee supplementation significantly reduced fasting blood sugar, insulin, and triglyceride levels. Furthermore, green coffee supplementation increased HDL (good cholesterol) levels. In Chinese adults, daily green tea consumption decreased risk of type 2 diabetes and decreased all-cause mortality in patients with diabetes. The associations for other types of tea were less clear. In addition, daily tea consumption was associated with a lower risk of diabetic microvascular complications (eye, nerve and kidney disease) but not macrovascular complications (heart disease, peripheral vascular disease and stroke).
- Cutaneous melanoma risk decreased 3% for drinkers of decaffeinated/partially caffeinated coffee and 4% for caffeinated coffee at 1 cup/day increments.
- No statistically significant association between caffeine intake or different types of coffee and the risk of ovarian cancer.
- Among breast cancer survivors, higher post-diagnostic coffee consumption was associated with better breast cancer and overall survival.

- The totality of eligible scientific papers (2021 review) supports the evidence that coffee intake is inversely associated with hepatocellular cancer risk and to a slight extent breast cancer risk among postmenopausal women. As to the association with other organs, including the esophagus, pancreas, colorectum, kidneys, bladder, ovaries and prostate, the results are less clear; reports reveal conflicting results or statistically non-significant data.
- 2020 study-Consumption of ≥2 cups/day of <u>decaffeinated</u> coffee was associated with 18% lower risk of overall colorectal cancer, 18% lower risk of colon cancer and 37% lower risk of rectal cancer.
- Consumption of ≥2 cups/day of <u>caffeinated</u> coffee was associated with 37% <u>higher</u> risk of rectal cancer but not with colorectal or colon cancer. FYI rectum and colon make up colorectal area.
- A large 2021 pooled analysis of two studies shows no association of coffee and decaffeinated coffee with colorectal cancer risk.
- A 2016 meta-analysis suggested that coffee consumption might be associated with a decreased risk of gastric cancer.
- Studies have consistently indicated that lung cancer risk is significantly increased by 47% in the overall population with the highest category intake of coffee compared with the lowest category intake. (Remember, a 200% increased risk means two people in 100 are affected instead of one). The study suggested that coffee intake was associated with an increased risk of lung cancer. If smokers and nonsmokers are separated, nonsmokers who drink more than three cups a day have a lower incidence of lung cancer by 15%.
- A 2019 study does not support a causal association between habitual coffee consumption and risk of atrial fibrillation.

Highlight Reel

- A 2020 study found no association between either coffee consumption or dietary caffeine intake with heart failure risk among U.S. male physicians.
- In comparison to no coffee intake, usual consumption of one to five cups a day is associated with a lower risk of death.
- Hypertensive patients with uncontrolled blood pressure should avoid consuming large doses of caffeine.
- Acute ingestion of high doses of caffeine (500 mg) did not induce arrhythmias in patients at rest and during a symptom-limited exercise test in patients with decreased systolic heart function and high risk for ventricular arrhythmias. Study provides further safety of caffeine in debilitated patients.
- Many clinicians continue to counsel patients with atrial or ventricular arrhythmias to avoid all caffeinated beverages, particularly coffee, despite an absence of evidence to support this approach.
- If, in individual cases where a clear temporal association between arrhythmic episodes and caffeine intake is apparent, then avoidance is sensible.
- Large-scale population-based studies and randomized controlled trials suggest coffee and tea are safe and may even reduce the incidence of arrhythmias.
- A regular intake of up to 300 mg/day appears to be safe and may even be protective against heart rhythm disorders.
- Contrary to common belief, the published literature (1994) provides little evidence that coffee and/or caffeine in typical dosages increases the risk of myocardial infarction, sudden death or arrhythmia. This belief is still true today based on 2021 literature.
- A 2016 study confirmed that drinking a single cup of coffee (containing 80 mg of caffeine) does not have a significant

impact on the blood pressure of healthy normotensive young adults one hour after the drink.

- In hypertensive individuals, caffeine intake produces an acute increase in blood pressure for more than three hours.
- Regular coffee consumption may be harmful to some hypertension-prone subjects. However, current evidence does not support an association between longer-term coffee consumption and increased blood pressure or between habitual coffee consumption and an increased risk of cardiovascular disease in hypertensive subjects.
- Coffee consumption was associated with a significant decrease in the risk for renal failure by 14% with a greater decrease in individuals who drank two or more cups a day compared to those who drank a cup or less a day. There was a significantly lower risk of incident end stage kidney disease in coffee drinkers by 18%, albuminuria (protein in urine) by 19% and death by 28%.
- The association of habitual coffee consumption with a lower risk of diseases, such as type 2 diabetes mellitus, chronic liver disease, certain cancer types, or with reduced all-cause mortality, has been confirmed in prospective cohort studies in many regions of the world.
- Coffee employs pathways in health promotion similar to vegetables and fruits. Coffee beans may be viewed as a healthy vegetable food and a main supplier of dietary phenolic phytochemicals. Coffee is entirely of plant origin. At present, there is no reason to assume that phenolic compounds of coffee are less "healthy" than comparable plant compounds. Coffee is the primary dietary source of phenolic acids and polyphenols.
- Coffee provides around 40% of polyphenols and around 70% of phenolic acids consumed.
- There seems to be one uniform response of cells when exposed to phenolic agents. The cellular response is an increased expression of a large number of genes involved in

antioxidative, detoxifying or repair mechanisms. Think of our body cells having a makeover at a spa.

- Caffeinated coffee, decaffeinated coffee, or caffeinated tea consumption was not significantly associated with survival to age 90 after adjusting for confounders.
- Findings from 2016 suggest a 26% lower risk of probable dementia or cognitive impairment in older women whose caffeine consumption was above median (261 mg or two to three cups a day).
- 2020 study suggests that caffeinated coffee and caffeine were associated with improved cognitive performance, while decaffeinated coffee was not associated with cognitive performance.
- Caffeine may be of potential use in prolonging the period of mild cognitive impairment in women prior to a diagnosis of dementia.
- Green tea consumption improves the prognosis for people who suffered a stroke or heart attack in the past but did not provide any additional benefit for those without a stroke or heart attack. Coffee did better. Coffee consumption was beneficial for decreasing mortality in everyone, except for stroke survivors.
- An umbrella review of 96 meta-analyses with 40 unique health outcomes showed that tea consumption of two to three cups per day decreased the risks of total mortality, cardiac death, coronary artery disease, stroke, and type 2 diabetes mellitus. Beneficial associations are also found for several cancers, skeletal, cognitive, and maternal outcomes. Harmful associations are found for esophageal and gastric cancer when the temperature of the tea is higher than 131-140 degrees F.
- A 2020 systematic review indicated that caffeine beneficially affects cognitive function and risk of dementia. This helpful effect is dependent on the caffeine source (e.g., coffee and

green tea), quantity (moderate), and gender (better response in females).

- The number of studies showing positive associations was 46 of 57 (81%) including 111,926 of 153,070 (73%) subjects, indicating that caffeine has a beneficial effect on the risk of dementia/cognitive decline. More than 70% of studies with mild cognitive impairment or any type of dementia, showed that caffeine has a helpful effect.
- Coffee drinking at midlife is associated with a decreased risk of dementia/Alzheimer's disease later in life. The lowest risk (65% decreased risk) was found in people who drank three to five cups a day.
- Daily caffeine intake in the morning and afternoon hours (150 mg three times a day) does not strongly impair nighttime sleep structure nor subjective sleep quality in healthy young good sleepers who regularly consume caffeine.
- A 2020 study looked at the efficacy of multiple repeated doses of caffeine (800 mg total per night) during 77 hours (3.2 days) of total sleep deprivation. While clearly superior to placebo, caffeine failed to sustain performance compared to normal baseline levels beyond the first few hours of sleep deprivation. Declining performance and frequency of attentional lapses continued to worsen with decrements exceeding more than 50% within the first 24 hours. Caffeine is an effective countermeasure to total sleep deprivation but does not replace sleep.
- Habitual short sleep duration has been associated with adverse health outcomes including obesity, type 2 diabetes, hypertension, cardiovascular disease, depression, and all-cause mortality. This decreased ability to sleep in older adults is often secondary to comorbidities and related medications (polypharmacy) rather than normal aging processes.

Highlight Reel

- Optimal sleep should be conceptualized as the amount of sleep needed to optimize outcomes (e.g., performance, cognitive function, mental health, physical health, quality of life, etc.). For example, nine hours of sleep per night could be best for athletic performance, while seven hours could be the best for academic achievement. Napping is increasingly seen as a public health tool and countermeasure for sleep deprivation in terms of reducing accidents and cardiovascular events and improving work performance.
- The results of a 2013 study suggest that 400 mg of caffeine (4 cups of coffee) taken at three hours before, or even 6 hours prior to bedtime significantly disrupts sleep. Even at six hours, caffeine reduced sleep by more than an hour. Four cups of coffee at night seems a lot.
- People who consume low or moderate amounts of caffeine (235 mg or about 2.5 cups a day) can exhibit withdrawal symptoms within 48 hours after caffeine intake.
- Caffeine withdrawal in the postoperative period may affect 10% to 55% of individuals with symptoms including headache, drowsiness, decreased alertness, flu-like symptoms, nausea/vomiting, and myalgias. Withdrawal can be effectively treated prophylactically with perioperative caffeine.
- Administration of caffeine results in faster emergence from sedation and anesthesia, particularly in individuals at high risk for post-extubation complications. Caffeine administration appears to be safe in moderate doses in the perioperative period and in the intensive care setting.
- The use of caffeine after elective colorectal surgery has been recommended to reduce the incidence of postoperative ileus (slow gut function). On the negative side, intraoperative or postoperative caffeine may increase the incidence of postoperative nausea/vomiting.

- Caffeine has been used in neonatal intensive care units to treat apnea-related syndromes with no long-term adverse effects. In infants, caffeine stimulates the respiratory center.
- Intraoperative caffeine was found not to affect the incidence of postoperative atrial fibrillation and reduced the time to spontaneous urination after indwelling bladder catheter removal.
- A 1996 national survey of 882 nurses found that 85% still practiced caffeine restriction in patients after an acute myocardial infarction. Caffeine use after an acute myocardial infarction may reduce the risk of cardiovascular mortality and does not increase the risk of atrial fibrillation after cardiac surgery.

  While there is routine screening and management for alcohol or smoking in the hospital, caffeine consumption or withdrawal is not routinely assessed.
- Caffeine can facilitate emergence from sedation or anesthesia. As caffeine is a central nervous system stimulant, there is a risk that early administration of caffeine could increase awareness during anesthesia.
- Coffee can be used in patients to enhance the recovery of gastrointestinal function after elective cesarean section.
- Coffee stimulates colonic motor activity. Its magnitude is similar to a meal.
- A 2015 study demonstrates that 100 mg on-demand caffeine can significantly improve premature ejaculation and satisfaction.
- In March 2013, 18 scientific and medical experts sent the FDA a report on energy drink consumption in children. This report concluded that "… there is neither sufficient evidence of safety nor a consensus of scientific opinion to conclude that the high levels of added caffeine in energy drinks are safe under the conditions of their intended use, as required by the FDA's "Generally Recognized as Safe" standards for food additives. To the contrary, the best

available scientific evidence demonstrates a robust correlation between the caffeine levels in energy drinks and adverse health and safety consequences, particularly among children, adolescents, and young adults." Furthermore, the Institute of Medicine has recommended that drinks containing caffeine not be sold to children at school.

- In 2014, the American Academy of Pediatrics released the following recommendation: "Due to the potentially harmful health effects of caffeine, dietary intake should be discouraged for all children. Because the actual stimulant content of energy drinks is hard to determine, energy drinks pose an even greater health risk than simple caffeine. Therefore, energy drinks are not appropriate for children and adolescents and should never be consumed."
- The Federal Substance Abuse and Mental Health Services Administration reported that from 2007 to 2011, the number of emergency room visits involving energy drinks doubled across the U.S., from 10,068 to 20,783.
- In 2010, the FDA removed pre-mixed alcohol-energy drinks from the market because caffeine was determined to be an unsafe additive to alcohol, in part because it promoted excessive drinking.
- Several studies have shown combining energy drinks with alcohol increased the urge to drink alcohol relative to drinking alcohol alone.
- Caffeine-containing products have a greater association with severe adverse events compared with non-caffeine-containing products. Exposure to pre-workout and weight loss products had greater odds of being associated with a more serious adverse event relative to noncaffeinated products.
- Excessive sugar-sweetened beverage consumption has been associated with being overweight and obese. The addition of low concentrations of caffeine to sugar-sweetened beverages significantly increases their consumption.

Regulating caffeine as a food additive may be an effective strategy to decrease the consumption of nutrient-poor high-energy foods and beverages.

- Energy drinks typically contain caffeine, taurine, glucuronolactone, vitamins, herbal extracts, proprietary blends, and/or amino acids. Proprietary blends and herbal extracts are usually a non-descriptive term used to mask agents that may be of a stimulatory nature. The drinks are available with or without sugar and may or may not be carbonated. Energy drinks often contain high concentrations of caffeine, typically between 70 and 200 mg of caffeine per 16 ounces (An eight-ounce cup of brewed coffee contains 95 mg of caffeine per cup, and a one-ounce shot of espresso contains 63 mg of caffeine). A single energy drink may be up to 32 ounces, implying up to 400 mg of caffeine, the equivalent of more than six shots of espresso.
- The amount of caffeine in over-the-counter products is limited to a maximum of 200 mg per drink, whereas there is no limit for energy drinks. Energy drinks can exceed 200 mg by stating that there is more than one serving per container.
- Between 2000 and 2012, the U.S. Poison Control Center reported 5,103 exposures to energy products and, among those, 552 adverse events: one fatal, 24 serious, and 527 moderate reactions. Importantly, 44.7% involved children younger than 6.
- According to the FDA's Center for Food Safety and Applied Nutrition Adverse Event Reporting System, between 2004 and 2012, 166 reports were received describing adverse events, including 18 deaths.
- The FDA's reporting system is estimated to capture only about 1% of the true number of adverse events associated with energy drinks; thus, the number of adverse events and deaths is likely to be much higher.

Highlight Reel

- Sudden cardiac death, coronary artery spasm, coronary artery thrombosis, coronary artery dissection, aortic dissection, ST-segment elevation myocardial infarction, stress cardiomyopathy (Takotsubo cardiomyopathy), seizures, and intracerebral hemorrhage have been noted in case reports. It is important to note that in many of these cases, confounding variables such as co-ingestions (e.g., drugs, alcohol), genetic predispositions, underlying cardiovascular abnormalities, and strenuous exercise were discovered, so specific causality cannot be attributed to energy drink consumption alone.
- Obesity is associated with energy drink consumption, secondary to caloric content, with a usual can containing 216-248 calories.
- The American Academy of Pediatrics in 2011 and the National Federation of State High School Associations in 2014 each recommend that energy drinks never be consumed by children or adolescents, or used for hydration before, during, or after physical activity.
- The American Beverage Association in 2017 recommended that energy drinks 1) be marketed separately from sports drinks, 2) not be sold or marketed in schools, and 3) not be marketed to children.
- A 2003 literature search revealed no negative reports or therapeutic benefits identified with taurine, ginseng, or guarana used in the amounts found in most energy drinks. Guarana comes from a plant which produces seeds containing small amounts of caffeine, theophylline, and theobromine (all three are ergogenic).
- Some 45% of deployed military personnel are reported to consume a minimum of one energy drink daily, with 14% having three or more a day.
- Despite energy drinks' widespread consumption, there are no systematic prospective studies of cardiovascular outcomes.

- Physical inactivity/sedentary lifestyle increase risk factors for more than 30 chronic diseases.
- Models of physical inactivity are so dramatic in the magnitude of health detriment that Human Institutional Research Boards would likely be hesitant, for ethical reasons, to approve random controlled trials lasting years if irreversible overt chronic disease were to occur because of physical inactivity. Therefore, studies to prove that long-term physical inactivity promote chronic diseases are unlikely to ever occur.
- Exercise provides a higher therapeutic index (benefits vs. side effects) than any drug therapy could provide. It requires the integration of almost every physiological system (brain, neural, vascular, liver, adipose, muscle, etc.).
- Physical activity diminishes mortality by 30% in the USA. Stated alternatively, physical inactivity increases mortality by 30%, or by 720,000 annual deaths (one death every 44 seconds).
- Drugs try to have laser focus with minimal side effects or collateral damage, whereas exercise benefits multiple sites. Weightlifting causes hypertrophy of muscles and prolonged daily running increases mitochondria, but neither activity does both. One must perform both types of exercise to prevent frailty.
- Energy expenditure was significantly greater when daily domestic tasks were performed without the aid of machines or equipment. An estimated 110 kcal/day was estimated to be expended by the combined impact of domestic mechanization. The annualization of 110 kcal/day is the caloric equivalent of 11.5 pounds per year.
- Modern humans have been able to engineer most physical activity out of daily life. Humans now have a choice not to be physically active.
- Infectious diseases were the No. 1 cause of death for over 95% of human civilization and has only been replaced by

heart disease, stroke, cancer and other chronic diseases in the past 60 years.

- People lose about 10 pounds of muscle mass per decade starting at age 50.
- Tanaka & Seals (2008) suggest that declines in endurance performance with increasing age appear to be a reduction in the absolute intensity and total volume of training undertaken. If older athletes simply increased their training load, then performance would increase. It could be argued that older athletes, particularly at the elite level, are already training at the maximum capability their age dictates or allows.
- The number of weekly training hours was negatively related to age, indicating a decrease of 0.76 hours of training per week per decade.
- FEV1 (Forced Expiratory Volume-1; amount of air expired in one second) decreases by 34 mL/year for both athletes and non-athletes. FVC (Forced Vital Capacity; total amount of air expired in a breath) is negatively associated with age by 36 mL/year. Other breathing measures worsen with age.
- A decrease in ventilatory function is a very important limiting factor with increasing age.
- Training can lower the physiological age of your lungs, but loss of lung function is inevitable. The harder a person exerts himself, the more likely this will probably be the rate-limiting issue.
- In a US population aged 55 to 74 years, chocolate consumption is associated with lower risks of death from all causes, cardiovascular disease, and Alzheimer's disease.
- Greater fitness in middle age (49 years) is strongly associated with lower health care costs 22 years later in life, independent of cardiovascular risk factors.
- The benefits of regular exercise have a dose–response effect. Higher levels of moderate-to-vigorous exercise (450 minutes or more/week, clearly above the minimum

international recommendations of 150 min/week) are associated with longer life expectancy.

- In 2017, The World Health Organization recommends that adults aged 18-64 engage in at least 150 minutes a week of moderate-intensity aerobic activities. Muscle-strengthening activities should be done on two or more days a week.
- The WHO (World Health Organization) recommends that more exercise is better, and it is estimated that maximal health benefits require up to ~ three to four times the current exercise recommendations. This was noted 2014 and 2016.
- Maximal risk reduction for all-cause mortality occurred at an exercise volume of three to five times current exercise recommendations.
- The most physically active group in middle age has a predicted life expectancy eight years longer than a sedentary group.
- Current studies suggest that 2.5 to 5 hours a week of moderate or vigorous physical activity confers maximal benefits; more than 10 hours a week may reduce these health benefits.
- Estimated daily step numbers have declined ~50% to ~70% since the introduction of powered machinery to our society.
- The average U.S. sedentary adult needs to burn at least 600 kcals more each day for appropriate physical activity.
- A threshold of ~60 minutes a day of moderate-intensity activity throughout a 13-year study was needed to gain <5 lbs. in 34,079 healthy US women consuming a usual diet.
- Men have a greater V02max than women because they have larger hearts, higher hemoglobin levels, less body fat, and greater muscle mass.

Highlight Reel

- Decrease in maximal oxygen consumption (i.e., V02max) is the predominant contributor to the decline in performance with advancing age.
- V02max declines by ~10% per decade after 30 years in healthy sedentary adults.
- Reduction in maximal heart rate seems to be the predominant mechanism for decreased performance.
- It is clear that exercise does not halt the aging process.
- The diminution in athletic performance is the result of the inherent aging process which cannot be prevented.
- Weight is a very important predictor of mortality risk for athletes and non-athletes especially after retirement.
- Consumption of six grams of chocolate per day (Hershey Kiss is 4.5 grams) was associated with a 39% lower risk of the combined outcome of myocardial infarction and stroke.
- The blood pressure-lowering effect of chocolate has been assessed in a number of intervention studies.
- Obesity, based on BMI, is sometimes overestimated in young people due to abundant muscle mass and underestimated in elderly people due to lack of muscle mass.
- Japan has the longest average life expectancy (84.79 years 2021). The low mortality rates from heart disease and cancer (particularly breast and prostate) are thought to reflect the low prevalence of obesity in Japan; low intake of red meat, high intake of fish, plant foods such as soybeans, and non-sugar-sweetened beverages such as green tea.
- Japan is in the top ten countries for tea drinking but not in the top 25 for coffee use.
- More than 60 diseases and 12 cancers are associated with obesity. Over 60% of obese Americans attempt weight loss each year. On June 21, 2013, the American Medical Association declared obesity a disease. Weight loss of 5-10% is clinically significant to reduce disease risk.

- Prevention and aggressive treatment of chronic diseases enable an individual to maintain functionality and age "successfully".
- By 2006, only 20% of American jobs required high levels of physical activity. This represented a huge drop from the 1960s when more than 50% of jobs met the current daily physical activity goals.
- Calories consumed by Americans increased 12% from 1971-74 to 1999-2002.
- Trained muscle consumes 9 kcals/lb./day and untrained muscle consumes 5-6 kcals/lb./day.
- From a biomechanics standpoint, 4 pounds of joint stress on our knees is decreased with every pound lost.
- The odds of sustaining musculoskeletal injuries is 15 percent higher for persons who are overweight and 48 percent higher for people who are obese, compared to persons of normal weight.
- The weight change from medicines may not always be noticed since it occurs against a background of progressive weight gain in the normal population. Weight gain can also be dose related emphasizing the basic principle of always trying to use the lowest dose to achieve the desired result.
- People underestimate calories by 30-50%, overestimate physical activity by 50%. This brings into question how reliable food questionnaires are since people may give answers that promote a healthier lifestyle then what is actually factual.
- Diabetic patients with no previous cardiovascular disease have the same long-term morbidity and mortality as nondiabetic patients with established cardiovascular disease. The 2000 OASIS study provided evidence for this foundation principle. "Diabetic patients with no previous cardiovascular disease have the same long-term morbidity and mortality as nondiabetic patients with established

cardiovascular disease after hospitalization for unstable coronary artery disease."

- It is well-known that too much sugar causes tooth decay, but it seems hard to convince people that too much sugar causes the same decay in many important organs we have.
- Risk factors at 70 years of age (smoking, BMI, blood pressure, lipids, fasting glucose) and chances of living to 90 years-old.
- No major risk factors: 51% reached 90 years of age
- One major risk factor: 33%
- Two risk factors: 30%
- Three risk factors: 20%
- Four risk factors: 18%
- Five risk factors: 7%

Narrative

I am not a coffee guy. I did not grow up on coffee. I have never had a cup of black coffee. I don't think I had a cup of coffee during high school or college. Coffee and tea are the most consumed drinks next to water in the world. Over 85% of the world drink coffee.

My first experience with coffee was probably in the doctor's lounge at a hospital at 6 a.m. as a third-year medical student. I had a cup of stale coffee in my hand because that was apparently the thing to do. We, medical students, were bottom feeders, and any way we could bond with our superiors was worth trying. A superior was someone 3 years older who had graduated from medical school to essentially be a minimum-wage worker who still did not know anything about medicine but was finally called "doctor." Our daily hospital entourage was led by an attending physician, whose job was to teach us and make sure we did not hurt anyone. Our entourage all dressed in perfectly pressed white coats, but the only one with confidence was the attending who spoke more like a drill sergeant than a teacher, barking out questions and criticisms.

Similar to the doctor's lounge as a meeting place to discuss issues, the first coffee houses were places to exchange information. In Arabia, coffee houses were known as "School of the Wise". From Arabia, coffee migrated to the Netherlands and then to other parts of Europe. The popular term "Java" comes from the name of the island that the Dutch grew coffee on. In middle school, we are taught about the "Dutch East India company" that developed in the early 1600s. The first coffee house opened in London in 1652. Coffee houses became intellectual hang-outs prompting the term "penny universities" since a penny would get you a cup of coffee and stimulating conversations. An 1892 article in the medical journal "The Hospital" noted that in France, coffee was considered "an intellectual drink" since it had a stimulating influence, decreased the need for sleep and increased the ability to do physical and mental work". It even mentioned the performance-enhancing effects of coffee "having the power of augmenting the functional activity of the muscles". In the same article, the French physician Dr G. See, compared alcohol and coffee "The muscular system and muscular energy are marvelously roused by coffee, and a man fatigued or overworked can find no more wholesome support, whereas alcohol produces in the muscles a dubious passing excitement, and in the end, a degeneration of all the organs of human activity". Since coffee seemed to have many positive attributes, many pharmacies during that time period sold coffee as a therapeutic medicine. Coffee started to compete with beer and wine at establishments.

If you asked me what Arabica, Robusta, Liberica and Excelsa were, I would probably say they are the names of the children of a professional athlete, but I would be incorrect. They are the four types of coffee beans. Liberica coffee still exists but does not play a role today in the coffee business. The Excelsa bean is used in less than 10% of coffee and is expensive and usually found in specialty shops. Basically, two types of coffee beans are traded globally. Arabica is the most common (63%) and Robusta second (37%) [5]. Since coffee commercially started in the Arab world, the name is not a surprise. Coffee plants actually originated in Ethiopia but the Arabic nation cultivated and started the coffee trade. Starbucks, Dunkin (formerly Dunkin Donuts) McDonalds, Tim Hortons, and most businesses use Arabica. Instant coffees like Folgers and Maxwell House are blends of Arabica and Robusta. Robusta is cheaper to grow and has almost double the caffeine content. The name comes from the hardy and resilient nature of the plant. Three memorable and popular Robusta coffee brands are Biohazard Coffee with 928 mg caffeine per 12 oz., Death Wish coffee which is a blend and has 728 mg caffeine per 12 oz and Cannonball coffee with a whopping 1202 mg caffeine per 12 oz. Coffee mugs are always a nice gift but I'm not sure the reaction one would get after receiving a "Death Wish" coffee mug. Most people think there are only two types of coffee beans; Arabica and Robusta and in practical terms, they are correct.

Coffee is a complex substance and the general consensus among experts is that caffeine is the key health-promoting ingredient in coffee. Caffeine is one of many polyphenols in coffee. Polyphenols are a large group of compounds that share a similar chemistry structure. They are abundantly found in fruits, vegetables, nuts, spices, chocolate, grains, etc. Your mother always told you to eat your fruits and vegetables because they were good for you. She was really saying that the polyphenols found in fruits and vegetables have therapeutic qualities. At present, there is no reason to assume that the phenolic compounds in coffee are less "healthy" than comparable compounds in fruits and vegetables. Coffee is the primary dietary source of phenolic acids and polyphenols. Coffee provides around 40% of polyphenols and around 70% of phenolic acids consumed.

When cells in our body are exposed to phenolic agents, a uniform response occurs. This cellular response is an increased expression of a large number of genes involved in antioxidative, detoxifying or repair mechanisms. Think of our cells going to a health spa and getting a makeover.

Other potentially important polyphenols in coffee include chlorogenic acid, trigonelline, cafestol, and kahweol. Both caffeinated and decaffeinated coffee contain a large amount of chlorogenic acid. A few small studies have shown cognitive benefits, but isolated clinical studies are limited. The other agents have anti-inflammatory, antioxidant, anti-diabetic, and anticarcinogenic activities, but clinical studies are also limited. Cafestol and kahweol are known to have an adverse effect in raising cholesterol levels.

Decaffeinated coffee has the same ingredients as regular coffee, but about 97% of the caffeine has been removed as required by the FDA to be called decaffeinated. Two studies in 2003, and 2006 by the same research team (McCusker et al.) showed that the caffeine concentration in the same coffee beverage from the same outlet on six consecutive days varied from 259-564 mg/dose. The second study looked at decaffeinated beverages at 10 different coffee establishments and the caffeine content varied from 0-13.9 mg/16-oz serving. Six samples of Starbucks decaf espresso and brewed decaf had caffeine concentrations of 3.0-15.8 mg/shot and 12.0-13.4 mg/16-oz serving. Caffeine content can vary due to the many steps from plant to cup. Someone that likes coffee but is extremely sensitive to caffeine needs to realize that decaffeinated coffee products have caffeine. With more than 1,000 bioactive compounds, no two cups of coffee are exactly the same chemically. Realistically, this does not change the flavor to a palatable level. Most coffee places and people pride themselves on the consistency of coffee brands and that's why many people stick to one particular coffee shop or chain.

Surveys tell us that people drink coffee because of habit, taste, energetic effect and socialization. The majority of consumers are not aware of the health benefits and will limit their caffeine intake due to concerns about the dangers of caffeine. 49% of European consumers believe coffee has negative health benefits. 61% of consumers believe that the correct number of cups of coffee per day is between three and four. Surprisingly, consumers are correct because this is the amount that probably provides the most benefits based on evidence.

I have always thought coffee came from a bean, but that is not exactly true either. Coffee comes from a tropical evergreen shrub/tree that bears a tart fruit known as a coffee cherry and the seeds of the fruit become coffee beans. A coffee tree is a fruit tree. Someone who eats a plant-based diet or encourages eating fruits and vegetables would be true to their beliefs in drinking coffee. Similar to eating vegetables and fruits, coffee shares many similar restorative benefits.

As of 2021, coffee has about 125 species with most species originating in Africa, Madagascar and a few in the Mascarene Islands. Brazil is currently the most significant coffee-exporting country. Just like the animal kingdom, new species of plants are discovered intermittently. Coffee comes from the genus Coffea. For comparison, man has seven species, and they are all extinct except for us. Man belongs to the Genus Homo and the species Sapiens which together means "wise man".

So why would a "wise man" who is not a coffee aficionado write a book or even look up articles about something that has had very little meaning to him for most of his life? The answer is running, more specifically, not being able to run fast enough to qualify for the Boston Marathon. Like many people, I pretend to be an athlete. I will not accept that my athletic ability probably peaked when I was 12 years old and about 75 pounds. Since I always ran to get into shape for other sports, I grew up running. When I was in 4th grade my gym teacher was clearly ahead of his time. He had students run 2 miles a day before classes in a tiny gym and kept track of everyone's miles with pins on a map that went from Buffalo to Toronto which was 100 miles away. The first one to reach that goal was not one person but a group of about five kids who never missed a day. This was not an affluent private school but just a typical elementary school down the street from my house. We even walked to school every day and I do not remember anyone ever taking a shower afterward running. We were just little kids, and the year was 1970. To make the story even better, two of the five kids were girls. The school took us to the Toronto Science Museum as a reward for free. I remember seeing a laser beam that was as big as a room and nowadays they can be the size of a keychain. Remember, at that time girls were not allowed to compete in many sports. In 1972, Title IX banned discrimination in higher education thus colleges could not exclude women from any activity — including sports. Woman were not allowed to run the Boston Marathon because it was felt to be too strenuous. The first woman, Bobbi Gibb, ran it as a bandit (unofficial entry, jumped into race) in 1966 and the first official woman was Katherine Switzer in 1967. She wrote KV Switzer on the applicant to conceal her name. In 2022, the Marathon celebrated the first 8 women who ran it. Presently, over 40 % of the 30,000 runners are women. Getting back to the stimulus for this book, I have noticed that my running ability has diminished a lot more than I would like over the past five years and, despite having a medical degree, I was dumbfounded.

I started to look up articles about athletic performance and aging. I came across several articles that touted caffeine as decreasing the risk of heart disease and also improving endurance performance. By drinking the caffeine equivalent of two to three cups of coffee, athletic performance especially in endurance events, could be boosted 2-4%. One may think 2-4% is not significant, but that can be the difference between qualifying and not qualifying for Boston. A performance improvement of less than 1% can make the difference between standing on the medal podium or not at the Olympic Games. In swimming, the difference between the top three medalists can be tenths of a second. I had potentially discovered the answer to my middle-aged running crisis.

Although caffeine has consistently been shown to improve athletic performance in many different sports and in professional, non-professional, trained and untrained athletes, it is not helpful for everyone. Athletes should gauge their physical response to caffeine during practice and competition, in addition to monitoring mood and potentially disrupted sleep patterns. The importance of mental health has to be considered. Side effects include anxiety, restlessness, tremors, gastrointestinal upset, palpitations, jitteriness, irritability and insomnia.

The present Covid 19 pandemic has tested our mental health and the importance of life balance. Fifty-percent of elite athletes face mental health issues sometime during their career. Famous athletes like Michael Phelps, Serena Williams, Simone Biles and Naomi Osaka have expressed their battles with anxiety and depression. Caffeine is not for everyone.

Several meta-analyses examining caffeine on a broad array of exercise tests showed performance enhancements as large as 16% to 51%. I suspect improvements at the higher percentage levels involved non-professional, untrained people. It seems that many athletes and agencies had come across the potential benefits of caffeine decades before me. The World Anti-Doping Agency (WADA) banned caffeine from the Olympics between 1984 and 2004. A threshold of 12 micrograms per milliliter (μg/mL) for urine caffeine concentration was set in 1987, and athletes who surpassed this threshold were penalized for doping. The International Olympic Committee and WADA removed the classification of caffeine as a controlled substance in 2004. Caffeine is still monitored by WADA, and athletes are encouraged to maintain a urine caffeine concentration below 12 μg/ml which corresponds to 10 mg/kg body mass (six to eight cups of coffee). Since 12 μg/ml is more than triple the intake reported to enhance performance, WADA monitors the proportion of urine samples with a caffeine concentration over 6 μg/ml. Caffeine is also categorized as a banned substance by the National Collegiate Athletic Association (NCAA), if urinary caffeine concentration exceeds 15 μg/ml. A positive drug test results in a one-year suspension from competition.

A 2019 study analyzed 7,488 urine samples from athletes competing in Olympic sports since 2004. The study analyzed specimens from 2004 (2,788 athletes), 2008 (2,543) and 2015 (2,157). About 25% were women. The median urine caffeine concentration in 2015 (0.9 μg/mL), 2004 (0.7 μg/mL), and 2008 (0.7 μg/mL) was just a fraction compared to the banned level. The vast majority of athletes had acceptable caffeine concentrations. About 75% of the athletes had caffeine present when tested. Endurance-sport athletes showed the highest urine caffeine concentrations. Whether this is just a reflection of increasing social use of coffee or to improve performance (or both) is not clear. Caffeine is a powerful ergogenic aid at levels that are considerably lower than the acceptable limit of the International Olympic Committee and could be beneficial in training and competition. Caffeine has consistently been shown to improve endurance by 2% to 4% across dozens of studies using doses of 3–6 mg/kg of body mass. It is recommended to ingest caffeine an hour before the event and this applies to both men and women. The use of coffee prior to competition may be problematic since caffeine concentrations vary between coffee blends and brands. Tablets or powder is more practical. Endurance sports have shown consistent benefit, whereas power sports (weightlifting, shotput, discus) have required higher doses such as 9 mg/kg or have not been consistently beneficial. There generally does not appear to be a difference in the ergogenic (performance-enhancing) effects of acute caffeine ingestion between habitual and non-habitual caffeine users. Many, but not all, studies support that conclusion. An interesting similar finding with caffeine seems to be the tolerant effect of chronic use in not increasing blood pressure in most people.

Epidemiologic studies have produced some contradictory findings regarding the association between blood pressure and coffee consumption. Almost 80% of consumers believe that drinking coffee increases blood pressure. Caffeine can acutely increase blood pressure in caffeine naïve people and some hypertensive individuals for an hour or two, but the effect is not seen in chronic coffee drinkers. A 2005 study showed an acute intake of caffeine stimulates a modest increase in blood pressure (both systolic and diastolic). In old studies from 1978 and 1987, volunteers who had abstained from caffeine-containing products were given a dose of 250 mg led to a 5–10% increase in both systolic and diastolic blood pressure for 1–3 hours. Tolerance to this effect developed, however, when caffeine was given three times a day for seven days. Although these studies are old, the conclusions are the same with present research. No elevation in blood pressure has been shown in recent long-term studies. This is important because the incidence of hypertension in the world is about 31%.

Without being contradictory, one can conclude that coffee may be harmful to some hypertension-prone subjects. Hypertensive patients with uncontrolled blood pressure should avoid consuming large doses of caffeine or any type of stimulatory agent like a decongestant. A conservative approach should be undertaken in each individual to see how caffeine interacts with him. Genetics can be important regarding caffeine and this will be discussed later.

Caffeine increases renal blood flow, glomerular filtration rate, and sodium excretion, resulting in increased urination. It exerts a minor diuretic effect, which is negated by exercise. Caffeine ingestion before exercise does not usually lead to dehydration, or electrolyte imbalance. Caffeine, especially in women, can aggravate urinary incontinence (leakage) in prone individuals. For women with pre-existing bladder symptoms, even moderate caffeine intake (200-400 mg/day) may increase the risk for irritable bladder.

Caffeine absorption is not influenced by age, gender, genetics, concomitant drugs or agents such as alcohol or nicotine. It is distributed to all body fluids including breast milk and to all tissues. Caffeine is rapidly absorbed by the small intestine within 45 minutes and its average peak value occurs at 30 minutes. After oral intake, the metabolism or breakdown of coffee is very different then the absorption.

Once caffeine is absorbed, several variables can affect the metabolism such as cigarette smoking, drugs, foods and genetics. Foods and drugs can inhibit or induce the effects of caffeine greatly. If a prescription or non-prescription drug has a significant interaction with caffeine, then there should be an appropriate time gap between the intake of the drug and coffee. Patients need to stop the use of coffee and other caffeine-rich products during warfarin (coumadin) therapy or drink consistent amounts daily so warfarin can be regulated accurately. Cigarette smoking doubles the rate of caffeine clearance by increasing liver enzyme activity, which may explain the higher rate of caffeine consumption among smokers. Smokers have to drink more coffee to obtain any potential benefits of coffee compared to non-smokers. Many epidemiological studies have investigated the association between coffee consumption and lung cancer risk, but the results are inconsistent. Lung cancer is one of the most prevalent malignancies in the world and is the leading cause of cancer death in the United States in both men and women. As reported by the World Health Organization, the steadily increasing proportion of elderly people in the world will result in ~50% increase in new cancer cases over the next 20 years.

Studies around 2010 to 2016 have consistently indicated that lung cancer risk is significantly increased by 47% in the overall population with the highest category intake of coffee compared with the lowest category intake. (Remember, a risk increase of 200% means two people in 100 are affected instead of one.) A 2016 meta-analysis of coffee and lung cancer looked at 17 studies involving 12,276 cases and 102,516 controls. The summary risk of lung cancer was 17% higher for coffee drinkers compared with nondrinkers and 31% higher for the highest category of coffee consumption (⩾3 cups per day) compared with the lowest category (⩽1 cup per day). Men had a 41% increased risk, women 16%, Americans 34%, Asians 49% and smokers 24%. This study is informative because when you separate data between smokers and non-smokers, nonsmokers who drink more than three cups/day have a lower incidence of lung cancer by 15%. In a 2016 meta-analysis, any coffee vs. no consumption in people who had never smoked was associated with an 8% lower risk of lung cancer. Other studies contradict this, so the question remains unanswered.

Bladder cancer is more straightforward. A 2019 study comprising 5,911 cases and 16,172 controls indicated that coffee consumption increased the risk for bladder cancer in never smokers by 30% in low to moderate drinkers and 52% in consumers > 4 cups/day coffee compared to non-coffee drinkers. Smokers already have increased risk of bladder cancer from tobacco. For smokers, the risk of mortality from cancer increased at all levels of coffee exposure, reaching significance above four cups a day. Having a cigarette and coffee in the morning is not a good start.

Caffeine is believed to exert its main effects on the central nervous system. Caffeine is close in structure to a compound called adenosine and is able to bind to the receptors that are specific to adenosine. Caffeine acts as a nonselective adenosine receptor antagonist. As a consequence, caffeine, does the opposite of adenosine.

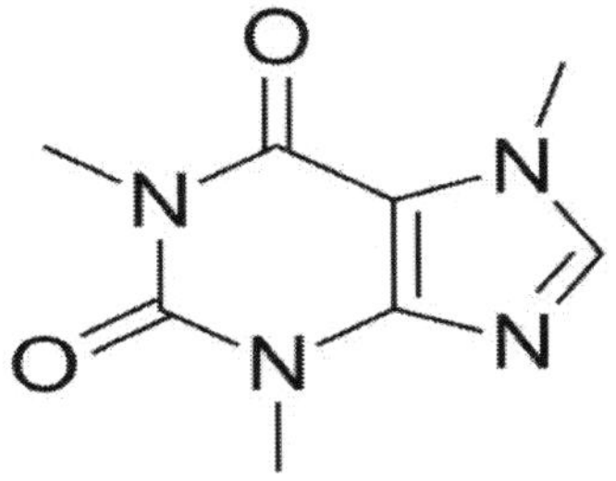

CAFFEINE 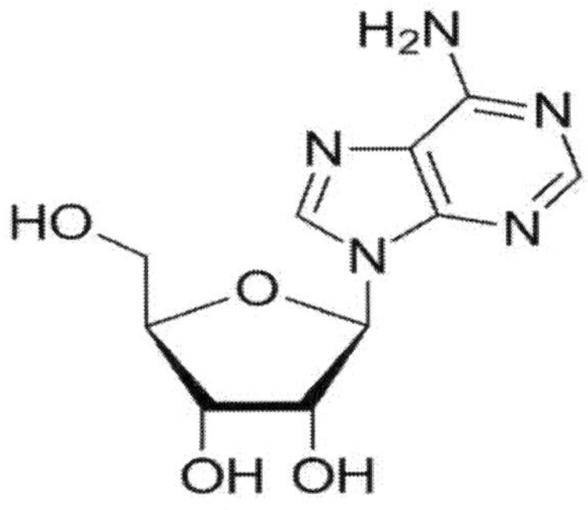 **ADENOSINE**

Adenosine is widely found in nature. Adenosine plays many important and different functions. In the cardiovascular system, adenosine produces either vasoconstriction or vasodilation of veins and arteries. There are four distinct adenosine receptors, A_1, A_{2A}, A_{2B} and A_3. Receptors A_1 and A_{2A}, which are highly concentrated in the brain, appear to be the main targets of caffeine. The major known effect of adenosine is decreasing the concentration of many CNS neurotransmitters, including serotonin, dopamine, acetylcholine, norepinephrine and glutamate. When adenosine receptors are activated, neural activity is decreased and you feel sleepy. When caffeine binds to the adenosine receptor, it blocks its activity, allowing neural activity to speed up making you more alert. It increases the concentration of these neurotransmitters. This results in positive effects on mood, motivation, focus, and alertness in most, but not all, individuals. Most prescription medicines that treat depression work by increasing or decreasing neurotransmitters.

More than 95% of caffeine is metabolized by the CYP1A2 enzyme system of the liver which has several genetically inherited versions. Some people are slow metabolizers of caffeine and may have increased symptoms and some are fast metabolizers where the benefits diminish with time. Because caffeine is a vasoconstrictor, slow metabolizers might experience prolonged vasoconstriction, and this could harm endurance performance (Guest, Corey, Vescovi, & El-Sohemy, 2018). The population that metabolizes "fast" may or may not notice the ergogenic (performance enhancing) effect of caffeine. There are examples of both fast and slow metabolizers helping and hurting the person. The best and simplest explanation is that multiple variables are involved in a person's response to caffeine and trial and error is usually necessary.

Another important aspect of caffeine metabolism involves the gene that codes for the adenosine A2A receptor. It's named the ADORA2A gene (ADenOsine Receptor A2A). Different versions of this gene (single-nucleotide polymorphisms) have been used to categorize individuals as having a high sensitivity, low sensitivity or normal sensitivity to caffeine. Alsene et al. in 2003 were the first group to document that people can have different anxiolytic responses to caffeine and this can be related to different ADORA2A genotypes. Not enough studies have been done to make generalizations about slow metabolizers or fast metabolizers of caffeine along with people who have the gene that make them more sensitive or less sensitive to caffeine. It should be noted that the half-life of caffeine is 4-6 hours but can vary between 2-12 hours in most adults; and it is not yet known with confidence the interaction that results from the altered caffeine metabolism with fast and slow metabolizers.

ADORA2A genotypes have "high" or "low" sensitivity to caffeine. CYP1A2 genotypes are "fast" metabolizers or "slow" metabolizers of caffeine.

It has been shown that genetically sensitive people to caffeine may voluntarily limit their caffeine intake and the potential health benefits of it.

Caffeine is considered a drug and is the most frequently ingested pharmacologically active substance in the world. The FDA lists caffeine as "generally recognized as safe" by experts. A drug is defined as a substance used to prevent or cure a disease or ailment or to alleviate symptoms. Simply put, a drug changes a person's mental or physical state. Caffeine is an ingredient in both beverages and foods and has been regulated by the Food and Drug Administration since 1958.

Caffeine can be sourced from:

- coffee beans
- cacao beans (seeds from a small tropical evergreen tree from which cocoa, cocoa butter, and chocolate are made)
- kola nuts (an African nut of the Cola evergreen tree)
- tea leaves
- yerba mate (a South American plant)
- guarana berry (a Brazilian plant whose seeds are high in caffeine).

The majority of adults in the United States consume caffeine regularly. There is a wide range of caffeine present in caffeinated coffees, ranging from 58 mg to 259 mg per serving. The average dose is 2.4 mg/kg per day for adults (about 2 cups of coffee). The average caffeine consumption in the United States is 76 mg/person/day (this number seems low since nondrinkers are included and US ranks around 25th in coffee consumption). In Canada, it is 210–238 mg/person/day and in Sweden and Finland, it exceeds 400 mg/day.

Although there is no specific daily allowance for caffeine, doses of up to 400 mg a day are considered safe. Special groups for which 400 mg a day may not be safe include pregnant women and children/teenagers (children and teenagers will be addressed later when energy drinks are discussed). The American College of Obstetricians and Gynecologists considers 200 mg of caffeine daily to be safe during pregnancy. The European Commission's Scientific Committee of Food Safety Authority and Health Canada both recommend that women consume no more than 300 mg of caffeine/day during pregnancy. A 2020 Korean study showed a significantly higher risk of bleeding in early pregnancy in women who drank 2 or more cups of coffee per day. A 2021 American study revealed that second trimester (weeks 13-26 weeks) caffeinated beverage intake within current recommendations was not associated with higher GDM (gestational diabetes mellitus, preeclampsia or GH (gestational hypertension). These findings may be reassuring for women with moderate caffeine intake, especially since the majority of women were minorities with an elevated risk of pregnancy complications.

One of the key mechanisms linking caffeine to improved performance is its effect on the concept of "rating of perceived exertion" (RPE). This is what allows one to train harder, feel better about training and increase chances of a rewarding outcome. It's like being "on your game" or "in the zone,". If something seems easier to do, the chances of continuing that behavior increases.

Narrative

Making someone feel better about exercise not only improves health but can also improve weight loss by increasing the number of calories burned. People will clearly exercise more often if they find it enjoyable. I have counseled patients on weight loss for more than eight years and my overwhelming perception is that patients despise exercise. Any tool to get past this roadblock is advantageous. Some people tell me that they exercise but do not sweat or that exercise makes them sweat and that's why they do not exercise. I would rather just have them tell me that they do not exercise because it is hard. This improved rating of perceived exertion with caffeine is a great quality and has been replicated in large numbers of studies across many different sports.

Exercise is formidable. Nobody likes to train or exercise, not even professional athletes. Find me a person who says he or she likes to exercise or train and you will have a person who does not train hard. Training is a job, and most people already work 40 hours per week. Exercise should be a total inconvenience to someone's schedule and life. It is not something you do, but something that you have to do. It should almost border on the rituals that an obsessive-compulsive person does to feel safe. It should be an automatic behavior like brushing one's teeth. Without sounding crazy, this is the point. I also believe that people will tell you the best part of exercising is the release of endorphins afterwards, but what someone usually does not confess about exercising is eating afterwards, maybe 45 minutes later. Eating and reading the newspaper after exercise will be the highlight of my day. The British running journalist Pat Butcher wrote: "The good ones pretend they don't train hard; the bad ones say they train like Olympic champions. They're never completely fit and never completely well. If an athlete ever admits to being ready for competition, without the slightest injury, raring to go and sure to win, you know it's time to send for the jacket with the laces up the back". To stress the point, when was the last time you saw a person running on the road with a smile? Almost never. You have a better chance of sighting "Bigfoot"!

One of the common negative effects of coffee is the higher chance of gastroesophageal reflux (heartburn). Caffeine, like most substances that enter the stomach, increases gastric acid secretion which is made of digestive enzymes and hydrochloric acid. GERD (gastro-esophageal reflux disease) is the unpleasant return of stomach acid contents into the esophagus. Because caffeine increases gastric acid secretion, negative effects of coffee upon various upper-gastrointestinal diseases have been accepted for decades. What is staggering to me is the lack of evidence supporting the common perception both in the general public and the medical field that coffee causes GERD and peptic ulcers. Surprisingly, there is no clear consensus in the literature between coffee consumption and the risk of GERD. Clearly, coffee can aggravate the stomach but there are many more guilty suspects. For example, the most common cause for reflux is obesity, especially in women. GERD is linked to spicy and high-fat foods, alcohol, high-salt diet, carbonated beverages, citrus, coffee, and chocolate. Low-level coffee consumption does not seem to aggravate GERD, while higher levels may increase the risk. Also, most studies show no association between coffee drinking and the risk of peptic (stomach) ulcers.

A large meta-analysis of risk factors of peptic ulcers reported that about 90% of peptic ulcer-related symptoms may relate to NSAID use (ibuprofen, etc.), infection by *Helicobacter pylori*, and tobacco smoking. A 2013 study of 8,013 healthy Japanese men and women showed no significant relationship between coffee consumption and the four major acid-related upper gastrointestinal disorders (gastric ulcer, duodenal ulcer, reflux esophagitis and non-erosive reflux disease). The key to accepting the research is the major role confounders like smoking, obesity, and Helicobacter infection play.

Barry J. Marshall and J. Robin Warren shared the Nobel Peace Prize in 2005 for their discovery of "the bacterium Helicobacter pylori and its role in gastritis and peptic ulcer disease".

Narrative

Conventional dogma before the discovery in 1982 was that stress and lifestyle mostly caused peptic ulcer disease. They uncovered that the bacterium is the cause for the vast majority of duodenal and gastric ulcers. They changed a chronic ailment to a cured condition about 80% of the time by simply taking a 10-14 day course of antibiotics and acid secretion inhibitors. Very few doctors and scientists would have believed that a bacterium caused many stomach disorders in the past. A very common disorder similar to GERD is functional dyspepsia. Functional dyspepsia applies to recurring signs and symptoms of indigestion that have no obvious cause. About 25% of the population suffer from functional dyspepsia worldwide. This syndrome is often associated with smoking, taking aspirin or NSAIDs, eating spicy food, and infection by *Helicobacter pylori.* No clear research answer is present between coffee and functional dyspepsia. The discovery of *Helicobacter* negated traditional teachings.

Coffee is very helpful in regulating bowels and can improve chronic constipation. A physician named Dr. I.N. Love in 1891 noted "coffee was one of the most valuable beverages and an admirable remedial agent as a direct stimulant, an antiseptic and an encourager of elimination". An encourager of elimination sounds like a core belief that inspired the Crusades of the Middle Ages. An idea that needs to stay in the Middle Ages are coffee enemas. It is a dangerous idea apparently practiced by some naturopaths. Why someone would have a coffee enema is outside the scope of my limited psychiatric understanding. It can lead to severe inflammation and death. The best route for coffee/caffeine is oral.

Distal colonic motility increases as rapidly as 4 minutes after coffee ingestion. Regular coffee stimulates the motility of the colon as much as cereals, 23% more than decaffeinated coffee or 60% more than a glass of water. Coffee stimulates the colon as much as having a meal. However, this effect varies with individuals. Coffee can be a low-cost strategy to accelerate postoperative recovery of intestinal function/motility after colorectal and gynecological surgery. A 2021 review and meta-analysis looked at postoperative ileus and included 13 trials concerning colorectal surgeries, cesarean sections, and gynecologic surgeries on a total of 1,246 patients. The regular intake of coffee promoted faster return of bowel function. Maybe, every recovery room needs a "Starbucks". Of course, that would be a very expensive cup of coffee since we all know that medical insurance companies would not pay for it.

A relatively new idea in medicine is the important role bacteria play in our health. The collective composition of the bacteria in our body is defined as the microbiota. The human intestine contains approximately 10-100 trillion microorganisms comprising up to 1,000 different species, weighing about 2 kilograms and carrying at least 100 times as many genes as the whole human genome. This population renews itself every three days and acts similar to a major human organ. There is growing evidence that healthy people have a different microbiome than unhealthy people. Coffee consumption promotes beneficial bacterial populations in our colon. An interesting example of the power of bacteria is the fact that 2 of the most expensive coffees in the world involve bacterial manipulation of the coffee cherry. Kopi Luwak coffee (Civet coffee) is probably the most recognized and costs around $160 per pound (average coffee price is about $12-39 per pound). The most expensive coffee is Black Ivory coffee from Northern Thailand and starts at about $1000 per pound. Both coffees start by feeding coffee cherries to either the Asian Palm Civet or elephants (Black Ivory coffee). Civets are small nocturnal mammals about 7 pounds that have the facial markings of a raccoon and are native to tropical Asia and Africa. The coffee cherries pass through the digestive systems picking up new flavors from enzymes, while breaking down unwanted proteins in the beans that cause a bitter taste. The stool is collected and remnants of coffee cherries gathered. The result is a very desirable coffee flavor. Unfortunately, this has led to the inhumane treatment of Civets.

Narrative

A negative aspect of coffee is caffeine withdrawal, which occurs as early as 12–24 hours after the last intake, with symptoms lasting between two days to more than a week. Symptoms include drowsiness, difficulty concentrating, mood disturbances, low motivation, flu-like symptoms, and headache. It is not surprising that when chronic caffeine users have surgery or a procedure, they develop a caffeine withdrawal headache postoperatively. Caffeine withdrawal in the hospital setting is an underappreciated syndrome. Withdrawal may occur upon abstinence from chronic daily exposure at doses as low as 100 mg/day and following only 3–7 days of consumption at higher doses. Some studies suggest caffeine withdrawal may contribute to intensive care unit delirium and that caffeine may promote wakefulness post-anesthesia. Administration of caffeine before can reduce the incidence of postoperative headache. While there is routine screening and management for alcohol or smoking when someone has surgery to prevent alcohol or nicotine withdrawal, caffeine consumption and potential withdrawal is not routinely considered. Routine resumption of coffee can easily alleviate this potential issue. (Nehlig, 2022)

In the 1988 Journal of Substance Abuse, 697 medical specialists were surveyed to determine whether there is any consensus on the harmful effects of caffeine. More than 75% of the specialists recommended reduction in caffeine in patients with anxiety, arrhythmias, esophagitis/hiatal hernia, fibrocystic breast disease, insomnia, palpitations, and tachycardia. I think the 1988 survey is absolutely correct and is also supported by professionals today but simply supports the notion that caffeinated coffee is not for everyone and highlights certain populations that have pre-existing conditions that may be aggravated by coffee intake. It's important to not make generalizations when the situation applies to small groups. Just because kryptonite is bad for Superman does not mean it's bad for everyone.

Athletes, coaches, trainers, and exercise physiologists are always looking for ways to improve performance, whether with different training methods, new equipment or ergogenic substances like caffeine. There is tremendous pressure to have an advantage on the playing field. Many professional and nonprofessional athletes will use legal and illegal supplements and drugs. Supplements are commonly consumed by athletes to enhance recovery and increase performance. The major issue with supplements is lack of quality control and lack of scientific evidence to support their claims. The three main categories of supplements prone to medical problems are those for sexual enhancement, weight loss, and sports. Creatine, a very popular and safe supplement for several decades, that has been supported well in the medical literature as an effective ergogenic aid. Dietary supplements exceed over 120,000 compounds The number one adulterant in dietary supplements are prescription drugs, followed by New Dietary Ingredients (NDI) not submitted to the FDA. Both are illegal and not simple supplements, but rather "tainted products marketed as dietary supplements". The death rate from supplements is clearly above zero percent due to contamination with legal and illegal substances. This is the risk with taking them. The FDA does not routinely review supplements. It will investigate a product only after multiple public complaints. I personally take glucosamine and have taken creatine. A person that wants to take a supplement should have it reviewed by a pharmacist, physician or reputable medical website and not by the salesperson. The best example of supplement abuse involves competitive body-builders. The doses of legal and illegal substances ingested and injected are truly incredible. The old idea that if one pill is good then 2 pills must be better is the philosophy and mind-set. A simple example how good intentions can lead to harm is green tea but it could be almost any substance. Supplements can have relatively high concentrations of a substance and someone could easily take more than directed leading to unpleasant side effects or damage. Green tea when ingested in large concentrated bolus amounts can lead to liver damage. This does not occur when consumed as brewed tea or extracts in beverages, or as a component of food. (Keller & Wallace, 2021)

Other simple athletic performance tools include quick-dry clothing, lighter protective equipment, more protective equipment and footgear. I remember watching NHL hockey games in the 1960s and 1970s and most goalies did not wear masks. Getting hit in the face with a 6-ounce frozen galvanized rubber projectile at 100 mph by an elite athlete at close range can "smart". Whether it is a baseball, hockey puck, boxing glove or a football helmet, these are dangerous projectiles. Wearing head protection has become mandatory in many sports.

A less dangerous phenomenon are footwear. The term "sneaker" almost doesn't exist anymore. The term sneaker was coined around 1880s due to the quiet nature of rubber soles. Sneakers customized for running did not become popular until the late 1970s. Nowadays, there are shoes specifically made for every sport, including ping-pong and pickleball. I make fun of my wife because she buys running shoes a lot, and I can't throw my shoes away until they have holes in them. Researchers will pay top elite marathon runners generously to test experimental running shoes to attempt to break the unconquerable 2 hours marathon time. The first shoe that breaks 2 hours in a non-enhanced marathon will make history and have a great marketing advantage. Non-enhanced means not using intermittent pace runners, very favorable wind and temperature conditions, downhill courses, or other potential variables to speed-up times. Eliud Kipchoge, a 34 years-old two-time Olympic gold marathon runner, ran a 1:59:40 marathon in Vienna, Austria on October 13, 2019 using 41 professional pacers and a laser to mark the most efficient running path. Because the conditions were enhanced, it is not an official record. Insider Inc., a news website, had an interesting interpretation on the difficulty of this; "Imagine running about the length of a football field in 17 seconds — then doing it 422 times in a row. That's what it takes to run a marathon in under two hours".

People take performance and competition very seriously. Remember, my quest to go from a slowpoke to a faster slowpoke. Competition for survival or sport has been around since evolution. Competition is important to our species.

A 1912 British medical article expressed an opinion about competition: "The Bureau of Medicine and Surgery has come to the conclusion that it is not so much the games and competitions themselves that do the harm, as the overtraining and too prolonged periods of preparation that the crack athletes indulge in. Long-distance racing is held to be the most injurious of all sports; and marathon racing is regarded as the worst of all. With these conclusions it is easy to sympathize: they contain a lesson which this country may well take to heart. Yet it is doubtful whether the mischief thus done is anything like so great in this country as in the States. It is an old observation that the American takes his sports much more seriously than we do, and thereby can often defeat his English competitor. To win is the great ambition over there, whereas to have a good game is the chief motive here."

Two sports that exceed normal athletic behavior are ice swimming and sauna competition with the difference in temperature close to 200 degrees Fahrenheit. Ice swimming takes place at less than 41 degrees and sauna competition is above 230 degrees (water freezes at 32 degrees and boils at 212 degrees).

The German ice swimmer Bruno "*Orca*" Dobelmann makes one smile just with his great name and nickname. One of the best-known ice swimmers is Lewis Gordon Pugh. He managed to swim a kilometer in 18:50 minutes in −1.7 °C (35 F) cold water at an open point in the ice at the North Pole. He suffered frostbite in his fingers. Just to put this extreme sport into perspective, a 2019 study of elite and sub-elite marathon swimmers came to the conclusion that water between 16°C (60.8 F) and 18°C (64.4 F) is too cold for elite marathon swimmers. An international swimming federation in

2017 made wetsuits compulsory at temperatures less than 64.4 F and optional below 68 F. Ice swimmers do not wear wetsuits or other protective equipment, only a bathing suit and swim cap.

On the opposite end of the thermometer, sauna competition usually starts at a temperature of 230 degrees. A normal recreational sauna is usually set at 150 to 195 degrees. A good brisket is smoked at 250 degrees. World records are in the 16-minute range. Severe skin burns and collapsing are the biggest side effects. You are not allowed to touch your skin in the competition and you have to sit in a designated position. You are disqualified if you cannot walk out of the sauna without assistance. The closest I come to this crazy stuff is running outside in 100 F degree weather or sitting in a 105 F jacuzzi while it's snowing outside.

People can do amazing things by devoting years to their passion. A woman can have a baby then resume training and compete at an elite level (Serena Williams). Professional basketball players shoot from distances that were considered "moon shots" years ago. A 95-year-old man can walk/run for 12 hours after completing his first marathon at age 90. Johnny Kelley can run 61 Boston Marathons, completing 58 in less than six hours. Athletes are always breaking records. There are athletes in their 60s who have times similar to the winners in the first modern-day Olympics back in 1896. A 73 years old man ran a marathon in 2 hours 54 minutes and the winner of the 1896 Olympics ran a slower marathon in 2 hours 58 minutes. More and more great achievements are being done by both older men and women in sports. If a person is not motivated after reading about a 95-year-old man who did his first marathon at age 90, then put this book down right now and grab a big cup of coffee for motivation.

Along with caffeine improving training and performance, it has also been shown to reduce mortality and morbidity. Mortality and morbidity can be confusing. Mortality is like "bringing out your dead" in the movie "Monty Python and the Holy Grail"; it deals with death rates. Morbidities are illnesses like hypertension, diabetes and heart disease that shorten a person's lifespan. In 'The Holy Grail", King Arthur faces off against the Black Knight in the woods. Arthur expects the knight to give up after he cuts his arm off. Instead, the knight says, "'Tis but a scratch" and continues fighting. After his second arm is cut off, he says, "Just a flesh wound." Multiple amputations would be considered a morbidity.

Coffee consumption is consistently associated with a lower risk of mortality from all causes of cardiovascular disease and stroke, with estimates indicating that the largest reduction occurs at three cups a day. Freedman et al. in a 2012 NEJM (New England Journal of Medicine) article considered seven specific causes of death and showed protective relationships between coffee consumption and lower mortality from heart disease, respiratory disease, stroke, injuries and accidents, diabetes, and infections. (Loftfield, et al., 2015)

In healthy people, habitual consumption of three to five cups of coffee per day is associated with a 15% reduction in the risk of a cardiovascular event. Usual consumption of one to five cups a day is associated with a lower risk of death compared to no coffee intake. In people who have already suffered a cardiovascular event, habitual consumption does not increase the risk of a recurrent cardiovascular event or death. It is safe to drink coffee after having a heart attack. A 1994 article pointed out that the published literature provides little evidence that coffee and/or caffeine in typical dosages increases the risk of myocardial infarction, sudden death or arrhythmia. This article's conclusions are still true in 2021. A 2019 study also does not support a causal association between habitual coffee consumption and risk of atrial fibrillation (irregular heart rate which increases risk of stroke). Studies have been done in different parts of the world with different ethnic populations, and the majority support the favorable mortality and morbidity nature of drinking caffeinated coffee. A 2018 article from Clinical

Electrophysiology, a specialist division of The Journal of the American College of Cardiology stated:

- Many clinicians continue to counsel patients with atrial or ventricular arrhythmias to avoid all caffeinated beverages, particularly coffee, despite an absence of evidence to support this approach.
- If, in individual cases where a clear temporal association between arrhythmia episodes and caffeine intake is apparent, then avoidance is sensible.
- Large-scale population-based studies and randomized controlled trials suggest coffee and tea are safe and may even reduce the incidence of arrhythmias.
- A regular intake of up to 300 mg/day caffeine appears to be safe and may even be protective against heart rhythm disorders.

The benefits of decreasing cardiovascular mortality and morbidity cannot be overstated since cardiovascular disease is the leading cause of death in the United States and the world. Great advances in diagnosing and treating cardiovascular disease have happened in my lifetime. Our lifespan has been increased by more than 20 years in the past century by better sanitation, antibiotics, vaccines and decreasing cardiovascular disease. If cardiovascular disease is the number one killer in the world, the number 2 killer is cancer. Lung cancer is usually the most common type of cancer death in the USA and the world. It is also the most preventable. Dr Robert Porter, a history professor of science at Stanford wrote an insightful article about tobacco and lung cancer published in 2012. A brief summarized version is noted.

> "In 1900, only about 140 cases of lung cancer were known in the published medical literature. Lung cancer was once a very rare disease, so rare that doctors took special notice when confronted with a case, thinking it as a once-in-a-lifetime oddity. Cases started increasing at an unprecedented level in the first half of the 1900's. Cigarettes were finally recognized as the cause of the lung cancer epidemic in the 1940s and 1950s. Unfortunately, the cigarette industry was very effective in the

art of denial and propaganda. In 1953, Ernst Wynder and Evarts Graham painted cigarette smoke tars onto the shaved backs of mice with *Life* magazine devoting several pages to the story. Researchers in the tobacco industry also became convinced of a cigarette–cancer link. Claude Teague in his confidential 1953 'Survey of Cancer Research', written for upper management at RJ Reynolds, makers of Camel cigarettes, concluded that tobacco was 'an important etiologic factor in the induction of primary cancer of the lung.' The American Cancer Society's National Board of Directors in 1954 announced 'without dissent' that 'the presently available evidence indicates an association between smoking, particularly cigarette smoking, and lung cancer.' If the US Surgeon General's report in 1964 was released in 1954 when the science data was conclusive, millions of lives would have been saved. In 1954, George Gallup surveyed the US public to ask: 'do you think cigarette smoking is one of the causes of lung cancer, or not?' 41% answered 'yes'. In 1960, a poll by the American Cancer Society, noted that only a third of all US doctors agreed that cigarette smoking should be considered 'a major cause of lung cancer'. This same poll revealed that 43% of American doctors were still smoking cigarettes on a regular basis. In the 1980s, Philip Morris was piloting a 'global strategy' to deny the reality of secondhand smoke hazards. Global tobacco use would be declining were it not for China, which now accounts for about 40 percent of all cigarettes sold and smoked. Hundreds of millions of Chinese remain poorly informed about the hazards of smoking. In 2011, a published survey from the Netherlands showed that only 61 per cent of Dutch adults agreed that cigarette smoke endangered non-smokers. The tobacco lobby has been successful over the last 70 years. One can argue that cigarettes have been the most effective WMD (weapon of mass destruction) in the history of human civilization. Cigarette makers make about a penny in profit for every cigarette sold, which means that the value of a life to a cigarette maker is about US$10 000".

In 2020 and 2021, COVID-19 was the third-leading cause of death. Please, do not buy this book if you do not believe in vaccines. Vaccines are one of humanity's greatest achievements and success stories since the 1880s. Unfortunately, people remain skeptical about science. Fill in the blank:

GET VACCINATED TOD_Y.

A 2014 survey performed by the World Cancer Research Fund (WCRF) revealed that as many as 36% of health professionals thought drinking coffee increased the risk of cancer. On June 15, 2016, The International Agency for Research on Cancer which is the cancer agency for the World Health Organization (WHO) and several large prospective trials concluded that caffeine is not carcinogenic. Studies published in recent years, including two large meta-analyzes in 2017, have shown protective associations between coffee consumption and the risk or development of 18 different types of cancer, including breast, prostate, oral, oral and pharyngeal, melanoma, skin and skin nonmelanoma, kidney, gastric, colorectal, endometrial, liver, leukemic and hepatocellular carcinoma, brain, and thyroid cancer, among others. Twelve publications demonstrated different findings with only a few cancers conveying an unfavorable association between coffee consumption and cancer. These were bladder, pancreatic, laryngeal, gastric and lung cancer. A literature search by Pauwels and Volterrani from January 2005 to December 2020 published in 2021 looking at coffee consumption and cancer noted that the totality of eligible scientific articles supports the evidence that coffee intake is inversely associated with risk of hepatocellular cancer and, to a slight extent, risk of breast cancer among postmenopausal women. As to the association with other organs, including the esophagus, pancreas, colorectum, kidneys, bladder, ovaries, and prostate, the results are less clear as reports reveal conflicting results or statistically nonsignificant data. The relationship with caffeinated coffee, decaffeinated coffee, caffeine, tea and cancer can easily be summarized as complicated. Cancer is a very large term used to describe the abnormal growth of cells. There are over 100 types of human cancers. Although cancers have many similar traits, they also have many unique traits. The drug protocols and modalities of treatment are very elaborate and change rapidly as research advances. Millions of years of evolution has made man a pretty formidable foe but conquerable. For example, studies about gastric cancers are conflicting but become more precise if we classify them based on their anatomical location. Cardia subtypes behave as esophageal cancers, while non-cardia types most often relate to the presence of Helicobacter pylori in addition to risk factors common to both types. When doing studies, more and more confounding variables have to be taken into account with research. It is no surprise that each cancer's relationship with coffee and caffeine has to be dealt with independently. A 2020 study exemplifies how it can be confusing.

- Consumption of ≥2 cups/day of decaffeinated coffee was associated with 18% lower risk of overall colorectal cancer, 18% lower risk of colon cancer and 37% lower risk of rectal cancer.
- Consumption of ≥2 cups/day of caffeinated coffee was associated with 37% higher risk of rectal cancer but not with colorectal or colon cancer.

(FYI rectum and colon make up colorectal area). In 2016, the International Agency for Research on Cancer (IARC) found the evidence between coffee consumption and digestive cancers to be inconsistent, with the exception of the liver.

The medical literature clearly supports the general statement that drinking coffee has a much greater likelihood of decreasing the risk of cancer than not drinking it.

Chronic liver disease is the fifth most frequent cause of death. Liver cancer is the fifth most common cancer in men and the ninth most frequent in women worldwide. In addition to the beneficial associations with liver cancer, all categories of coffee exposure were associated with lower risk for a range of liver outcomes. Coffee consumption was associated with a 29% lower risk of non-alcoholic fatty liver disease, a 27% lower risk for liver fibrosis, and a 39% lower risk for liver cirrhosis. Because caffeine is an antioxidant and anti-inflammatory, caffeine can potentially improve liver tests such as alanine aminotransferase (ALT), aspartate aminotransferase (AST), γ-glutamyl-transferase (GGT) and bilirubin. Coffee reduces the risk of chronic liver disease including viral hepatitis B and C, and alcohol-induced liver disease. (Rodak, Kokot, & Kratz, 2021) The beneficial associations between drinking coffee and liver conditions stand out as consistently having the highest magnitude compared with other outcomes. A 2017 meta-analysis with more than 2.2 million people concluded that drinking more than two cups of coffee per day was associated with a 35% reduction in the risk of hepatocellular carcinoma. A 2020 meta-analysis also concluded a significant protection against liver cancer occurred at a coffee consumption of 2 cups/day. In all these studies, the degree of protection increased with larger amounts of coffee consumed. Coffee reduced the risk of liver cancer recurrence and improved survival even in patients that underwent liver transplantation. Coffee consumption has been linked to a reduction in pancreatitis. (inflammation of the pancreas mainly induced by alcohol). In prospective cohort studies, coffee intake was significantly associated with a 17% risk reduction of gallbladder stones, but only in women, not in men. Gallstones occur more frequently in women. In a group of 72,680 Swedish adults (45-83 years old), the risk of developing gallbladder cancer was decreased by 24%, 50%, or 59% for the consumption of 2 cups, 3 cups, or ≥4 cups per day. These data reflect a strong beneficial association between coffee consumption and gallbladder cancer risk. (Nehlig, 2022)

Coffee also has valuable associations with metabolic conditions including type 2 diabetes, metabolic syndrome, gallstones, gout, and renal stones. Summary estimates indicate that the largest relative risk reduction is associated with intakes of three to four cups a day. Importantly, increase in consumption beyond this intake does not seem to be associated with increased risk of harm; rather, the magnitude of the benefit is reduced.

Since caffeine improves "perceived exertion", it also can have an effect on mood. A 1996 study of 86,626 US female registered nurses looked at caffeine consumption and suicide. Compared with non-drinkers of coffee, the risk of suicide in women was 66% lower in women who consumed two to three cups per day and 58% lower in women who consumed four or more cups per day. A strong inverse relationship was similarly found for caffeine intake from all sources and risk of suicide. A 2014 study involving 208,424 (43,599 men, 164,825 women) showed a 45% lower risk of suicide for those consuming 2-3 cups/day and 53% lower risk of suicide for those consuming ≥ 4 cups/day compared to ≤ 1 cup/week of caffeinated coffee (< 8 oz/237 ml).

Suicide is usually the second most common cause of death in ages 10-34 years-old. This is a very heartbreaking statistic. Accidents are usually always first (National Vital Statistics System).(Poole, et al., 2017)

Along with suicide risk, caffeine can help depression in some people. Something as simple as drinking a single cup of coffee daily has been clinically shown to improve depression in a statistically significant manner in multiple studies. Treating oneself to coffee regularly probably competes with "an apple a day to keep the doctor away". They both have beneficial polyphenols. Compared with the lowest level of consumption, **coffee** consumption decreased risk for depression by 24%; **caffeine** consumption decreased risk by 28%. The association between caffeine consumption and depression became significant when the caffeine consumption was between 68 and 509 mg/day. Both coffee and caffeine consumption were significantly associated with decreased risk of depression.

Another simple method of improving depression is to walk 30 minutes per day five days a week. A British study by Dimeo in 2001 involving 10 days of walking for 30 minutes a day resulted in a decrease in the Hamilton Scale for Depression and self-assessed intensity of symptoms. (Booth, Roberts, & Laye, 2012)

Walking is one of the most underrated activities in human history. So many good things result from walking. No one doubts the physical and mental benefits of walking and it would be an endless debate on which aspect it helps more. Forget the idea that walking on two feet separates us from many animals, but instead cherish all the great inspirational songs about walking;

"Walk Like a Man" by Frankie Valli and The Four Seasons
"Walking on Broken Glass" by Annie Lennox
"Walk This Way" by Run DMC and Aerosmith
"Walk on The Wild Side" by Lou Reed

No one can deny the health benefits of listening to "Born to Run" by Bruce Springsteen. Not being able to walk diminishes so many systems in your body that mortality is greatly increased.

When someone stops walking, it is the beginning of the end.

A devastating disease that effects almost every family is diabetes. Almost a third of people are not aware that they have it because symptoms are not always present until damage has occurred to their hearts or eyes or organs. Unintentional weight loss or constant thirst is a common symptom. It was pretty easy to diagnose a future good friend of mine after he walked into my office carrying 2 water bottles. A 2005 systematic review notes that habitual coffee consumption is associated with a 28-35% lower risk of type 2 diabetes. A 2014 review with more than 1.1 million people in different studies with follow-up from 10 months to 20 years revealed that coffee consumption decreased the risk of type 2 diabetes in a dose-related manner. Both caffeinated and decaffeinated coffee was associated with reduced diabetes risk. Since coffee does not decrease glucose levels by itself, the ability of habitual coffee drinking to lower the risk of type 2 diabetes may be a result of long-term preservation of liver cells and pancreatic beta-cells. Beta-cells make insulin and liver cells store glucose. If coffee can help preserve beta-cell function, that would be a very remarkable finding.

The 2020 National Diabetes Statistics Report showed that more than 10% of the population has diabetes and more than 32% has prediabetes. Prediabetes is present when a person has a fasting glucose between 100 and 125 mg/dl and diabetes is defined when the sugar is 126 mg/dl or higher. Prediabetes is important to look for and treat. It is not benign. Most topics with "pre" before them mean something significant. Just think of the words pretrial, premature, prenuptial, precancer, pre-op, preeclampsia and prehistoric. In multiple studies, prediabetes is shown to have a cause-effect relationship to cardiovascular disease and all-cause mortality.

The estimated lifetime risk of developing diabetes for babies born in 2000 is 32.8% for males and 38.5% for females, with Hispanics having the highest estimated lifetime risk (males, 45.4% and females, 52.5%) among ethnic groups. If coffee can decrease the risk of diabetes, that would be beneficial to tens of millions in the USA and more than a billion people worldwide. The reason diabetes is such a serious disease is that it leads to premature heart disease. Type 2 diabetes is estimated to cost men 11.6 life-years and women 14.3 life-years A person with diabetes has the same mortality statistics as a person who has had a heart attack. (Booth, Roberts, & Laye, 2012)

The 2000 OASIS study provided evidence for this foundation principle "Diabetic patients with no previous cardiovascular disease have the same long-term morbidity and mortality as nondiabetic patients with established cardiovascular disease after hospitalization for unstable coronary artery disease."
This is why doctors constantly encourage good compliance in people afflicted with diabetes and why all people with diabetes are recommended to take a statin cholesterol medication and a baby aspirin. Taking a statin and a baby aspirin improves longevity for people with heart disease. Heart disease is the No. 1 killer in the USA and the world (7.7 billion people in the world and about a third have heart disease).

Looking at another global killer, Alzheimer's type dementia is the most common neurodegenerative disease that affect millions of people but has no definitive curative treatment. There are several types of dementia; Alzheimer's is the most common at more than 80% of cases. Pathologically, Alzheimer's disease results in loss of synaptic integrity (connections) and neurons by deposition of plaques composed of amyloid beta (Aβ). Li et al. in 2015 described a potential mechanism whereby caffeine protects against amyloid beta (Aβ) generation. Other types include vascular dementia resulting from multiple strokes, Lewy Body dementia, and frontotemporal dementia. Lewy Body dementia has abnormal proteins deposited in certain parts of the brain and typically presents as a person in his 50s with onset of Parkinson-like features and dementia within a year. One can differentiate Parkinson's disease from Lewy Body disease since dementia either presents late in the course or does not present at all in Parkinson's and presents early on with movement issues with Lewy Body. Drug treatment is usually disappointing. Drugs such as donepezil (Aricept), rivastigmine (Exelon patch), galantamine (Razadyne), and memantine (Namenda) delay progression of symptoms at best and need to be taken essentially on faith. When problems such as aggression or inappropriate behavior develop, antipsychotics and anti-depressants can help. People afflicted with Lewy Body should not be given anti-psychotics since they can worsen symptoms dramatically. The number of studies showing that caffeine has a beneficial effect on the risk of dementia/cognitive decline was 46 of 57 (81%), including 111,926 of 153,070 (73%) subjects. More than 70% of studies for mild cognitive impairment or any type of dementia showed that caffeine had a beneficial effect. This helpful effect is dependent on the caffeine source (e.g., coffee and green tea), quantity (moderate), and gender (better response in females). Lindsay et al. in 2002 stated that coffee consumption at midlife correlated with a 31% reduced risk of Alzheimer's disease in 10,236 Canadian participants over the age of 65 years. Eskelinen and co-workers in 2009-10 looked at long-term coffee consumption at midlife and Alzheimer's disease/dementia risk. After an average follow-up of 21 years, in 1,409 individuals (534 men and 875 women) aged 50 years in 1972-1977, moderate coffee drinkers (three to five cups every 24 hours) had lower risk of Alzheimer's disease by 62-64% and dementia by 65-70% in comparison with low coffee consumers (zero to two cups per 24 hours). Acute caffeine ingestion has been shown to enhance functional performance, manual dexterity and readiness to exert effort in healthy older adults aged 61-79 years-old. Higher coffee consumption was independently associated with better physical performance in men with a mean age of 87 years. A 2019 European study with 11,963 people aged ≥60 years showed that habitual coffee consumption was associated with a lower risk of falling in older adults in Spain and the United Kingdom. (Rodak, Kokot, & Kratz, 2021)

The other common neurodegenerative disorder, Parkinson's disease, also has no effective cure. Prescribed medications help alleviate symptoms and improve the quality of a patient's life. Deep-brain stimulators are very helpful in lessening debilitating tremors and bradykinesia (slow movement) in select patients. Most medicines stimulate dopaminergic neurotransmission since Parkinson's disease depletes dopamine levels. Levodopa, i.e., a

precursor of dopamine, is still considered the most active drug that controls Parkinson's disease manifestations.
A 2014 meta-analysis noted a linear dose relationship for decreased Parkinson's risk with tea and caffeine consumption; the strength of protection reached a maximum at about three cups a day for coffee. The risk of Parkinson's disease was reduced by about 30–38% in one recent systematic review and meta-analysis of caffeine drinkers. Four different meta-analysis from 2002 to 2014 came to the same conclusion. A five-time lower risk of developing Parkinson's disease was noted in 45-68 years old people by drinking greater than 421 mg of caffeine per day (3-4 cups). This was reported by Ross et al. based on 27 years of follow-up. Hu et al., in a nearly 13-year control study involving about 14,500 people (approximately 62 years old), showed that Parkinson's risk decreased by 45% for subjects drinking one to four cups and 59% for subjects drinking more than five cups of coffee per day. The findings did not differ between men and women. Several studies showed that decaffeinated coffee consumption was not associated with neurodegenerative disorders, providing further evidence that caffeine is the active agent. (Socała, Szopa, Serefko, Poleszak, & Wlaź, 2020)

Unlike coffee/caffeine, where there are multiple studies repeatedly showing very similar conclusions, tea does not tout such an impressive record of studies. Regular tea consumption was associated with decreased prevalence and progression of coronary artery calcium (a marker of cholesterol plaque in coronary arteries) along with a decreased incidence of cardiovascular events. The American Heart Association supports the regular consumption of tea.

Tea consumption worldwide is highest for black tea, followed by green tea, oolong tea, and white tea. Tea is divided into unfermented (green and white), semi-fermented (oolong), fully fermented (black), and post-fermented (dark). Unfermented teas contain more polyphenol compounds (remember benefits of fruits and vegetables), then fermented teas. The predominant polyphenols are called catechins; they have long, confusing names such as epigallocatechin gallate, epicatechin, epigallocatechin, and epicatechin-3-gallate. They have antioxidant, anti-inflammatory, anti-microbial, anti-cancer, and neuroprotective benefits, but most of the research is preclinical (not studied in humans yet and therefore inconclusive results for our health). Approximately one-fifth of Americans report drinking tea on a daily basis. A consistent intake of tea at levels around 2 cups per day seems to have the potential to decrease cardiovascular (CVD) risk. One to three cups of black or green tea improves cardiovascular mortality by 2-27%. Tea polyphenols seem to decrease LDL cholesterol, systolic blood pressure, and diastolic blood pressure across both healthy and hypertensive populations (Keller, Wallace 2021). Drinking 2 to 3 cups of coffee and 2 to 3 cups of tea per day was associated with a 32% lower risk of stroke and a 28% lower risk of dementia compared to non-drinkers. Higher consumption of green tea and coffee was associated with reduced all-cause mortality in patients with type 2 diabetes. Their combined effect appeared to be additive in patients with type 2 diabetes. In Chinese adults, daily green tea consumption decreased risk of type 2 diabetes and decreased all-cause mortality in patients with diabetes. The associations for other types of tea are less clear. Other studies, unfortunately, have shown contradictory results. Although there are many epidemiological studies showing that tea has neuroprotective effects, several inconsistent results are also reported. For instance, a 2009 survey including 1,409 participants (71% ages 65-79 years) showed that drinking coffee was related to the prevention of Alzheimer's disease, while drinking tea was not.

A 2018 study focused on 29,876 men and women aged 40-69 years old without a history of heart disease, stroke or cancer showed no significant positive or negative association between tea and the incidence of stroke or coronary artery disease in either men or women. Favorable relationships seem to be more statistically significant and stronger with coffee than tea. (Chen, et al., 2018)

Narrative

As a general statement, tea consumption clearly does more benefit than harm to health.

Because energy drinks have caffeine as the main ingredient, and teenagers and young adults drink them regularly, I have reviewed energy drinks. Energy drinks are beverages that typically contain caffeine, taurine, glucuronolactone, vitamins, herbal extracts, proprietary blends, and/or amino acids. They are available with or without sugar and may or may not be carbonated, thus the range of products is broad. Proprietary blends and herbal extracts are usually a non-descriptive term used to mask agents that may be of a stimulatory nature. Similar to supplements, asking a pharmacist is a great source for medical information.

Between 2000 and 2012, the U.S. Poison Control Center reported 5,103 exposures to energy products and among those 552 adverse events: one fatal, 24 serious, and 527 moderate reactions. Importantly, 44.7% of the adverse events were in children younger than 6. According to the FDA's Center for Food Safety and Applied Nutrition Adverse Event Reporting System, between 2004 and 2012, 166 reports were received describing adverse events, including 18 deaths. Together the FDA and Poison Control have more than 700 adverse events. The FDA's reporting system is estimated to capture only about 1% of the true number of adverse events associated with energy drinks; thus, the number of adverse events and deaths is likely to be much higher. In many studies, the combination of alcohol and energy drinks results in higher rates of binge drinking, reductions in perceived intoxication, faster rates of self-paced alcohol consumption, or increases in risk-taking behavior. Other data negates this idea.
In 2010, the FDA removed pre-mixed alcohol-energy drinks from the market because caffeine was determined to be an unsafe additive to alcohol, in part because it promoted excessive drinking.

In March 2013, 18 scientific and medical experts sent the FDA commissioner a report summarizing the research findings on energy drink consumption by children. This report concluded: "... there is neither sufficient evidence of safety nor a consensus of scientific opinion to conclude that the high levels of added caffeine in energy drinks are safe under the conditions of their intended use, as required by the FDA's 'Generally Recognized as Safe' standards for food additives. To the contrary, the best available scientific evidence demonstrates a robust correlation between the caffeine levels in energy drinks and adverse health and safety consequences, particularly among children, adolescents, and young adults". Furthermore, the Institute of Medicine has recommended that drinks containing caffeine should not be sold to children at school. Simply stated, caffeine-containing products have a greater association with severe adverse events compared with non-caffeine-containing products. (Temple, et al., 2017)

Energy drinks were first introduced in 1987. When I played sports in high school (1974-78), energy drinks did not exist. Lemon-lime Gatorade was the popular drink; it did not contain caffeine and came in glass bottles. Gatorade was invented in 1965 by Dr J. Robert Cade to help the Florida Gators football team deal with dehydration in the very hot weather. That simple idea started a multi-billion dollars industry and helped save millions of lives when babies suffered from diarrhea in underdeveloped countries.

I have been an anti-energy drink person, but I can see some benefit, mostly in sports. I think teenagers drink them too often and don't need more energy. If young people need energy drinks to get through the day, that idea makes me sad.

Chances are higher that energy drinks may promote more negative rather than positive outcomes. My research has softened my militant view, and I am even considering trying energy drinks to help improve my feeble athletic ability. I still have not bought an energy drink yet, but I'm thinking about it. I would be a hypocrite if I drank them and yet criticized them. Maybe, I have a future in politics. The great thing about learning is it helps you make the most informed decisions. Sometimes first impressions are not accurate. Coffee was like that many times in history.

When coffee was introduced in Venice in 1615, some people referred to it as the "bitter invention of Satan." The local clergy condemned coffee, and the controversy was so great that Pope Clement VIII intervened. He decided to taste the beverage and found the drink so satisfying that he gave coffee papal approval. A good word from the Pope is never a bad thing.

When coffeehouses starting popping up everywhere in Europe in direct competition with beer and wine, many businesses and politicians were not very happy and did their best to limit them. In 1777, Frederick the Great of Prussia used his power to limit coffee intake only to the aristocracy. He declared:
"It is disgusting to notice the increase in the quantity of coffee used by my subjects, and the amount of money that goes out of the country as a consequence. Everybody is using coffee; this must be prevented. My people must drink beer. His Majesty was brought up on beer, and so were both his ancestors and officers. Many battles have been fought and won by soldiers nourished on beer, and the King does not believe that coffee-drinking soldiers can be relied upon to endure hardships in case of another war".

Frederick the Great encouraged free speech, religious tolerance and many noble democratic ideas but apparently not coffee. His speech reminds me of the Supreme Court hearing for Brett Kavanaugh when he was nominated in 2018 and confessed his liking of beer.

Just like the Pope approving coffee, doctors look at the potential benefits and side effects or risks when prescribing medicines and or treatments. For example, Drug A may improve a medical condition by 20% and improve survival by 2 years after the person has taken the drug for 5 years. A great example of a beneficial treatment is exercise. The benefits of exercise outperform prescription medicines by leaps and bounds. Also, drugs try to have laser-focus pharmacology to maximize benefit and limit harm. Exercise works more globally and hits many body systems all at the same time in an advantageous orchestral manner. Exercise is so profound that a study dividing people into an exercise group and a non-exercise group could never be approved by a Human Institutional Research Board since the negative repercussions of the non-exercise group would be too vast to allow it to be considered ethical. No "Pepsi Challenge" can compete with exercise. If I have learned anything over 30 years in medicine, the power of exercise is paramount.

When I picture an older couple sitting at a kitchen table in pajamas drinking coffee slowly and reading the newspaper in the morning, I assume that breakfast will come next followed by more sitting and then eventually going back to bed for a little while. What about a different scenario? What about the couple fueling themselves before a long, hard challenge and making sure they have their "game face" on by having coffee. Truly, they would be "the greatest generation."

A famous researcher named Jerry Morris wrote a paper in 1949 showing that the drivers of London's double-decker buses and government clerks were more likely to die from heart disease than conductors and postmen. He made the connection between the more physically active conductors and postmen and the more sedentary bus drivers and clerks that physical activity protects against heart disease and sedentary activity promotes heart disease. He was awarded a gold medal at the 1996 Olympics in recognition of his work on exercise and heart disease.

Morris died at age 99. In his 10th decade of his life, he wrote, "We in the West are the first generation in human history in which the mass of the population has to deliberately exercise to be healthy. Modern humans have been able to engineer most physical activity out of daily life. Humans now have a choice not to be physically active". I came across a quote written more than 100 years ago that describes how some people feel about exercise; it applies to present times: "There is a considerable class to whom exercise is a disagreeable sort of medicine which is taken in holiday doses only."

Physical inactivity causes substantial increases in risk factors for more than 30 chronic diseases. The volume of evidence is overwhelming. Physical activity diminishes mortality by 30% in the United States. Expressed alternatively, physical inactivity increases mortality by 30%, or by 720,000 annual deaths (one every 44 seconds). Physical inactivity is defined as "a physical activity level less than that required for optimal health and prevention of premature death." The idea of prevention of premature death delivers the message succinctly. For "substantial health benefits," the 2008 federal guidelines recommend exercising 150 minutes a week (30 minutes five times per week). In reality, the best amount of exercise is really three to four times that amount (450 minutes a week), but our society has become so sedentary that more success will be achieved by promoting 150 minutes per week.

Arem and associates in 2015 combined data with a study population of 661,137 individuals. They concluded that maximal risk reduction for all-cause mortality occurred at an exercise volume of three to five times current exercise recommendations.

Lear et al. analyzed a 2017 cohort of 130,843 individuals from 17 countries. Individuals in the high physical activity group had a 35% decreased risk for all-cause mortality and 25% reduced risk for major cardiovascular disease compared to the low physical activity group.

The average U.S. sedentary adult needs to burn at least 600 calories more each day for appropriate physical activity. Estimated daily step numbers have declined ~50% to ~70% since the introduction of powered machinery to our society.

By 2006, only 20% of American jobs required high levels of physical activity. This represented a huge drop from the 1960s when more than 50% of jobs met the current daily physical activity goals.

The Institute of Medicine suggests that 60 minutes a day (420 minutes a week) of moderate-intensity activity may be needed to prevent a transition from a normal weight to an overweight or obese level. A 2010 JAMA (Journal of American Medical Association) study involving 39,876 women aged 51-61 years old showed that normal weight women successfully maintained their weight and gained less than 5 pounds throughout a 13-year study by exercising the equivalent of 60 minutes a day of moderate-intensity activity.

An article in the Journal of Applied Physiology in 2000 using MRI technology revealed a reduction in relative skeletal muscle mass starting in the third decade and a noticeable decrease in absolute skeletal muscle mass at the end of the fifth decade. People need to grasp the idea that we need to work harder to maintain ourselves because our bodies start to weaken in our mid-30s instead of our 40s or 50s. If one eats the same amount every year and does not increase energy expenditure either through work or exercise, they will gain weight each year typically starting at 35 years-old. Six pounds of muscle are lost per decade, metabolic rate decreases 3% per decade, and 16 pounds of fat are gained per decade by the 40-50 years-old age bracket. Low muscle strength increases all-cause mortality in 13 studies using subjects > 65 years of age. Sedentary lifestyle speeds up aging of skeletal muscle by 24 years. The development of frailty was more than twice as likely among men who were overweight and more than five times more likely in obese men in midlife compared to men with normal weight at midlife (around 47 years-old). Preventing old-age frailty should be recognized as an important goal of treating obesity in midlife.

Narrative

Below is an example that provides a good reason to maximize the multiple benefits of coffee in regards to morbidity and mortality.

Dr. J.A. Dempsey, pulmonary researcher, states: "The design of the pulmonary system is clearly intended for the exercising state. The system shows remarkable capability for true adaptation. At the same time, there are limits to the system's capabilities. The healthy pulmonary system may become a so-called 'limiting factor' at least during short-term maximum exercise in the highly trained. No organ system has limitless functional capacity". Most organ systems in our bodies deteriorate about 1% each year starting at about 35 years-old or earlier. We can slow down or possibly lessen the deterioration with exercise but the decline is inevitable in everyone. By waiting until our health decays, we are losing valuable ground.

Elite athletes exercise more than any group. Elite athletes have longer lifespans than the general population and provide the best example for the medical benefits of exercise. A 2015 Finnish study looked at 2,363 elite athletes and followed them for 50 years, comparing them to 1,657 healthy men serving as controls. Median life expectancy for endurance athletes was 79.1 years and for team-sport athletes 78.8 years. Control-group subjects lived 72.9 years, essentially 6 years less. Boxers had 4.2 times the risk of dying from dementia (probably from chronic traumatic encephalopathy). Most studies on elite athletes involve men only which is slowly changing to include women also.

An interesting 2018 study looked at the gene versus environment debate by comparing 900 former elite athletes who represented Finland in competition with their brothers. Median age at death was 79.9 years for endurance athletes with their brothers dying at 77.5 years. Mixed sports athletes died at 75.9 years and their brothers at 73.7 years. Power-sport athletes died at the same age as brothers, 72.2 years. Former elite athletes live longer than their brothers. Publications involving 80 identical twins unequivocally show that if one twin has lower physical activity, he exhibits increased risk for chronic diseases.

Elite athletes also provide the best argument against the idea that extended exercise/training is detrimental to health. When does someone exercise "too much"? At some level of training, it will be counterproductive and harmful to an athlete's mental and physical welfare. The amount of training is probably both sport-sensitive and athlete-sensitive. Some epidemiological studies reported an increased risk of disease and/or mortality at the highest exercise volumes, suggesting that health benefits may plateau or even decline in extreme exercisers. Fortunately, this "Extreme Exercise Hypothesis" has more data negating it than supporting it. (Eijsvogels, Thompson, & Franklin, 2018)

Atrial fibrillation (irregular heart rate increasing risk of stroke) has been associated with higher-intensity exercise regimens, faster competitive finishing times and absolute number of endurance races completed. Long-term endurance exercise – more than 2,000 hours and/or more than 20 years of training – displays a strong correlation with atrial fibrillation even in individuals without cardiovascular risk factors. The harder one trains or the longer duration of training exposes higher and longer levels of catecholamines which can increase the risk of rapid arrythmias or new arrythmias. Catecholamines help the body respond to positive or negative stress and include epinephrine (adrenaline), norepinephrine (noradrenaline), and dopamine. To counter that argument, better conditioning lessens the negative effects of catecholamines. A conditioned athlete may have a resting heart rate of 42 beats per minute which increases to 128 with workouts and an unconditioned person may have a resting heart of 84 which increases to 156 with vigorous activity. The athlete can triple his heart rate and it is still lower than the unconditioned person who does not even double his heart rate. With more than 10 hours of vigorous exercise a week, the risk of developing atrial fibrillation begins to exceed that of a sedentary group. Non-supporting evidence notes that up to 90% of all exercise-related sudden cardiac deaths occur in recreational athletes rather than competitive athletes. Cardiac anomalies may be present in a small proportion of the most-active veteran athletes, and the combination of high-intensity physical activity in the presence of known or occult cardiovascular disease seems to be the major cause of exercise-related fatalities. In athletes older than 35, more than 80% of sudden cardiac deaths are caused by coronary artery disease; whereas among younger athletes (less than 35 years old), congenital abnormalities of the heart muscle, coronaries and conduction system are the most common cause. The current body of data is not strong enough to recommend that recreational athletes reduce their exercise dose. Current studies suggest that 2.5 to 5 hours a week of moderate or vigorous physical activity confers maximal benefits; more than 10 hours a week may reduce these health benefits. Exercising between 5-10 hours per week is probably very athlete dependent and is the norm and safe in some non-elite recreational athletes. The people at risk are unconditioned sedentary people that overdue activity and do not start exercise in a gradual manner. A 2021 article from the journal "Resuscitation" looked at potential triggers of sudden cardiac death (SCD). Physical exercise is second on the list. Just think of all the unconditioned overweight/obese people and realize that half have heart disease and it is not hard to appreciate the ranking. Also, because 85% of the population drink coffee, it is probably not surprising that coffee consumption is on the list. Potential triggers for SCD are different than well-documented medical diseases like diabetes, COPD (tobacco), hypertension, obesity, cholesterol, family history etc. that significantly increase heart disease. Triggers are acute events and disease are chronic risk factors. The potential triggers are:

- 14.5% episodic alcohol consumption
- 9.4% physical exertion
- 6.9% cocaine
- 6% episodic coffee consumption
- 3% psycho-emotional stress in the previous month

- 1.7% amphetamines
- 0.9% cannabis
- 0.3% influenza infections

Along with exercise being a great health promoter, medical advances over the past 50 years have increased our lifespan. Our lifespan has gone from

- 1860: 39.4 years
- 1900: 47.3 years
- 1960: 69.7 years
- 2020: 78.9 years

Hopefully, the next chapter in medicine will improve not only our longevity but our health span – the number of years we have a good quality of life. We want to limit or compress the number of years of poor health. A 2020 study by Urtamo followed healthy Finnish businessmen between 46-55 years old and the number who survived to age 90 by tabulating the presence of five risk factors at age 70. The risk factors were smoking, body mass index, blood pressure, lipids and fasting glucose. The results were

- no major risk factors, 51% reached age 90.
- one risk factor, 33%.
- two risk factors, 30%.
- three risk factors, 20%.
- four risk factors, 18%.
- five risk factors, 7%.

People are living longer, and the number of centenarians (100 years or older) and supercentenarians (110 or older) are growing. Centenarians are about one in 10,000 people, supercentenarians are very rare. Worldwide, the number of centenarians fluctuates between half a million and a million with five women for each man (finally, a statistic in this book that makes sense). Centenarians are more likely to be widowed women that live alone. In general, centenarians are healthier throughout their 80s and 90s compared with others. Although these centenarians are living longer than most of their group, they are doing so in poor health, which is discouraging to hear. More than half of centenarians live with a chronic disease, about 20% with one or more disabilities and 10% with cognitive impairment. A total of 55% remained cognitively intact over the study period, confirming that dementia is not an inevitable condition of living longer lives. Women are characterized by more disability and disease than their male counterparts._Men are felt to live with less disability than women at this age due to more financial security. I suspect this will change in the future as women climb the success ladder rapidly.

Living to a hundred years is a remarkable feat. Exceptional longevity should really refer to people older than 90 but it does not. Remember, the normal range for a given test is based on the results seen in 95% of the population. People in their nineties are in the 5th percentile of the survival curve in the Western world and are considered outside the "normal range." Nevertheless, it is often the memorable age of 100 that is regarded as the threshold of exceptional longevity. Numerous studies demonstrate that biological relatives of centenarians have a substantial survival advantage. Having a parent live to 100 is a strong independent predictor of survival to age 100.

This brings to mind the old question, what plays a larger role: genetics or environment? My personal opinion is environment. Comparison of lifespans for adult relatives reveals a survival advantage of brothers and sisters of centenarians: brothers lived 2.6 years longer, and sisters lived 2.9 years longer. Being a farmer is the best indicator of longevity for men. Some early-life characteristics (birth in the Northeast region of the United States and birth in the second half of the year) turned out to be significant predictors of exceptional longevity (for men but not women). Only a few factors were related to exceptional longevity of women: parental longevity and, surprisingly, the availability of radio in the household in 1930. Having a radio indicated household wealth, which may explain the latter finding. Earlier studies found that radio listening increased the quality of life and decreased depression.

Listening to the radio before TV was invented was very popular and was a method of socialization. Having a hearing impairment limited communication and increased feelings of isolation. It was stigmatizing and handicapped educational potential. It was and still is a significant hardship at any age and increases the chances of accidents and trauma. Hearing loss is the fifth leading cause of disability in the world. A 2021 study looked at coffee consumption and risk of disabling hearing impairment over a 10 years period in 36,923 participants (16,142 men and 20,781 women) [mean age 56.6 years]. Men who consumed one or more cups/day had a 28% lower risk of hearing impairment compared with those who consumed <1 cup/day of coffee. No association was found between coffee and hearing function among women. 36,923 participants is a very respectable number for a study. It would be interesting if they separated the men into married, never married, or ever-married along with coffee consumption and hearing impairment. Loud noises like yelling and broken dishes can damage fragile hair cells! (Gavrilov & Gavrilova, 2015)

In 2014, Dr. Andrew Cohen wrote an article in the Journal of the American Geriatric Society regarding the 100th anniversary of the first textbook on geriatrics, titled "*Geriatrics*", written by Dr. Ignatz Nascher, a physician and pharmacist in New York City. I would not call the article a celebration of the first book, but a commentary on early observations over a hundred years ago. Cohen writes: "This is not a book that is nice about old age, and it is not generous to the elderly. It begins with a description of their appearance, often 'repellent': flabby, slouching, with excessive hair and blue lips, a 'tout ensemble' of decay that arouses "repugnance".

The aged are further described as generally careless, apathetic, and gloomy. Their lives "for all practical purposes ... are useless." Their helplessness instills "a spirit of irritability if not positive enmity" in the young. Most noxious is their self-interest, a theme to which the author returns repeatedly. An old man "demands constant attention and complains of the slightest neglect, he becomes indignant and suspicious, he develops an "overwhelming interest in self … which gradually subordinates every other interest in life. Certain passages make the modern reader cringe."

Dr. Cohen credits the author with the concept that medications can have uncertain effects in the elderly and polypharmacy should be avoided. An excellent paragraph by one of the founders of pediatrics, Dr. Abraham Jacobi, describes a more sympathetic description of elderly people: "The recovery from every new disease contracted at any period of life is handicapped by the tissue changes left behind from the previous accidents or ailments. There are few persons of advanced years without a permanent blemish – one or many – which make the diagnosis of any additional illness or comorbid condition more difficult, treatment more uncertain, and complete recovery more doubtful."

His description makes me think that every wrinkle a person has tells a story. Maybe, Dr. Nascher is telling us not to repeat the mistakes of the past when we see an older person that is weathered by age and illness. Many older medical books promoted stereotypes of older people that were not productive in helping them.

Aging from the time of birth to old age is a roller-coaster that gets faster while we tolerate the speed less and less. There is no such thing as the "golden years." We are not "fine wine that gets better with age". We need to think of our bodies as billions of tiny test tube racks with chemical reactions occurring instantaneously and constantly. Chemical reactions allow our muscles to contract along with digesting our favorite foods. As we get older, we are unable to do the chemical reactions with the speed or accuracy as before. The reactions become less efficient. We make mistakes. Test tubes break. Reagents for the reactions stop working or are not the right solutions and more and more maintenance is required. Our little lab that we call ourselves goes from "state of the art" to a crowded messy garage. This crowded garage eventually stops working.

A 2015 study looked at coffee's ability to decrease spontaneous strand breaks in our DNA (genes). DNA is the genetic material that separates one species from another. DNA strand breaks essentially lead to malfunctions in making proteins. Proteins are important in all the chemical reactions our body requires to keep us working well. The study analyzed the impact of 84 healthy men consuming either a placebo drink or about two cups of a dark-roast coffee blend daily for four weeks. The coffee group had 27% decreased spontaneous DNA strand breaks. The study concluded that regular coffee consumption significantly contributes to DNA integrity. Despite coffee improving our DNA integrity, no study or coffee infusion has been shown to improve the integrity of politicians. Unfortunately, some ideas are just outside the realm of speculation or faith.

We do not have a choice when it comes to aging. Our mothers and grandmothers were right in the importance of eating fruits and vegetables and I'm saying let's add some coffee for good health. A 2014 study looked at 24 years-old and 60 years-old men who engaged in the same eight-week training program to assess if equal benefits were attained. The young improved their conditioning (V02max) by 13% and the older men by 6%. The young increased maximal power output by 20%, the older men by 10%. Maximum heart rate remained unchanged in the old, but was significantly decreased in the young. The benefits in the young group were about twice as large as the older group. Working out as we get older is similar to the catchphrase "Two steps forward, one step back". Strangely, Vladimir Lenin coined the phrase "One Step Forward, Two Steps Back" as a title of a 1904 revolutionary pamphlet. With aging inevitable and the diminished level of return from exercising, only one conclusion is sensible. Tom Hanks in the 2000 movie "Castaway" is deserted and alone on a remote island. He eventually realizes that he has no control and states "I know what I have to do now. I gotta keep breathing. Because tomorrow the sun will rise. Who knows what the tide could bring? This is what we do. We keep breathing and go to work and raise our family. We do this on our best day and we do this on our worst day. Sometimes, life can be that simple and hopefully comforting. In the past, when I did some high-altitude marathons like Pike's Peak, I would try to comfort myself by repeating that all I need to do is "breath and move" and that would give me some confidence and relief when I was short of breath. The best advice for aging is to keep fighting.

An important aspect of coffee is not only creating a thirst for knowledge at coffeehouses but also by enriching a sense of community and togetherness among people. Coffeehouses were not only for intellectuals but also for the average "Joe" to get a cup of "Joe" and just hang-out. The importance of these "third places" has been brought to the spotlight with the Covid-19 pandemic. People did not realize how important these simple, plain, inexpensive, non-threatening places are to our mental health. Because of difficult economics, these places that lessen stress, loneliness and isolation are closing across the United States. Many "mom-and- pop" businesses cannot survive financially. Starbucks has used this idea very successfully. "Third places" was first coined by Dr Ray Oldenburg, a doctor of sociology, in his 1989 book "The Great Good Place". First place is home, second place is work, and third place is wherever you feel comfortable at. Going out to get coffee or breakfast as a routine is very important for mental health. Humans are a social being.

Near the end of the book, one of the articles describes getting older in spartan-like terms and grabbed my attention. "Human aging is a condition satisfying four principles: it is intrinsic, universal, progressive and usually detrimental to the host" I guess describing death as usually detrimental to the host is probably not a good example of "owning" a statement and maybe a little overly optimistic?

Before I present articles explaining how coffee/caffeine and exercise will not only save me but hopefully others, I have to reveal an essay written by Sir Graham Hills about a condition for which there is no cure, only a palliative method of treatment for a particular addiction. I hope my genetics have passed this on to my children and their children's children: CURIOSITY. Also, I do want to promise that I will not use the word "journey" in the book to describe anything. Enough said.

Chapter 1: Caffeine Basics

Before someone can run, they need to learn how to walk first. These articles start the education process.

Regulatory status of caffeine in the United States

•Caffeine has been regulated by the Food and Drug Administration since 1958.
•Caffeine is generally recognized as safe by experts.
•The regulatory history of caffeine is complex and not typical of most food ingredients.
•In 1978, the FDA concluded it was "inappropriate to include caffeine among the substances generally recognized as safe," noting that "at current levels of consumption of cola-type beverages, the dose of caffeine can approximate that known to induce central nervous system stimulation."
•In 1980, the FDA "found no evidence to show that the use of caffeine in carbonated beverages would render these beverages injurious to health."
•In 2010, the FDA issued a warning letter to manufacturers of caffeinated alcoholic beverages, resulting in the removal of such products from the marketplace.
•Because the amount of caffeine in plant-based products, such as coffee or chocolate varies, quantitative labeling is difficult (how much caffeine is present).

Major Sources of Caffeine in Today's Marketplace

•A serving of espresso (about one ounce or 30 mL) provides 64 mg of caffeine.
•An 8-ounce cup (237 mL) of automatic drip coffee provides 145 mg of caffeine.
•Tea beverages contain 20–80 mg of caffeine per 8 ounces.
•Chocolate candy may contain 11–115 mg caffeine per 1-ounce serving. Cocoa beverages contain about 5 mg caffeine per 6-ounce serving.
•Carbonated soft drinks with caffeine typically have about 30–40 mg per 12-oz serving.
•Caffeine-containing energy drinks typically contain 17–224 mg caffeine per serving.

FDA concerns about caffeine

•The FDA is concerned about the indiscriminate use of caffeine as an ingredient in food.
•There is an ongoing debate about caffeine's health risks to children and adolescents, largely related to incomplete development of the nervous system in youth.
•The mean daily exposure to caffeine for the total population ranged from 142.1 to 150.8 milligrams (Rosenfeld, Mihalov, Carleson, & Mattia, 2014)

Consumers' Perceptions of Coffee Health Benefits and Motives for Coffee Consumption and Purchasing

- Consumers' beliefs in the health benefits of coffee are unclear.
- A minority of consumers believed that coffee could have positive health effects.
- Consumers drink coffee because of habit, taste, energetic effect and socialization.
- Only about 16-25% of U.S. consumers know about coffee's health benefits. 66% are prone to limiting their caffeine consumption.

Chapter 1: Caffeine Basics

- 49% of European consumers believe coffee has negative health effects.
- Coffee drinking is not considered a health-oriented behavior, even if scientific evidence indicates that coffee can be part of a healthy diet.
- Adverse effects of coffee drinking were mainly limited to pregnancy and to women at increased risk of bone fracture.
- Level of education did not explain the perception of health benefits of coffee consumption.
- Almost 80% of consumers believe that drinking coffee increases blood pressure, more than half think that it decreases depression and headache, and one-fourth that it decreases the risk of cardiovascular diseases.
- 61% of consumers believe that the correct number of cups of coffee per day is between three and four. Surprisingly, consumers are correct because this is the amount that probably provides the most benefits based on evidence.
- 80% believe that decaffeinated coffee has a similar impact to caffeinated coffee on human health.
- The vast majority of consumers (74%) are willing to pay a price premium for coffee with health benefits.
- The history of coffee started in the 15th century.
- Its consumption first grew in Arabic countries and then expanded to Persia, Egypt, Syria, and Turkey. It was known as the "wine of Araby", and drunk as a substitute for alcohol, which was prohibited according to the Islamic religion.
- In the 17th century coffee arrived in Europe (e.g., Italy, England, France, Austria). Consumers increasingly drank it in coffee houses that become competitors for pubs, with coffee becoming a substitute for beer and

wine. During the 18th century it became common in North America.

- Brazil is currently the most significant coffee-exporting country.
- During its long history, coffee has been criticized for various reasons:
  - stimulated critical thinking (Mecca)
  - considered Satanic (Italy)
  - considered a toxic substance used to bring about death (unsuccessfully in Sweden)
  - threatened beer consumption and therefore local agricultural production (Prussia).
- Drinking a specific coffee brand (e.g., Starbucks) represents a status symbol and way of life for some consumers.
- Despite recent studies showing that coffee can have positive health effects, consumers are still cautious on drinking coffee. (Samoggia & Riedel, 2019)

<u>Health Effects of Coffee: Mechanism Unraveled?</u>

- The association of habitual coffee consumption with a lower risk of diseases, such as type 2 diabetes mellitus, chronic liver disease, certain cancer types, or with reduced all-cause mortality has been confirmed in prospective cohort studies in many regions of the world.
- The radical-scavenging and anti-inflammatory activity of coffee constituents is too weak to account for such effects.
- We argue that coffee as a plant food has similar beneficial properties to many vegetables and fruits. Recent studies have identified a health-promoting mechanism common to coffee, vegetables and fruits, i.e., the activation of an adaptive cellular response characterized by the upregulation of proteins involved

in cell protection, notably antioxidant, detoxifying and repair enzymes. (Kolb H, 2020)

We conclude that coffee employs similar pathways of promoting health as assumed for other vegetables and fruits. Coffee beans may be viewed as a healthy vegetable food and a main supplier of dietary phenolic agents.

Thinking of the beneficial aspects of coffee in the same regard as fruits and vegetables reminds me of the 2003 Will Ferrell movie "Elf" where he plays Buddy, an adult man raised by elves who was brought up on a different meal plan than ours. "We elves try to stick to the four main food groups: candy, candy canes, candy corn and syrup."

Coffee for Cardioprotection and Longevity

Coffee contains hundreds of biologically active compounds and promotes long-term health benefits. Coffee improves all-cause mortality and lowers the risk of many cardiovascular diseases and cardiovascular death. Coffee's effects on arrhythmias and hypertension are neutral. Coffee consumption is associated with improvements in type 2 diabetes, depression, and obesity. Chronic coffee consumption also appears to protect against some neurodegenerative diseases and is associated with improved asthma control and lower the risks for liver disease and cancer. Habitual intake of three to four cups of coffee appears to be safe. The potential negative aspects of caffeine include anxiety, insomnia, headaches, nervousness, and palpitations. Coffee may also increase risk of fracture in women, increase risk for low birth weight and preterm labor in pregnancy. (O'Keefe, DiNicolantonio, & Lavie, 2018)

The Safety of Ingested Caffeine: A Comprehensive Review

- **Caffeine is the most widely consumed psychoactive drug in the world.**
- The amount of caffeine in chocolate varies by the percentage of cocoa it contains. Dark chocolate has more caffeine than milk chocolate.
- Caffeine is a constituent of many over-the-counter pain relievers and prescription drugs because the vasoconstricting and anti-inflammatory effects of caffeine act as a complement to analgesics, in some cases increasing the effectiveness of pain relievers by up to 40%.
- Caffeine is used to counteract drowsiness (NoDoz and Vivarin each contain 200 mg of caffeine).
- Between 50 mg and 200 mg of caffeine is added to some weight-loss supplements (Dexatrim, Hydroxycut, and Nutrisystem Energi-Zing Shake).
- **Average daily caffeine intake is about 180 mg/day, about two cups of coffee.**
- **Trends in caffeine consumption have been stable among adults and children aged 2-19 years old for the past two decades.**
- Caffeine intake usually begins in childhood, most often in chocolate, soda, and chocolate milk. As children become adolescents, they increase consumption of soda and begin to add beverages with greater caffeine content, such as coffee and energy drinks. Average caffeine intake increases from about 50 mg/day in childhood (aged 2–11 years) to 180 mg/day in adulthood.

Pregnancy

- The half-life of caffeine is on average 8.3 hours longer during pregnancy.

Infancy

- By age 6 months, infants eliminate caffeine at the same rate as adults.
- **Cigarette smoking doubles the rate of caffeine clearance by increasing liver enzyme activity, which may explain the higher rate of caffeine consumption among smokers.**

Cognitive effects

- The impact of caffeine appears to be greater under conditions that would negatively affect performance, such as sleep deprivation.
- Caffeine consumption may decrease the risk of Parkinson's disease and Alzheimer's disease.

Pain Relief

- The vasoconstricting action of caffeine has been associated with pain relief. (decreased blood supply decreases swelling and pain). Several studies have reported that acute dietary caffeine consumption can reduce pain.
- In March 2013, 18 scientific and medical experts sent the FDA commissioner a report summarizing the research findings on energy drink consumption in children. This report concluded that "… *there is neither sufficient evidence of safety nor a consensus of scientific opinion to conclude that the high levels of added caffeine in energy drinks are safe under the conditions of their intended use, as required by the FDA's Generally Recognized as Safe standards for food additives. To the contrary, the best available scientific evidence demonstrates a robust correlation between the caffeine levels in energy drinks and adverse health and safety consequences, particularly among children, adolescents, and young adults". Furthermore, the Institute of Medicine has recommended that drinks containing caffeine not be sold to children at school. In addition, The American Academy of Pediatrics' Committee on Nutrition and the Council on Sports Medicine and Fitness recently concluded that "rigorous review and analysis of the*

literature reveal that caffeine and other stimulant substances contained in energy drinks have no place in the diet of children and adolescents".

Reproductive effects

- The 2016 Nurse's Health Study shows pre-pregnancy coffee consumption at levels of fewer than four servings a day is associated with an increased risk of spontaneous abortions.
- No clear association has been found between moderate doses of caffeine ingestion during pregnancy and birth defects.
- Several studies have reported maternal caffeine consumption and low birth weight.

Cancer

- **The International Agency for Research on Cancer and several large prospective trials have concluded that caffeine is not carcinogenic.**

Unstable bladder

- Excessive caffeine intake (more than 400 mg/day) may increase the risk of detrusor instability (unstable bladder) in women. For women with preexisting bladder symptoms, even moderate caffeine intake (200-400 mg/day) may increase the risk for unstable bladder. In addition, caffeine intake of three to four cups caused early urgency and frequency of urination in men and women with overactive bladder.

Hydration and diuresis

- **Caffeine has a diuretic effect which is not likely to have adverse consequences for healthy adults.**

Children and adolescents

- Two 2014 studies suggest an association between caffeine consumption and anger, violence, sleep disturbances, and alcohol/drug use in youth.
- The consumption of highly caffeinated energy drinks has been associated with elevated blood pressure,

altered heart rate, and severe cardiac events in children, adolescents, and young adults, especially those with underlying cardiovascular diseases.

Caffeine and alcohol

- An increasingly popular form of caffeine consumption is mixing alcohol with energy drinks. **In 2010, the FDA removed pre-mixed alcohol-energy drinks from the market because caffeine was determined to be an unsafe additive to alcohol, in part because it promoted excessive drinking.**
- In many studies, the combination of alcohol and energy drinks results in higher rates of binge drinking, reductions in perceived intoxication, faster rates of self-paced alcohol consumption, or increases in risk-taking behavior. Other studies negate this idea.

Caffeine-related diagnoses

The American Psychiatric Association's Diagnostic and Statistical Manual-IV included four caffeine-related diagnoses:

- **Caffeine intoxication**- recent consumption of caffeine, usually in excess of 250 mg, and five (or more) of the following: restlessness, nervousness, excitement, insomnia, flushed face, diuresis, gastrointestinal disturbance, muscle twitching, rambling flow of thought and speech, tachycardia or cardiac arrhythmia, periods of inexhaustibility, psychomotor agitation.
- **Caffeine-induced anxiety and sleep disorder**- significant symptoms occur in association with caffeine intoxication or withdrawal.
- **Caffeine-related disorder not otherwise specified**- symptoms that do not fit into the aforementioned categories.
- **Caffeine withdrawal disorder** occurs when an individual experiences impairment after abrupt cessation of caffeine intake, including headache,

difficulty concentrating, fatigue, nausea, flu-like symptoms, and changes in mood. These symptoms typically begin 12–24 hours after caffeine cessation and may continue for three to seven days. Avoidance of caffeine withdrawal may motivate individuals to consume more caffeine. This could result in chronic, excessive consumption of caffeine. When this results in impairment, an individual may meet the criteria for caffeine use disorder.

- The criteria for caffeine use disorder include 1) persistent desire or unsuccessful effort to control caffeine use, 2) "*use despite harm*" and 3) withdrawal.

Recommendations on safe intake levels and limits on intake

- Intake of caffeine up to 400 mg/day is not associated with adverse effects.
- The European Commission's Scientific Committee of Food Safety Authority and Health Canada both recommend that women consume no more than 300 mg of caffeine/day during pregnancy.
- The total amount of caffeine contained in some energy drinks can exceed 500 mg (equivalent to 14 cans of caffeinated soft drinks or five cups of coffee) and is high enough to be toxic in children and young adults.
- The American Academy of Pediatrics released the following recommendation: "*energy drinks are not appropriate for children and adolescents and should never be consumed (2014).*"

The Federal Substance Abuse and Mental Health Services Administration reported that from 2007 to 2011, the number of emergency room visits involving energy drinks doubled across the U.S. from 10,068 to 20,783. However, for adults aged 40 years and older, emergency room visits involving energy drinks nearly quadrupled during that same period (from 1,382 to 5,233). (Temple J. L., 2017)

Chapter 1: Caffeine Basics

Caffeine as a Factor Influencing the Functioning of the Human Body—Friend or Foe

- Chawla et al. in 2015 stated that average caffeine consumption in the United States is 76 mg/person/day. In Canada, it is 210–238 mg/person/day and exceeds 400 mg in Sweden and Finland.
- Caffeine is rapidly absorbed within 45 min and its average peak value occurs at 30 min.
- **Individual variation in response to caffeine consumption is connected with genetic aspects. There are two genes especially linked with caffeine metabolism—*CYP1A2* and *ADORA2A*. The *CYP1A2* gene is mainly responsible for caffeine metabolism.**
- Sachse et al. determined that there are "fast metabolizers", "normal metabolizers", and "slow metabolizers".
- The *ADORA2A* gene encodes adenosine receptor $A_{2A}R$. Variations categorize people as "high responders to caffeine" and "low responders to caffeine".
- Caffeine is so close in structure to adenosine that it is able to bind to the receptors that are specific to adenosine. **It is a nonselective adenosine receptor antagonist.**
- Caffeine antagonizes Adenosine Receptors: A_1, A_{2A}, A_3, and A_{2B}. As a consequence, caffeine, does the opposite of adenosine.

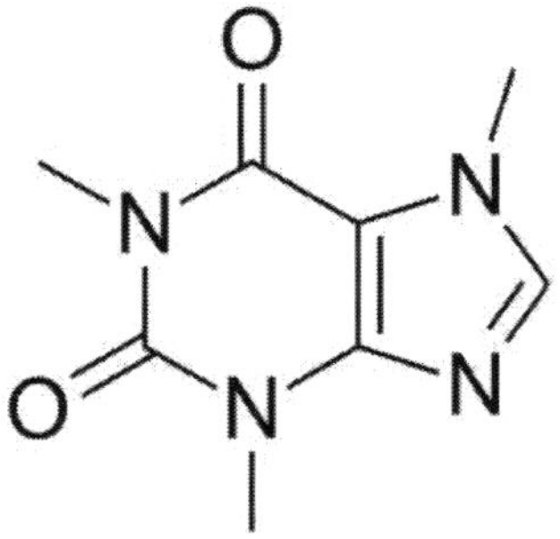

CAFFEINE 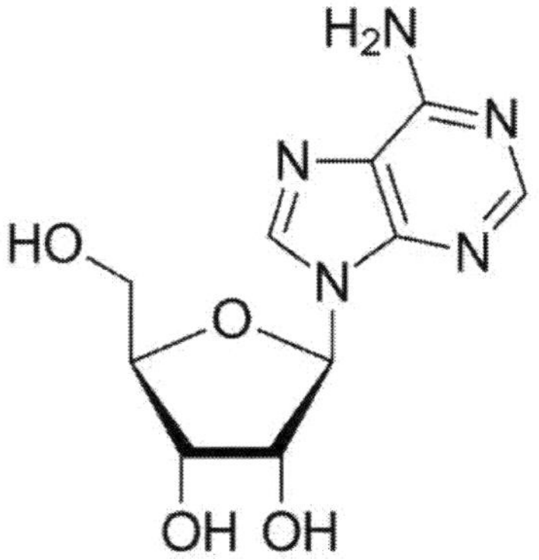 **ADENOSINE**

- Caffeine has multiple targets in the brain. Caffeine, through antagonism of ARs, affects sleep, cognition, learning, and memory, and modifies several brain diseases.
- Alzheimer's disease (AD) is caused by loss of synaptic integrity and neurons, deposition of amyloid plaques composed of amyloid beta (Aβ). Li et al. described a mechanism whereby caffeine protects against Aβ generation.
- The neuroprotective effect of caffeine has been demonstrated by Maia et al. in a 2002 study among 54 patients with AD who consumed 73.9 ± 97.9 mg/day of caffeine during the 20 years before diagnosis of AD in relation to individuals without AD who consumed 198.7 ± 135.7 mg/day during the corresponding 20 years of their lifetimes. Authors showed that caffeine consumption was associated with lower risk for AD.
- Kolahdouzan and Hamadeh in 2017 also stated that caffeine is protective in AD at 3–5 mg/kg body weight.
- Ritchie et al., in 2007, showed that consumption of at least three cups of coffee per day is associated with less decline in verbal memory.

- A 2009 study by Eskelinen et al. with 1409 subjects, aged 50 years, showed that midlife coffee drinking reduced risk of dementia and AD by 62–70% in people who drank 3–5 cups of coffee per day, compared to low coffee consumers (0–2 cups). Tea drinking was not associated with risk of dementia/AD.
- Lindsay et al. stated that coffee consumption correlated with 31% reduced risk of AD in 10,236 Canadian participants over the age of 65 years.
- Dong et al. in 2010-2014 that included a total of 2,513 participants aged 60 years or older. The authors observed no significant association between **decaffeinated** coffee intake and several aspects of cognitive performance.
- Ross et al. in 2000 looked at 8004 Japanese-American men (aged 45–68 years) drinking at least 28 ounces (421 mg of caffeine) of coffee, had 5-times lower risk of PD, and this risk decreased as coffee consumption increased.
- Liu et al. in 2012 examining 187,499 men and 130,761 women showed that higher caffeinated coffee consumption was associated with lower PD risk in a dose-dependent manner.
- Palacios et al. in 2012, showed that caffeine consumption decreased risk of PD more for men than for women.
- Lucas et al. in 2014, concluded that two cups of caffeinated coffee per day had 24% lower risk of depression than those who did not drink coffee.
- Richards and Smith found that the incidence of depression decreased as the dose of caffeine intake increased.
- Iranpour and Sabour, found that 4,737 adult women who consumed more caffeine had a lower risk of depression.

- Bertasi et al., showed that high caffeine intake is associated with higher levels of anxiety in a 2021 study of 114 college students.
- Botella et al. in 2021, examined 3,323 students (11–17 years old) and showed that the effect of caffeine on anxiety is significant mainly in boys and also dose related.

Digestive System

- Caffeine increases gastric acid secretion, relaxes smooth muscles, and stimulates the secretion of hydrochloric acid, causing higher risk of inflammation of the stomach.
- Caffeine can potentially improve liver tests such as alanine aminotransferase (ALT), aspartate aminotransferase (AST), γ-glutamyl-transferase (GGT) and bilirubin levels.
- **Coffee stimulates colonic motor activity. Its magnitude was similar to a meal.**
- Caffeine is inversely associated with the risk of cirrhosis, hepatocellular carcinoma, especially among people with the hepatitis C virus and other liver diseases. Modi et al. with 177 patients revealed an association between caffeine consumption and lower risk of liver fibrosis, especially in patients with HCV infection who drank two cups per day.

Caffeine and Digestive Tract Cancer

- A 2013 meta-analysis conducted by Li et al. consisting of 25 case-control and 16 cohort studies showed that the risk of **colorectal (colon and rectal)** cancer was reduced by 15% for the highest coffee drinkers compared to low or non-drinkers, and the authors concluded that the risk of **colon cancer (not rectal)** was reduced by 21%.

- Tian et al. in 2013, reported a significant decrease in the risk of colorectal and colon cancer among subjects consuming at least four cups of coffee a day.
- Bravi et al. in a meta-analysis showed that the risk of hepatocellular carcinoma was reduced by 40% for any coffee consumption versus no consumption.

Circulatory System

- Caffeine stimulates a modest increase in blood pressure (both systolic and diastolic). In volunteers who abstained from caffeine-containing products, a dose of 250 mg led to a 5–10% increase in both systolic and diastolic blood pressure for 1–3 hours. Tolerance to this effect developed, however, when caffeine was given three times a day for seven days.

Caffeine and Arrhythmia

- A 2021 meta-analysis of 22 studies conducted by Greenland showed that drinking at least five cups of coffee per day may enhance the risk of myocardial infraction or coronary death.

Urinary Tract

- Caffeine may increase urine production, and excessive caffeine intake (more than 400 mg/day) may increase the risk of detrusor instability (unstable bladder) in women.
- Jura et al. in 2011 conducted a prospective cohort study of 65,176 women (37–39 years old) without urinary incontinence. The authors associated risk for urgency incontinence with high caffeine intake and showed that this risk was higher in patients who consumed more than 450 mg of caffeine, and 25% of incident urgency incontinence may be attributable to caffeine consumption.
- In 2012, Hirayama et al. showed that caffeine was not associated with a higher risk of urinary incontinence in

a group of 683 men and 298 women (aged 40–75 years) from Japan.

The Association between Caffeine Consumption and All-Cause and Cause-Specific Mortality.

- In a 2019 meta-analysis conducted by Li et al., composed of 21 cohort studies, the consumption of caffeinated coffee was associated with decreased all-cause mortality. (Rodak, Kokot, & Kratz, 2021)

Caffeine

Caffeine can be sourced from

1. coffee beans
2. cacao beans (seeds from a small tropical evergreen tree, from which cocoa, cocoa butter, and chocolate are made)
3. kola nuts (African nut of Cola evergreen tree)
4. tea leaves
5. yerba mate (South American plant)
6. guarana berry (Brazilian plant whose seeds are high in caffeine).

- The FDA has approved caffeine in the treatment of apnea (diminished breathing) of prematurity and prevention and treatment of bronchopulmonary dysplasia (lung damage) in premature infants.
- Non-FDA approved uses include treating migraine headaches, post-spinal tap headaches and enhancing athletic performance, especially in endurance sports.
- Caffeine seems to increase systolic blood pressure by approximately 5 to 10 mmHg in individuals with infrequent use. However, there is little to no acute effect on habitual consumers. This is very good news to daily coffee drinkers.

Chapter 1: Caffeine Basics

- Caffeine increases renal blood flow, glomerular filtration, and sodium excretion, resulting in increased urination.
- Caffeine is a potent stimulator of gastric acid secretion and gastrointestinal (GI) motility (i.e. some people move their bowels like clockwork after morning coffee).
- Metabolism (breakdown) of caffeine primarily occurs in the liver via an enzyme system called the cytochrome P450 oxidase system, specifically enzyme CYP1A2.
- The half-life of caffeine is about five hours in the average adult (50% is gone after five hours).
- **Cigarette smoking decreases the effect of caffeine.**
- Caffeine is considered a pregnancy class C drug (Class C indicates inadequate studies performed; one has to look at benefit vs. risk). Many Class C drugs, such as diabetic and asthma medications, are taken by pregnant women. 60% of all medications are class C, making it confusing.
- Reports of severe intoxication are not very common since gastrointestinal upset and nausea usually occur first.

The American College of Obstetricians and Gynecologists considers 200 mg of caffeine daily to be safe during pregnancy. (Evans, Richards, & Battisti, 2021)

<u>**Coffee consumption and health: umbrella review of meta-analyses of multiple health outcomes**</u>

All-cause mortality

- Three cups a day lowered all-cause mortality risk by 17% compared with no consumption.
- High vs. low intake of <u>decaffeinated</u> coffee was also associated with lower all-cause mortality.

- We identified 16 unique outcomes for associations with decaffeinated coffee. Decaffeinated coffee was beneficially associated with all-cause and cardiovascular mortality with the largest benefit with two to four cups a day and of similar magnitude to caffeinated coffee.
- A 2017 large cohort study of 521,330 participants followed for a mean period of 16 years in 10 European countries revealed that the highest quarter of coffee consumption, when compared with no coffee consumption, was associated with a 12% lower risk of all-cause mortality in men and a 7% lower risk in women.
- A 2017 North American cohort of 185,855 participants were followed for a mean duration of 16 years. After adjustment for smoking and other factors, consumption of four or more cups of coffee a day had an 18% lower risk of mortality. Subgroups included African Americans, Japanese Americans, Latino, and white populations. Associations were also similar in men and women. Mortality from heart disease, cancer, chronic lower respiratory disease, stroke, diabetes, and kidney disease was also beneficially associated with coffee consumption.

Cardiovascular disease

- Coffee consumption was consistently associated with a 19% lower risk of mortality from all causes of cardiovascular disease, 16% lower risk of coronary heart disease, and 30% lower risk of stroke with estimates indicating largest reduction at three cups a day (2016).
- Increasing consumption to more than three cups a day was not associated with harm, but the beneficial effect was less pronounced.
- Women were protected from cardiovascular disease and coronary heart disease risk more than men with higher

levels of consumption. The benefit was less involving stroke risk.

- A 45% lower risk of mortality after myocardial infarction was found in high vs. low coffee consumption.
- A 2014 study revealed 15% lower risk of cardiovascular disease, 10% lower risk of coronary heart disease, and 20% lower risk of stroke, with the largest benefits from drinking three to five cups a day. There was no clear benefit with high vs. low decaffeinated consumption and cardiovascular disease (2014).
- A 2015 British study showed an 11% beneficial effect on stroke with coffee.
- A 2012 study found an 11% benefit with heart failure at four cups a day.

Cancer

- A 2011 meta-analysis of 40 cohort studies showed an 18% lower incidence of cancer for high vs. low coffee consumption, along with a 13% benefit for any coffee consumption vs. no consumption.
- For smokers, the risk of mortality from cancer increased at all levels of coffee exposure, reaching significance at more than four cups a day. In a 2016 meta-analysis, any coffee vs. no consumption in people who had never smoked was associated with an 8% lower risk of lung cancer.
- A 2009 meta-analysis of two studies showed that high vs. low consumption of decaffeinated coffee was associated with a lower risk of lung cancer.
- High vs. low coffee consumption was associated with a lower risk of prostate cancer, endometrial cancer, melanoma, oral cancer, leukemia, non-melanoma skin cancer, and liver cancer.

- For prostate, endometrial, melanoma, and liver cancer, there were also significant dose-response relations indicating benefit.
- No significant association was found between coffee consumption and gastric, colorectal, colon, rectal, ovarian, thyroid, breast, pancreatic, esophageal, or laryngeal cancers and lymphoma or glioma.

Liver and gastrointestinal outcomes

- In addition to beneficial associations with liver cancer, all categories of coffee exposure were associated with lower risk for a range of liver outcomes. Any consumption vs. no coffee consumption was associated with a 29% lower risk of non-alcoholic fatty liver disease, a 27% lower risk for liver fibrosis, and a 39% lower risk for liver cirrhosis.
- In a 2016 study, coffee consumption was associated with a 31% lower risk of cirrhosis with high vs. low consumption and exposure to one extra cup a day with a 26% lower risk of death from cirrhosis.
- Coffee consumption significantly decreased risk of gallstones.

Metabolic disease

- A 30% lower risk of type 2 diabetes was found for high vs. low consumption. The risk was still lower for each dose between one and six cups. Decaffeinated coffee had similar associations of comparable magnitude.
- For metabolic syndrome high vs. low coffee consumption was associated with 9% lower risk.
- High vs. low consumption was significantly associated with a lower risk of renal stones and gout.

Neurological outcomes

- Coffee consumption was consistently associated with a lower risk of Parkinson's disease.

- Decaffeinated coffee was associated with a lower risk of Parkinson's disease but did not reach statistical significance.
- 27% lower risk of depression and cognitive disorders, especially for Alzheimer's disease with caffeinated coffee.

Antenatal exposure to coffee

- High vs. low consumption was associated with a 31% higher risk of low birth weight, 46% higher risk of pregnancy loss, 22% first trimester preterm birth, and 12% second trimester preterm birth.
- No significant association was found for third trimester preterm birth, neural tube defects, and congenital malformations.
- High vs. low coffee consumption and any consumption during pregnancy increased risk of childhood leukemia.

Coffee consumption is more often associated with benefit than harm for a range of health outcomes across multiple measures of consumption, including high vs. low, any vs. none, and one extra cup a day. The benefit associated with coffee consumption was supported by lower risk for all-cause mortality, cardiovascular mortality, and total cancer.

Overall, there is no consistent evidence of harmful associations between coffee consumption and health outcomes, except for those related to pregnancy and for possible risk of fracture in women. (Poole, et al., 2017)

Systematic review of the potential adverse effects of caffeine consumption in healthy adults, pregnant women, adolescents, and children

- Caffeine consumption of less than 400 mg/day in adults is not associated with overt, adverse effects.

- Intakes of 300 mg/day or less in pregnant women and 2.5 mg/kg or less per day in children and adolescents remain acceptable. (Wikoff, et al., 2017)

Caffeine content of specialty coffees

We evaluated the caffeine content of caffeinated and decaffeinated coffee from coffee shops.

- The coffees sold as decaffeinated were found to have caffeine concentrations less than 17.7 mg/dose.
- There was a wide range in caffeine content in caffeinated coffees ranging from 58 to 259 mg/dose.
- The mean (SD) caffeine content of the brewed specialty coffees was 188 (36) mg for a 16-oz cup.
- A wide range of caffeine concentrations (259-564 mg/dose) in the same coffee beverage obtained from the same outlet on six consecutive days **was noted.** (McCusker, Goldberger, & Cone, Caffeine content of specialty coffees, 2003)

Caffeine content of decaffeinated coffee

Because of medications, medical conditions or caffeine sensitivity, some people need to restrict caffeine intake. In an effort to abstain from caffeine, patients may substitute decaffeinated for caffeinated coffee. Decaffeinated beverages are known to contain caffeine in varying amounts. The FDA requires that 97% of the caffeine content be removed to be called decaffeinated.

- **The present study determined the caffeine content in a variety of decaffeinated coffee drinks.**
- In phase 1 of the study, 10 decaffeinated samples were collected from different coffee establishments. In phase 2 of the study, Starbucks espresso decaffeinated (N=6) and Starbucks brewed decaffeinated coffee (N=6) samples were collected from the same outlet to evaluate variability of caffeine content of the same drink.

- The 10 decaffeinated coffee samples from different outlets contained caffeine in the range of 0-13.9 mg/16-oz serving.
- The caffeine content for the Starbucks espresso and the Starbucks brewed samples collected from the same outlet were 3.0-15.8 mg/shot and 12.0-13.4 mg/16-oz serving, respectively.

Patients that are very sensitive to caffeine effects should know that most decaffeinated coffee has some caffeine. (McCusker, Fuehrlein, Goldberger, Gold, & Cone, 2006)

The Effect of Coffee on Pharmacokinetic Properties of Drugs: Review

- Coffee can have a significant interaction with certain prescription and non-prescription drugs. There should be an appropriate time gap between the intake of drugs and coffee based on drug properties.
- Coffee inhibits vitamin D receptors which is important in the absorption of calcium in building bone; this results in an increased risk for osteoporosis.
- One study shows that women who consumed more than two cups of coffee per day had a 69% higher risk of fracture over the next 12 years compared to women who did not consume coffee and caffeinated beverages.
- Patients need to stop the use of coffee and other caffeine-rich products during coumadin therapy or drink consistent amounts daily so coumadin can be regulated accurately. (Belayneh & Molla, 2020)

Dietary Polyphenol Intake in US Adults and 10-Year Trends: 2007-2016

- Due to antioxidant, anti-inflammatory, anticancer, and antiviral properties of dietary polyphenols, research suggests that intake is protective against major chronic diseases.

- This study explored usual dietary polyphenol intake among 9,773 adults aged 20 years and older from 2007-2016 and 2013-2016.
- The usual intake of polyphenols did not change significantly from the two periods. Foods and beverages contributed 99.8% of polyphenol intake, with coffee (39.6%), beans (9.8%), and tea (7.6%) as major dietary contributors. (Huang, Braffett, Simmens, Young, & Ogden, 2020)

Chapter 2: Coffee/Caffeine and Exercise

Coffee/caffeine can promote greater achievements in performance or simply provide the initial stimulus to finally go to the gym. Both are admirable.

Caffeine and exercise: metabolism, endurance and performance

Caffeine is a powerful ergogenic aid at levels that are considerably lower than the acceptable limit of the International Olympic Committee and could be beneficial in training and competition. Caffeine does not improve maximal oxygen capacity directly but could permit the athlete to train at a greater power output and longer. Caffeine has also been shown to increase speed. These effects have been found in activities that last as little as 60 seconds or as long as two hours. The effects of caffeine on strength are unclear. Many studies suggest no effect on maximal ability, but better endurance and less fatigue. Caffeine ingestion before exercise does not lead to dehydration, electrolyte imbalance, or any other adverse effects. The ingestion of caffeine as coffee has inconsistent concentrations, making powder or tablets more practical. It appears that male and female athletes have similar caffeine pharmacokinetics. The limited information available suggests that caffeine non-users and users respond similarly and that withdrawal from caffeine may not be important. Caffeine may work, in part, by creating a more favorable environment in active muscle. (Graham, 2001)

Kudos to T E Graham, I could not have said it better.

Acute Effects of Caffeine Intake on Psychological Responses and High-Intensity Exercise Performance

- Cognitive function (mindset) plays an important role in athletic performance. It has been observed that caffeine supplementation leads to a more favorable mood profile, which positively influences exercise performance and reduces the rate of perceived exertion during exercise
- 15 male undergraduate students with weightlifting training experience participated. The study design was randomized, double-blind, placebo-controlled, cross-over. Caffeine intake was restricted 24 hours before the study onset.
- Acute caffeine supplementation has positive effects on several mood and psychological responses, along with performance. Caffeine supplementation reduces the rating of perceived exertion. These responses favor an optimal psychological state. (Domínguez, et al., 2021)

Caffeinated Drinks and Physical Performance in Sport: A Systematic Review

- Caffeine shows well-supported ergogenic properties in a multitude of exercises.
- caffeine is a socially accepted drug recently endorsed by the International Olympic Committee.
- Moderate doses of caffeine (3–6 mg/kg) produce benefits to physical performance with low side effects.

Chapter 2: Coffee/Caffeine and Exercise

Systematic review of 37 articles published from January 2000 to August 2020

34 studies with 692 participants (416 males, 208 females, and 68 undetermined), with an age range from 12 to 45 years old. Studies involved multiple sports.

1. Caffeinated drinks improve performance.
2. Effectiveness may be reduced in players with habituation to caffeine.
3. It may be recommended to reduce the daily consumption of caffeine days before an event to maximize the acute benefit of caffeine intake.
4. Similar benefits in men and women athletes.

(Jiménez, Díaz-Lara, Pareja-Galeano, & Del Coso, 2021)

Exploring the minimum ergogenic dose of caffeine on resistance exercise performance: A meta-analytic approach

- Explore the minimum ergogenic dose of caffeine on resistance exercise.
- Twelve studies with caffeine supplementation from 0.9 to 2 mg/kg.

These findings highlight that the minimal ergogenic doses of caffeine are even lower than previously suggested. Such doses of caffeine can be consumed through a regular diet, because for most individuals, a dose of approximately 1 to 2 mg/kg is equivalent to a dose of caffeine in one to two cups of coffee (Grgic, 2022)

International society of sports nutrition position stand: caffeine and performance (2010)

- Caffeine enhances performance in trained athletes in low-to-moderate dosages (~3-6 mg/kg) (two to four cups) and does not enhance further performance at higher dosages (greater or equal to 9 mg/kg).

- Caffeine exerts a greater ergogenic effect when consumed in an anhydrous state (powder) as compared to coffee.
- Caffeine can enhance vigilance during bouts of extended exhaustive exercise, as well as periods of sustained sleep deprivation.
- The literature is equivocal on strength-power performance with caffeine supplementation.
- The scientific literature does not support caffeine-induced diuresis during exercise. (Goldstein, et al., 2010)

International society of sports nutrition position stand: caffeine and exercise performance (2021)

Caffeine legality in sport

- The International Olympic Committee and World Anti-Doping Agency removed the classification of caffeine as a "controlled" substance in 2004. Caffeine is still monitored by WADA, and athletes are encouraged to maintain a urine caffeine concentration of less than the limit of 12 μg/ml, which corresponds to 10 mg/kg body mass. This is more than triple the intake reported to enhance performance.
- Caffeine is a banned substance by the National Collegiate Athletic Association if urinary caffeine concentration exceeds 15 μg/ml.

Mechanism of action

- **Caffeine is believed to exert its effects on the central nervous system via the antagonism of adenosine receptors, leading to increases in neurotransmitter release, motor unit firing rates, and pain suppression. There are four distinct adenosine receptors, A_1, A_{2A}, A_{2B} and A_3. A_1 and A_{2A}, which are highly concentrated in the brain, appear to be the main targets of caffeine.**

Chapter 2: Coffee/Caffeine and Exercise

- **The major known effects of adenosine are to decrease the concentration of many central nervous system neurotransmitters, including serotonin, dopamine, acetylcholine, norepinephrine and glutamate. Caffeine, which has a similar molecular structure to adenosine, binds to adenosine receptors after ingestion and therefore increases the concentration of these neurotransmitters. This results in positive effects on mood, vigilance, focus, and alertness in most, but not all, individuals.**
- **The attenuation of pain during exercise from caffeine supplementation may result in a decrease in the rating of perceived exertion (how hard you feel your body is working during exercise).**
- A meta-analysis identified 21 studies using 74% males between 20-35 years-old showed a 5.6% reduction in rating of perceived exertion during exercise following caffeine ingestion. An average improvement in performance of 11% was reported across all exercise modalities.

Caffeine and endurance exercise

- **Caffeine has consistently been shown to improve endurance by 2% to 4% across dozens of studies using doses of 3–6 mg/kg body mass.**
- Caffeine has been shown to be of benefit in cycling, running, cross-country skiing, and swimming.

Caffeine and sport-specific performance

- **Basketball**: Increased jump height, but only in those with fast metabolizer version of the CYP1A2 gene, increased number of free throws attempted and free throws made, increased number of total and offensive rebounds.
- **Soccer:** Increased total distance covered during the match, increased passing accuracy, and jumping height,

but did not enhance performance in the "T test" (very reliable agility and speed test) in female soccer players, did not improve match play in young soccer players.

- **Volleyball**: Increased number of successful actions and decreased imprecise actions, did not improve performance in multiple sport-specific tests in professional females, nor performance in competition.
- **Football**: Did not improve performance for anaerobic exercise tests at the NFL Combine.
- **Rugby**: Increased the number of body impacts, running pace, and muscle power during jumping, but did not impact agility.
- **Field hockey:** Increased high-intensity running and sprinting, and may offset decrements in skilled performance associated with fatigue.
- **Ice hockey**: Has limited impact on sport-specific skill performance and rating of perceived exertion, but may enhance physicality during scrimmage.
- **Combat sports**: Increased number of offensive actions and throws.
- **Cross-country skiing**: Reduced time to complete a set distance and improved time to task failure.

In summary, although reviews of the literature show that caffeine ingestion is, *on average*, helpful for a wide range of sport-specific tasks, its use might not be appropriate for every athlete. Athletes should gauge their physical response to caffeine during practice, and competitions along with mood and sleep patterns.

Genetics

- More than 95% of caffeine is metabolized by the CYP1A2 enzyme, which is used to categorize individuals as fast, slow, or normal metabolizers.
- Individuals with the slow metabolizer genotype have an elevated risk of myocardial infarction, hypertension and elevated blood pressure, and pre-diabetes, with increasing caffeinated coffee consumption, whereas

those with the fast metabolizer genotype show no such risk.

- The ADORA2A gene (ADenOsine Receptor A2A) is another genetic modifier of the effects of caffeine.
- It can contribute to increased anxiety after caffeine ingestion.
- In elite athletes, 50% face mental health issues sometime during their career. Caffeine is not for everyone.

Training status

- Trained and untrained individuals experience similar improvements in performance following caffeine ingestion.

Caffeine and cognitive performance

- Lieberman et al. examined the effects of caffeine on cognitive performance during sleep deprivation in U.S. Navy SEALs. Caffeine doses of 100 mg, 200 mg, or 300 mg, were used with results significant in both the 200 and 300 mg caffeine doses.
- Multiple studies demonstrate the effects of caffeine on vigilance and reaction time in a sleep-deprived state.
- It is unlikely that caffeine would be more effective than actually sleeping (you cannot "out-caffeinate" poor sleep).

Caffeinated chewing gum.

- Five studies in well-trained cyclists suggest that caffeine chewing gums may be beneficial.

Caffeine mouth rinsing

- The findings are equivocal.

Caffeinated nasal sprays and inspired powders

- Two separate trials showed no significant improvements.

Caffeine and carbohydrate

- **A 2011 systematic review and meta-analysis of 21 investigations concluded the co-ingestion of**

carbohydrate and caffeine significantly improved endurance performance when compared to carbohydrate alone.

Caffeine within brewed coffee

- There is difficulty standardizing caffeine content in brewed coffee. (Guest, International society of sports nutrition position stand: caffeine and exercise performance, 2021)

<u>Wake up and smell the coffee: caffeine supplementation and exercise performance-an umbrella review of 21 published meta-analyses</u>

Ergogenic effects of caffeine on muscle endurance, muscle strength, anaerobic power and aerobic endurance were substantiated by moderate quality of evidence coming from moderate-to-high quality systematic reviews. The magnitude of the effect of caffeine is generally greater for aerobic as compared with anaerobic exercise. (Grgic, et al., 2020)

<u>Effects of Different Doses of Caffeinated Coffee on Muscular Endurance, Cognitive Performance, and Cardiac Autonomic Modulation in Caffeine Naive Female Athletes</u>

Seventeen elite resistance-trained female team sport athletes, non-caffeine consumers, were studied.

- The ingestion of both 3mg/kg and 6mg/kg (three to four cups of coffee) increased lower body muscular endurance and cognitive performance with no harmful effects.
- 6mg/kg caffeinated coffee reduced muscle pain perception. (Karayigit, et al., 2021)

<u>Caffeine and Exercise: What Next?</u>

Chapter 2: Coffee/Caffeine and Exercise

- Several meta-analyses examining caffeine effects on a broad array of exercise tests showed performance enhancements from 16% to 51%.
- Caffeine exerts acute cognitive benefits, especially in sleep-deprived subjects. This has been explored in military personnel, athletes, and the general public.
- General caffeine guidelines recommend the consumption of 3-6 mg/kg of caffeine, typically 60 minutes before the start of exercise.
- Caffeine ingestion can impair the ability both to fall asleep and to achieve high-quality sleep.
- Drake and colleagues reported that 400 mg of caffeine, ingested six hours prior to bedtime, disrupted several aspects of sleep.
- The downstream metabolites of caffeine may have additional ergogenic effects.
- Because caffeine is a vasoconstrictor, slow metabolizers might experience prolonged vasoconstriction, harming endurance performance.
- Caffeine lessens the negative effects of jet lag on performance and sleepiness.
- Several studies show the effects of caffeine to be similar in both sexes.
- Bell and McLellan reported in 2003 that 5 mg/kg of caffeine enhanced performance, and this ergogenic effect was maintained in a second exercise bout performed six hours later (remember, caffeine lasts one to six hours).
- Hodgson et al. reported in 2013 that both caffeine and coffee at a dose of 5 mg/kg, were similarly efficacious in enhancing performance above placebo in a cycle ergometer test.
- Two 2016 studies compared the use of coffee and anhydrous (powder) caffeine for strength and sprint performance, reporting similar ergogenic effects.

- The use of coffee prior to competition may be problematic since caffeine concentrations vary between coffee blends and brands.
- Pasman et al. in 1995 used doses of 5, 9, and 13 mg/kg, and reported that all doses were equally effective in enhancing cycling performance.
- Graham and Spriet in 1995 compared the effects of 3, 6, and 9 mg/kg on performance, observing that only the two lower doses enhanced performance.
- Desbrow et al. in 2012 compared the effects of 3 vs. 6 mg/kg and reported that both doses enhanced aerobic endurance equally.
- Pallarés et al. reported that a dose of 9 mg/kg was ergogenic for high-load resistance exercise (90% of 1 RM), while doses of 3 and 6 mg/kg were not.
- Sabol et al. in 2019 found that caffeine doses of 2, 4 and 6 mg/kg were all effective in enhancing lower-body ballistic exercise performance; however, only a dose of 6 mg/kg enhanced upper-body ballistic exercise (ballistic-explosive movement like throwing a medicine ball).
- Tallis and Yavuz reported that 6 mg/kg of caffeine enhanced isokinetic (bikes, treadmills) force production, but (3 mg/kg) did not.
- Research has demonstrated that caffeine is effective in enhancing exercise performance in elderly adults.
- **A review by Shabir et al. reported a placebo effect of caffeine on performance in 13 out of 17 studies.**

(Pickering & Grgic, 2019)

Placebo Effect of Caffeine on Substrate Oxidation During Exercise

The purpose of this experiment was to investigate the placebo effect of caffeine on fat oxidation (breaking down fat into energy) during exercise in 12 young males in their twenties.

Experimental Design

- A deceptive, double-blind and crossover design was used. Each participant underwent three trials. In the two first trials participants ingested either 3 mg/kg of a placebo or 3 mg/kg of caffeine. In the third trial, participants ingested a placebo, but they were informed they had received 3 mg/kg of caffeine. Before the experiment, participants were informed about research related to acute effects of caffeine intake on fat oxidation rate. This was to create the belief that caffeine has a well-proven capacity to increase fat oxidation during exercise.
- There was no effect on resting heart rate or blood pressure.

Discussion

- Both trials increased the rate of fat oxidation over the placebo.
- This investigation indicates that the expectation of having received caffeine was equally effective as the actual administration of caffeine on fat oxidation during exercise.

The placebo effect has been associated with opioid, endocannabinoid, serotonin, and dopamine systems, while the most common view is that various neurotransmitter systems are in fact involved at the same time in the placebo effect. This especially applies to the placebo effect of caffeine, as the main effect of this substance on the brain is to block adenosine receptors, resulting in higher concentrations of serotonin, dopamine, and norepinephrine. (Gutiérrez-Hellín, et al., 2021)

<u>Dispelling the myth that habitual caffeine consumption influences the performance response to acute caffeine supplementation</u>

There has been a long-standing paradigm that habitual caffeine intake may influence the ergogenic of caffeine supplementation. This study investigates the influence of habitual caffeine intake on performance to acute caffeine supplementation.

- A double-blind, crossover, counterbalanced study was performed. Forty male endurance-trained cyclists were divided into three groups, according to their daily caffeine intake: low (58 mg/d), moderate (143 mg/d), and high (351 mg/d). Cyclists completed three trials after ingestion of: 6 mg/kg caffeine, placebo, and no supplement.

Low, moderate, and high caffeine consumers showed similar absolute and relative improvements in cycling time-trial performance following acute supplementation of 6 mg/kg caffeine. (Gonçalves, et al., 2017)

Challenging the Myth of Non-Response to the Ergogenic Effects of Caffeine Ingestion on Exercise Performance

- The extent of the ergogenic response to acute caffeine ingestion might greatly vary among individuals. The existence of non-responders has been reported in several previous investigations.

The ergogenic effect of acute caffeine intake (3 mg/kg) was measured eight times over a placebo in the same individuals and under the same conditions by an incremental cycling test to fatigue. The ergogenic response to caffeine varied from 9% to 1% among individuals, but all participants increased cycling power at least three to eight times out of eight.

This data shows that all individuals responded to caffeine when caffeine was compared to a placebo on multiple and repeated testing sessions. (Del Coso, Lara, Ruiz-Moreno, & Salinero, 2019)

Chapter 2: Coffee/Caffeine and Exercise

This article reminds me of the Winter Olympics in 1980 when the USA hockey team upset greatly favored Russia. The coach, Herb Brooks, said in the movie "*Miracle on Ice,*" "*If we played Russia 10 times, they may beat us nine times, but not this time.*"

<u>**Caffeine Increases Work Done Above Critical Power, but Not Anaerobic Work**</u>

We investigated whether caffeine ingestion could increase total work done.

- Nine men (age 26.6 ± 5.3 yr) cycled until exhaustion at different exercise intensities on different days after ingesting either caffeine (5 mg/kg) or a placebo.
- Time to exhaustion was 34% longer with caffeine compared with placebo; this was accompanied by greater work done. Caffeine was associated with a higher tolerance to maintain exercise at maximal rate. (Silveira, et al., 2018)

Athletes get anxious about whether they will be able to push themselves hard during an event; caffeine may provide a higher probability of achieving that goal. Athletes or anyone who has an important event worries whether he or she will perform well. Caffeine may help with focus or drive to allow the person to better achieve the goal.

<u>**Caffeine withdrawal and high-intensity endurance cycling performance**</u>

Twelve well-trained male cyclists, who were caffeine consumers, participated in a double-blind placebo-controlled cross-over design with four experimental trials. Caffeine dose was 3 mg/kg/day.

- Average heart rate throughout exercise was significantly higher following acute caffeine administration compared with placebo.

A 3 mg/kg dose of caffeine significantly improved exercise performance irrespective of whether a four-day withdrawal period was imposed on habitual caffeine users. (Irwin, et al., 2011)

The effects of different doses of caffeine on endurance cycling time trial performance

Sixteen well-trained male cyclists were studied using a randomized, placebo-controlled, double-blind crossover design.

- Exercise performance was significantly improved with both caffeine treatments compared to placebo (4.2% improvement with 3 mg/kg and 2.9% with 6 mg/kg).

A caffeine dose of 3 mg/kg appears to improve cycling performance in well-trained cyclists.
Doubling the dose to 6 mg/kg body mass does not confer any additional improvements in performance (6 mg/kg was still better than placebo). (Desbrow, et al., 2012)

The metabolic and performance effects of caffeine compared to coffee during endurance exercise

Eight trained male cyclists/triathletes (mean age 41 yrs.) took part in a single-blind, crossover, randomized study, completing a 45-minute target time trial.

- One hour prior to exercise, each athlete consumed drinks with caffeine (5 mg/kg), instant coffee (5 mg/kg), instant decaffeinated coffee or a placebo.

Significantly faster performance times (about 5%) were similar for both caffeine and coffee compared to decaf and placebo. This provides evidence that the caffeine in coffee, and not the other components in coffee, improves performance. (Hodgson, Randell, & Jeukendrup, 2013)

Chapter 2: Coffee/Caffeine and Exercise

Effects of caffeine supplementation on physical performance and mood dimensions in elite and trained-recreational athletes

Eighteen men were enrolled. Eight were elite athletes of the Spanish national senior male boxing team. The remaining 10 subjects were undergraduate recreational athletes.

- Study design was crossover, randomized, double-blind, placebo-controlled. Half of the athletes were randomly assigned to caffeine (6 mg/kg) or placebo.
- Caffeine seems to modify the rating of perceived exertion, reducing the rating for a given load.
- Supplementation with 6 mg/kg of caffeine improved performance.
- Caffeine supplementation led to considerable improvements in factors contributing to mood state such as tension, vigor and vitality perception, but only in the elite athletes. (Jodra, et al., 2020)

The effects of different doses of caffeine on maximal strength and strength-endurance in women habituated to caffeine

Twenty-one healthy, resistance-trained female students (age 23.0), with a daily caffeine intake of 5.8 ± 2.6 mg/kg (about three cups) participated in a randomized, crossover, double-blind design.

- Each participant performed three experimental sessions after ingesting either a placebo, 3 mg/kg, or 6 mg/kg of caffeine. In each experimental session, the participants underwent a 1RM (one maximum repetition) test and a maximum repetition test at 50% 1RM in the bench press exercise.
- Both caffeine doses significantly improved 1RM compared to placebo.
- The 6 mg/kg dose significantly improved 1RM compared to 3 mg/kg.

An acute dose of 3 mg/kg and 6 mg/kg of caffeine improves maximum strength but not maximum number of repetitions in young female lifters who are daily moderate coffee drinkers. (Filip-Stachnik, et al., 2021)

Coffee Ingestion Improves 5 km Cycling Performance in Men and Women by a Similar Magnitude

A total of 38 participants (19 men, 19 women) completed a 5 km time trial following the ingestion of coffee providing 3 mg/kg- of caffeine, or placebo.

- Coffee ingestion significantly increased salivary caffeine levels and significantly improved 5 km time trial performance in men and women by a similar magnitude. Checking caffeine levels provided more evidence that caffeine promoted performance. (Clarke, Kirwan, & Richardson, 2019)

Caffeine intake and its effect on the maximal aerobic speed corridors 800 -meter athletes

Study evaluated the effects of caffeine intake (3 mg/kg) on time to exhaustion and blood lactate levels in 800-meter runners.

- Crossover, randomized blind study involved seven (20 ± 3 years), elite 800-meter runners. They conducted a test to exhaustion on a treadmill where they ingested a capsule with either caffeine (3 mg/kg) or placebo.

Caffeine intake showed a significant increase in time to exhaustion relative to placebo. Regarding the blood lactate, no significant differences were noted. Lactate levels were drawn to see whether different efforts were present between runners. (Rosales Soto, Monsálves Álvarez, Yáñez Sepúlveda, & Durán Agüero, 2015)

Chapter 2: Coffee/Caffeine and Exercise

The Effects of Pre-exercise Caffeinated Coffee Ingestion on Endurance Performance: An Evidence-Based Review

- Significant improvements in endurance performance were observed in five of nine studies, which were on average 24.2% better over controls for time to exhaustion trials, and 3.1% for time to completion trials.
- Three of six studies found that coffee reduced perceived exertion significantly more than control conditions.

Moderate evidence supported the use of coffee to improve performance in endurance cycling and running.
Coffee providing 3.0-8.1 mg/kg of caffeine may be used as a safe alternative to anhydrous caffeine (powder) to improve endurance performance. (Higgins, Straight, & Lewis, 2016)

Coffee Ingestion Enhances 1-Mile Running Race Performance

Double-blind, randomized, cross-over, and placebo-controlled design, 13 trained male runners completed a 1-mile race 60 minutes following the ingestion of 9 mg/kg coffee, 9 mg/kg decaffeinated coffee, or a placebo.

- 1-mile race performance was enhanced by 1.9% and 1.3% compared with placebo and decaffeinated coffee, respectively. (Clarke, Richardson, Thie, & Taylor, 2018)

In 2010, I missed qualifying for the Boston Marathon by 2 seconds while running it. Qualifying for Boston at Boston is hard because the course is not fast because of all the hills. One percent can mean a lot. I suspect several dozen runners were just like me in missing the time by a few

seconds. Improving my marathon time by 1% is essentially 2 minutes, and that is significant.

<u>The Effect of Acute Caffeine Ingestion on Endurance Performance: A Systematic Review and Meta-Analysis</u>

A systematic review of 46 randomized placebo-controlled studies investigating the effects of caffeine on endurance performance.

- Caffeine has a small effect on endurance performance when taken in moderate doses (3-6 mg/kg) as well as on overall improvement in mean power output (3.03%) and time-trial completion time (2.22%).

Differences in responses to caffeine ingestion have been shown, with two studies reporting slower time-trial performance, while five studies reported lower mean power output during the time trial. (Southward, Rutherfurd-Markwick, & Ali, 2018)

<u>Effect of caffeine on sport-specific endurance performance: a systematic review</u>

21 studies examining time-trial endurance (>5 minutes) performance.

- The mean improvement in performance with caffeine ingestion was 3.2 +/- 4.3%; however, this improvement was highly variable between studies (-0.3 to 17.3%).

Caffeine ingestion can be an effective performance aid for endurance athletes when taken before and/or during exercise in moderate quantities (3-6 mg/kg body mass). (Ganio, Klau, Casa, Armstrong, & Maresh, 2009)

<u>Caffeine's Effects on an Upper-Body Resistance Exercise Workout</u>

Examine the effects of caffeine on an upper-body resistance exercise workout. Fifteen men (mean age, 23.1, weight 196 lbs.) were studied.

- Visit 1: 1-repetition maximum for bench press, incline bench press, and dumbbell bench press exercises.
- Visit 2: Subjects consumed either 800-mg caffeine or a placebo. Subjects then completed three sets to failure of each exercise using 80% of their 1RM.
- Visit 3 was the same as visit 2; however, participants consumed the opposite treatment as visit 2.
- Participants completed significantly more repetitions per set for the bench press (4.80 vs 4.42) and incline bench press (4.91 vs 4.36) in the caffeine condition compared with the placebo condition.
- Higher arousal and vigor scores were found in the caffeine condition.

Results suggest that caffeine has an ergogenic effect on strength performance and workout perception. Ingesting 800 mg caffeine is about six to seven cups of coffee, a relatively high amount of caffeine (about 11.4 mg/kg). The subjects tolerated relatively high-dose caffeine without any undesirable side effects. (Salatto, Arevalo, Brown, Wiersma, & Coburn, 2020)

<u>The effect of caffeine ingestion on functional performance in older adults</u>

The study evaluated the effect of acute caffeine ingestion on functional performance, manual dexterity and readiness to exert effort in older adults.

- A total of 19 healthy volunteers (10 females and 9 males aged 61-79 years) performed tests of functional fitness and manual dexterity following ingestion of caffeine (3mg/kg) or placebo in a randomized order.

Acute caffeine ingestion was shown to positively enhance functional performance, manual dexterity and readiness to exert effort in healthy older adults (61-79 years). (Duncan, Clarke, Tallis, Guimarães-Ferreira, & Leddington Wright, 2014)

<u>**Caffeine consumption around an exercise bout: effects on energy expenditure, energy intake, and exercise enjoyment**</u>

The study evaluated whether combining exercise and caffeine supplementation was more effective for weight loss.

- Fourteen recreationally active participants (mean BMI: 22.7) completed a resting control trial, a placebo exercise trial, and a caffeine exercise trial (3 mg/kg of caffeine 90 minutes before and 30 minutes after exercise) in a randomized, double-blinded design.
- Trials were four hours in duration with an hour of rest, an hour of cycling at ~65% maximum and a two-hour recovery.

Exercise and caffeine (3 mg/kg) resulted in significantly greater calorie burning than exercise alone and also led to exercise being perceived as less difficult and more enjoyable. (Schubert, et al., 2014)

Caffeine can help weight loss by increasing the calories burned with exercise and also promote the perception that exercise is easier. People will clearly exercise more often if they find it enjoyable. Helping people lose weight has been a part of my practice for over eight years, and my overwhelming perception is how much patients despise exercise. Any tool to improve that roadblock is very productive.

<u>**Dose-dependent effect of caffeine supplementation on judo-specific performance and training activity: a randomized placebo-controlled crossover trial**</u>

Pre-exercise supplementation with caffeine (3, 6, or 9 mg/kg) and placebo in 22 highly trained male judoists was examined. The group was divided into caffeine consumers (160 mg/day) or non-consumers (less than 160 mg/day).

- The study protocol involved five separate testing sessions using the Special Judo Fitness Test, three judo sparring combats and rate of perceived exertion.
- Six and 9 mg/kg caffeine doses improved performance, while 9 mg/kg increased combat activity.
- The 3 mg/kg caffeine dose did not have any positive effect.
- The ergogenic effect of caffeine is not only dose-dependent but also related to customary caffeine-consumption.
- Among caffeine non-consumers, 6 mg/kg caffeine was equally efficient to 9 mg/kg in enhancing performance, while in habitual caffeine consumers, only 9 mg/kg was more effective. (Durkalec-Michalski, Nowaczyk, Główka, & Grygiel, 2019)

I learned a new word. A judoist is a person who does judo. Take that to your spelling bee.

Coffee Increases Post-Exercise Muscle Glycogen Recovery in Endurance Athletes: A Randomized Clinical Trial

Glucose is the primary energy source for exercise. Glucose is released when needed and converted to glycogen when not needed. Because muscle glycogen stores do not completely recover after a few hours of exercise, it is important that athletes maximize their glycogen re-synthesis rate. An example of glycogen depletion occurs when a marathon runner develops fatigue and loss of energy and "*hits the wall*".

- This study was a randomized, double-blind, crossover clinical trial with 14 healthy endurance-trained adult men, cyclists (*n* = 11) and triathletes (*n* = 3).
- The total caffeine provided with the three doses of coffee + milk treatment was 8 mg/kg.

- They were all regular coffee consumers with caffeine intake of 296 ± 111 mg. per day.
- The consumption of coffee with sweetened milk improved the muscle glycogen re-synthesis during the 4-h recovery period when compared to the consumption of sweetened milk. The improvement did not meet statistical significance with a P value of 0.22. This equals a 22% chance that these findings were random.
- Although it did not meet statistical significance, this is probably an effective strategy to improve muscle glycogen recovery.
- These findings add to the current knowledge on the ergogenic properties of coffee (Loureiro, et al., 2021)

Clinically, I have always thought that chocolate milk was the perfect recovery drink. Now, I will add some coffee to it.

Effect of Caffeine on Golf Performance and Fatigue during a Competitive Tournament

Twelve male golfers (34.8 ± 13.9 yr.) with a U.S. Golf Association handicap of 3-10 participated in a double-blind, placebo-controlled, crossover design in which they played a 36-hole tournament and were randomly assigned a caffeine-containing supplement or placebo.

- Caffeine or placebo was consumed before and after nine holes during each 18-hole round.
- Total score (76.9 vs 79.4), greens in regulation (8.6 vs 6.9), and drive distance (239.9 yards vs 233.2) were statistically better with caffeine than placebo.
- Golfers reported more energy ($P = 0.025$) and less fatigue ($P = 0.05$) with caffeine and no substantial difference in heart or breathing rate, peak trunk acceleration, or putting posture ($P > 0.05$).

> A low-moderate dose (1.9 ± 0.3 mg/kg) (about two cups) of caffeine consumed before and during a round of golf improves golf-specific measures of performance and reduces fatigue in skilled golfers. (Mumford, et al., 2016)

Despite being a fan of the movie "Caddyshack" with Rodney Dangerfield, all the coffee in the world could not motivate me to wear those ridiculous plaid golf pants some people wear when they play. Rodney Dangerfield died in 2004. Everyone knows his catchphrase: "*I don't get no respect.*" But I like his line: *"My wife and I were happy for 20 years. Then we met."*

Women Experience the Same Ergogenic Response to Caffeine as Men

This study aimed to determine whether 1) consumption of caffeine improves performance in women and 2) do gender differences exist in response.

- Twenty-seven endurance-trained cyclists and triathletes (11 women and 16 men) participated in this randomized, double-blind, placebo-controlled, crossover study. Ninety minutes before the trials, participants ingested either 3 mg/kg of anhydrous caffeine or a placebo.
- Performance improvement was similar for women (mean 4.3%) and men (mean 4.6%). Plasma caffeine concentrations were similar between sexes before exercise, but significantly greater in women after exercise ($P < 0.001$).

Ingestion of 3 mg/kg of caffeine significantly enhanced endurance exercise performance in women similar to that of men. The current recommendations for caffeine intake, derived almost exclusively from studies with men, may also be applicable to women. (Skinner, et al., 2019)

Chronic ingestion of a low dose of caffeine induces tolerance to the performance benefits of caffeine

This study examined four weeks of caffeine supplementation on endurance performance.

- Eighteen low-habitual caffeine consumers (<75 mg/day) were randomly assigned to ingest caffeine (1.5-3.0 mg/kg/day; titrated) or a placebo for 28 days. Trials consisted of 60 minutes of cycle exercise at 60% max followed by a 30-minute performance task.

People with chronic low dose caffeine usage develop tolerance. Therefore, individuals with low habitual intake should refrain from caffeine supplementation temporarily to maximize performance benefits from acute caffeine ingestion. (Beaumont, et al., 2017)

Effects of caffeine on inspiratory muscle function

Fifteen (eight males, seven females) healthy adults participated in a double-blind, placebo-controlled, crossover design.

- During the initial visit, participants were familiarized with inspiratory muscle measurements. For the second and third visits, participants ingested either a 5 mg/kg dose of caffeine or placebo capsule.
- After one hour, they completed at least 12 maximal inspiratory maneuvers.

Caffeine ingestion significantly increased short-term inspiratory muscle function. (Nicks & Martin, 2020)

Effects of Caffeine on Performance During High- and Long-Jump Competitions

Using a crossover, double-blind design, six well-trained high jumpers and six well-trained long jumpers performed a simulation of a high jump and long jump competition 60 minutes after ingesting a capsule containing either 5 mg/kg of caffeine or a placebo. The velocity during the approach run of the long jump was also monitored using photocells.

- Caffeine improved high jump performance by 5.1% (P = .008).
- Caffeine had no effect on long jump distance but increased the velocity during the last 10 meters of the long jump, and the percentage of "foul jumps" was higher. (Santos-Mariano, et al., 2021)

The jumpers who had more fouls probably experienced the old cliché' "*a little too much caffeine.*"

Effect of Carbohydrate and Caffeine Ingestion on Badminton Performance

Investigate the effect of ingesting carbohydrate and caffeine solutions on measures that are central to success in badminton. Twelve male badminton players were recruited. Participants consumed either:

- 7 mL/kg body mass of water (Placebo)
- 6.4% carbohydrate solution (CHO)
- a solution containing a caffeine dose of 4 mg/kg
- 6.4% carbohydrate and 4 mg/kg caffeine (C+C).

The ingestion of a caffeinated carbohydrate solution before and during a badminton match significantly improved performance. (Clarke & Duncan, 2016)

Badminton is the fastest racket sport in the world.
The fastest shuttlecock speed was 206 mph.
Jai Alai ball has been clocked at 188 mph.
Tennis ball can go about 163 mph.
Baseball about 105 mph.

Effects of acute caffeine ingestion on resistance training performance and perceptual responses during repeated sets to failure

Fourteen moderately resistance-trained men (20.9 years, 171 pounds) ingested a dose of caffeine (5 mg/kg) or placebo prior to three sets of bench press and three sets of leg press exercises.

- Caffeine ingestion resulted in a significant increased number of repetitions in bench press and leg press compared to placebo.
- The sum of repetitions performed in the three sets was 11.6% higher in bench press and 19.1% in leg press. (Da Silva, et al., 2015)

Caffeine and Exercise Performance: Possible Directions for Definitive Findings

- Higher doses of caffeine (above 6 mg/kg) are associated with strength and power performance improvement when compared to moderate doses
- Dodd et al. in 1991 were the first to show the effects of caffeine tolerance on humans. The performance effect of 3-5 mg/kg of caffeine was negated by heavy habitual caffeine users.
- Beaumont et al. also evidenced this tolerance to caffeine habituation in aerobic performance.
- A contrary study by Gonçalves et al. involved 40 male recreational cyclists, 14 low caffeine consumers (±58 mg/day), 12 moderate consumers (±143 mg/day) and 14 heavy consumers (±351 mg/day). Caffeine supplementation (6 mg/kg) showed an improvement in performance regardless of usual caffeine consumption.
- Lara et al. investigated the chronic administration of caffeine (3 mg/kg) or placebo during 20 days in both a cycle ergometer test and 15-second Wingate test. The results showed that chronic caffeine consumption had an ergogenic effect, but after four days of continuous use of caffeine, the ergogenic effects had lessened compared to the initial performance tests.
- Alsene et al. in 2003 were the first to show that people can have different anxiolytic responses to caffeine due to different ADORA2A genotypes for adenosine

receptors. (Martins, Guilherme, Ferreira, de Souza-Junior, & Lancha, 2020)

The studies looking at whether chronic caffeine use limits the ergogenic effect of acute caffeine intake are equivocal.

Chapter 3: Coffee/Caffeine, Tea and Morbidity/Mortality

What's the world coming to when the expression "an apple a day keeps the doctor away" is stolen by dentists and they say "an apple a day keeps the dentist away" in advertisements?

A study in 2015 showed that apple eaters do better than non-apple eaters in needing less health care, but the result did not reach statistical significance. Apple eating is beneficial when it comes to prescription costs. Apple eaters show statistically significant lower yearly prescription needs per year of $228. How do you like those apples?

Drinking coffee/caffeine does a lot better than apples in regards to health.

<u>Health Effects of Coffee: Mechanism Unraveled?</u>

Coffee is evolving from a luxury stimulant drink to a health promoting beverage.

- Positive health outcomes include lower incidences of type 2 diabetes mellitus, kidney stones, Parkinson's disease, gout, liver fibrosis, non-alcoholic fatty liver disease, liver cirrhosis, liver cancer and chronic liver disease. This is the conclusion of an umbrella review of meta-analyses of multiple health outcomes, even after extensive correction for a large number of possible confounding factors, and also the result of the EPIC (European Prospective Investigation into Cancer and Nutrition Study) trial analyzing coffee consumption versus mortality.

- The lower risk of type 2 diabetes with habitual coffee consumption may be mediated by the polyphenols and other agents in coffee rather than caffeine since the benefits are present in decaffeinated coffee also.
- Beneficial effects of coffee probably employ the same pathway as "healthy" vegetables or fruits (polyphenols)

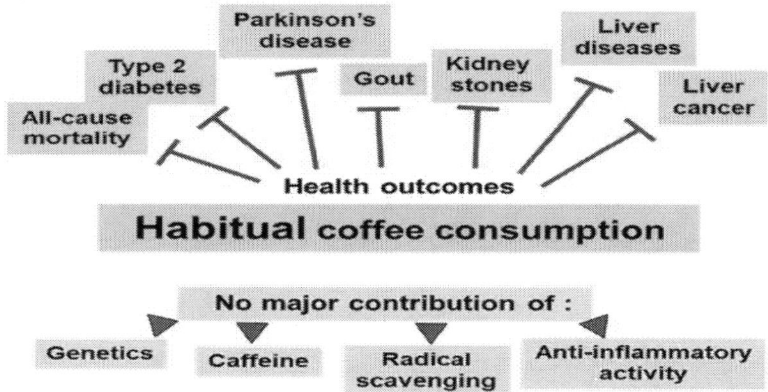

- Although radical scavenging by coffee components is still a quite common belief, the concentrations of coffee constituents are too low for efficient radical scavenging and therefore this contribution is small.
- Besides caffeine, the major constituents of coffee are of a phenolic nature. Phenolic acids are found in all food groups and they are abundant in fruits, vegetables, cereal grains, oilseeds, beverages and herbs. They exert antioxidant activity and are important compounds in cell signaling pathways. The health benefits of the groups are usually attributed to their phenolic compounds

Chapter 3: Coffee/Caffeine, Tea and Morbidity/Mortality

Coffee is entirely of plant origin. At present, there is no reason to assume that phenolic compounds of coffee are less "healthy" than comparable compounds. Coffee is the primary dietary source of phenolic acids and polyphenols. Coffee provides around 40% of polyphenols and around 70% of phenolic acids consumed.
There seems to be one uniform response of cells when exposed to phenolic agents. The cellular response is an increased expression of a large number of genes involved in antioxidative, detoxifying or repair mechanisms. (Kolb, Kempf, & Martin, Health Effects of Coffee: Mechanism Unraveled?, 2020)

Safety of coffee consumption after myocardial infarction: A systematic review and meta-analysis

Evaluate the impact of coffee consumption in patients with previous myocardial infarction (MI), in relation to all-cause and cardiovascular mortality, as well as other Major Adverse Cardiovascular_Events (MACE) such as stroke, heart failure, recurrent MI and sudden death.

- Literature search of six prospective cohort studies.

Consumption of coffee was associated with lower risk of cardiovascular mortality and was not associated with an increased risk of all-cause mortality, recurrent MI, stroke, and MACE. It is safe to drink coffee after having a heart attack. (Ribeiro, et al., 2020)

Coffee consumption after myocardial infarction and risk of cardiovascular mortality: a prospective analysis in the Alpha Omega Cohort

Examine caffeinated and decaffeinated coffee in relation to cardiovascular disease (CVD) mortality, ischemic heart disease (IHD) mortality, and all-cause mortality in patients with a prior myocardial infarction (MI).

- 4,365 Dutch patients who were aged 60-80 y (21% female) and had experienced an MI <10 y before study enrollment. At baseline (2002-2006), dietary data including coffee consumption was collected.

Median follow-up was 7.1 years. Most patients (96%) drank coffee, and the median total coffee intake was 375 mL/d (~3 cups/d).

Coffee consumption decreased CVD mortality
31% for >2-4 cups/d compared with 0-2 cups/d
28% for >4 cups/d compared with 0-2 cups/d.

Coffee consumption decreased IHD mortality (CAD)
23% for >2-4 cups/d compared with 0-2 cups/d
32% for >4 cups/d compared with 0-2 cups/d.

Coffee consumption decreased all-cause mortality
26% for >2-4 cups/d compared with 0-2 cups/d
18% for >4 cups/d compared with 0-2 cups/d

Similar associations were found for decaffeinated coffee and for coffee with additives.
Drinking coffee, either caffeinated or decaffeinated, may lower the risk of CVD and IHD mortality in patients with a prior MI. (van Dongen, Mölenberg, Soedamah-Muthu, Kromhout, & Geleijnse, 2017)

<u>**Coffee consumption and all-cause and cause-specific mortality: a meta-analysis by potential modifiers**</u>

Meta-analysis through March 8, 2019 of 40 studies including 3,852,651 subjects and 450,256 all-cause and cause-specific deaths.

- 3.5 cups/day decreased all-cause mortality by 15%.
- 2.5 cups/day decreased CVD mortality by 17%
- 2 cups/day decreased cancer mortality by 4%

- The inverse association was maintained irrespective of age, overweight status, alcohol drinking, smoking status, and caffeine content of coffee.
- Europe and Asia showed stronger inverse associations than US.

Moderate coffee consumption (e.g. 2-4 cups/day) was associated with reduced all-cause and cause-specific mortality, compared to no coffee consumption. (Kim, Je, & Giovannucci, 2019)

<u>Light to moderate coffee consumption is associated with lower risk of death: a UK Biobank study</u>

To study the association of daily coffee consumption with all-cause and cardiovascular (CV) mortality and major CV outcomes. A subgroup had cardiovascular magnetic resonance (CMR) imaging.

- 468,629 participants with median follow-up of 11 years.
- without clinically manifested heart disease at the time of recruitment.
- age (56.2 ± 8.1 years, 44.2% male).
- 22.1% did not consume coffee regularly.
- 58.4% had 0.5-3 cups per day (light-to-moderate).
- 19.5% had >3 cups per day (high).
- In analysis, we adjusted for CV risk factors.

Compared to non-coffee drinkers:

- light-to-moderate (0.5-3 cups per day) coffee drinking had 12% statistically significant lower risk of all-cause mortality.
- 17% statistically significant lower risk of CV mortality.
- 21% statistically significant lower risk of stroke.

30,650 had CMR imaging. Both coffee consuming categories had dose-dependent increased left and right ventricular end-diastolic, end-systolic and stroke volumes, and greater left ventricular mass.

Coffee consumption of up to three cups per day was associated with favorable CV outcomes and likely

healthy pattern of heart MRI imaging (Simon J, et al., 2022)

Associations of coffee drinking with physical performance in the oldest-old community-dwelling men The Helsinki Businessmen Study (HBS)

- We explored coffee consumption and physical performance among 126 independent men with mean age 87 years.
- Coffee consumption (around 2 cups) was positively associated with higher gait speed ($p = 0.003$), SPPB (Short Physical Performance Battery – timed 4-minute walk, repeated sit to stand chair test, and balance test) score ($p = 0.035$), and chair rise points ($p = 0.043$).

Higher coffee consumption was independently associated with statistically significant better physical performance in men with mean age 87 years. (Jyväkorpi, Urtamo, Kivimäki, & Strandberg, 2021)

Coffee Consumption and the Risk of All-Cause and Cause-Specific Mortality in the Korean Population

Examine coffee consumption and all-cause mortality and cause-specific mortality risks in the Korean population.

- Prospective cohort study had a median follow-up period of 9.1 years. 173,209 participants aged 40 years and older with 110,920 participants without diabetes, cardiovascular disease (CVD), or cancer.
- 1 to 3 cups/day had a 38% reduced risk of CVD mortality.

Coffee consumption is associated with a decreased risk of all-cause mortality and moderate coffee consumption (approximately 3 cups/day) is associated with a decreased risk of CVD mortality in a Korean population. (Kim, Tan, & Shin, 2021)

Chapter 3: Coffee/Caffeine, Tea and Morbidity/Mortality

Beverage habits and mortality in Chinese adults

This study examined the association between coffee, black and green tea, sugar-sweetened beverages (soft drinks and juice), and alcohol and all-cause and cause-specific mortality.

- A prospective data analysis with 52,584 Chinese men and women (aged 45-74 years) free of diabetes, cardiovascular disease, and cancer at baseline (1993-1998) and followed through 2011.
- Higher coffee and black tea intake decreased mortality in never-smokers.
- Light to moderate alcohol intake decreased mortality regardless of smoking status.
- Heavy alcohol intake was positively associated with mortality in ever-smokers.
- There was no association between sugar-sweetened beverages, green tea and mortality. (Odegaard, Koh, Yuan, & Pereira, 2015)

Caffeinated Coffee Consumption and Health Outcomes in the US Population: A Dose-Response Meta-Analysis and Estimation of Disease Cases and Deaths Avoided

We conducted a meta-analysis up to September 2019 of prospective studies investigating caffeinated coffee and incidence/mortality of cardiovascular disease, type 2 diabetes, hepatocellular carcinoma, endometrial cancer, melanoma, and nonmelanoma skin cancer. We selected diseases positively associated with coffee consumption. Twenty-six studies and 3,713,932 participants.

Coffee drinkers:

- 10% lower risk of cardiovascular disease
- 10% lower risk of type 2 diabetes
- 15% lower risk endometrial cancer

- 11% lower risk of melanoma
- 8% lower risk of nonmelanoma skin cancer
- 7% lower risk of hepatocellular carcinoma (not statistically significant)

The death risk decreased in all areas studied by 7% to 15% with increasing coffee consumption.
For cardiovascular disease, the largest risk reduction observed was with 3-4 cups/d (~120 mL/cup). (Di Maso, Boffetta, Negri, La Vecchia, & Bravi, 2021)
This study was a little atypical in that it did not tout the great benefits of coffee protecting against hepatocellular cancer.

<u>Association of Coffee Consumption with Overall and Cause-Specific Mortality in a Large US Prospective Cohort Study</u>

The PLCO (prostate, lung, colorectal, ovarian) Cancer Screening Trial enrolled 78,234 women and 76,704 men aged 55–74 years from 10 centers between 1993 and 2001.

- Significant inverse associations between coffee and death from heart disease, chronic lower respiratory diseases, diabetes, influenza and pneumonia, and intentional self-harm.
- Similar associations with caffeinated or decaffeinated coffee.
- No association between coffee and cancer mortality.

Nine years of follow-up may have been too short to assess cancer deaths. (Loftfield, et al., 2015)

<u>Association of Coffee Consumption with Total and Cause-Specific Mortality in Three Large Prospective Cohorts</u>

We examined consumption of total, caffeinated, and decaffeinated coffee with risk of total and cause-specific mortality among 74,890 women in the Nurses' Health

Study, 93,054 women in the Nurses' Health Study II, and 40,557 men in the Health Professionals Follow-up Study.

- Compared with nondrinkers, coffee consumption of one to five cups per day was associated with lower risk of mortality, whereas coffee consumption of more than five cups per day was not associated with improved mortality.
- Statistics are a little different when separating smokers from non-smokers. Removing smokers and comparing coffee drinkers to nondrinkers, mortality for coffee drinkers was
    - 1 or less cup per day (risk improved 6%).
    - 1.1 to 3.0 cups per day (risk improved 8%).
    - 3.1 to 5.0 cups per day (risk improved 15%).
    - more than 5.0 cups per day (risk improved 12%).
- Significant beneficial associations were observed for caffeinated and decaffeinated coffee.
- Significant inverse associations were found between coffee consumption and deaths from cardiovascular disease, neurologic diseases, and suicide.
- No significant association between coffee consumption and total cancer mortality was found. (Ding, et al., 2015)

Higher consumption of total coffee, caffeinated coffee, and decaffeinated coffee was associated with lower risk of total mortality.

Consumption of coffee and tea and risk of developing stroke, dementia, and poststroke dementia: A cohort study in the UK Biobank

Investigate the associations of coffee and tea separately and in combination with the risk of developing stroke, dementia, and poststroke dementia.

- prospective cohort study included 365,682 participants (50 to 74 years old). Participants joined the study from 2006 to 2010 and followed to 2020.
- coffee intake of 2 to 3 cups/d or tea intake of 3 to 5 cups/d or their combination intake of 4 to 6 cups/d were linked with the most protection against stroke and dementia.
- drinking 2 to 3 cups of coffee and 2 to 3 cups of tea per day was associated with a 32% lower risk of stroke and a 28% lower risk of dementia compared to non-drinkers.

Intake of coffee alone or in combination with tea was associated with lower risk of poststroke dementia. (Zhang, Yang, Li, Li, & Wang, 2021)

<u>Moderate coffee consumption is associated with lower risk of mortality in prior Acute Coronary Syndrome patients: a prospective analysis in the ERICO cohort</u>

This study examined the association between coffee consumption and all-cause mortality in patients with a prior acute myocardial infarction or unstable angina.

- 928 patients with Acute Coronary Syndrome (ACS) with 4 years' follow-up.
- Moderate coffee consumption (1-2 and 2-3 cups/day) had 13% and 22% lower rate of total mortality.
- After stratification by smoking status, the analysis revealed lower risk of mortality in never and former smokers, drinking 1-2 and 2-3 cups/day.

Among current smokers there was an unfavorable association between >3 cups/day and mortality (Miranda, Goulart, Lotufo, &Marchioni, 2021)

<u>Coffee Consumption and All-Cause, Cardiovascular, and Cancer Mortality in an Adult Mediterranean Population</u>

Chapter 3: Coffee/Caffeine, Tea and Morbidity/Mortality

Association between usual coffee consumption and all-cause, cardiovascular (CV), and cancer mortality over an 18-year period in 1,567 Spanish participants. Mean age in 40s.

- Compared with no-consumption, ≤1 cup per day had a 27% lower risk and >1 cup per day had a 44% lower risk of all-cause mortality.
- A 59% lower cancer mortality was observed with more than 1 cup per day compared with nondrinkers.
- Caffeinated coffee was associated with 34% and 41% lower all-cause mortality at 12 years and 18 years of follow-up respectively.
- Moderate consumption of coffee, particularly caffeinated coffee (range 1-6.5 cups per day), was associated with a lower all-cause and cancer mortality over an 18-year follow-up period.
- No significant association was found between coffee consumption and CV mortality (Torres-Collado, et al., 2021)

Coffee consumption and the risk of cerebrovascular disease: a meta-analysis of prospective cohort studies

We investigated the effect of coffee on stroke risk.

- Seven large-scale, long-term cohort studies of a healthy population.
- 8% reduction in the risk of overall stroke with coffee consumption.
- In studies with a clear definition of hemorrhagic and ischemic stroke, coffee consumption reduced the risk of ischemic stroke by 17% and hemorrhagic stroke by 10%. (Chan, Hong, & Bai, 2021)

FYI stroke can be separated into two subtypes: 80% ischemic (lack of blood flow), 20% hemorrhagic (head bleed).

Habitual coffee consumption and risk of falls in 2 European cohorts of older adults

Examine habitual coffee consumption and the risk of ≥1 fall, injurious falls, and falls with fracture in older people.

- 2,964 participants aged ≥60 years from Spain and 8,999 participants aged ≥60 y from the UK.
- In the Spain study, habitual coffee consumption was assessed in 2008-2010, and falls were ascertained up to 2015.
- In the UK study, coffee was measured with food records starting in 2006, and falls were assessed up to 2016.

Habitual coffee consumption was associated with lower risk of falling in older adults in Spain and the United Kingdom. (Machado-Fragua, et al., 2019)

Association between coffee and green tea intake and pneumonia among the Japanese elderly: a case-control study

Because Japan is aging at a pace unparalleled in other countries, prevention of pneumonia is very important since the risk of pneumonia increases with age.

- This study investigated the association between coffee, green tea intake, and pneumonia in the elderly. This hospital-based, matched case–control study was conducted at 24 hospitals in Japan. Study patients were 65 years-old or older and newly diagnosed with pneumonia. As a control, patients with the same sex and age (range of 5 years) who visited the same medical institution at the same time for a disease other than pneumonia were selected. 199 cases and 374 controls were enrolled.

Our study found a significant reduction in the risk for pneumonia in elderly individuals who drank ≥ 2cups/day of coffee compared to non-coffee drinkers. The intake of green tea was not related to pneumonia. (Kondo, et al., 2021)

Everyone should get Pneumococcal vaccinations starting at 65 years-old.

Coffee and Caffeine Consumption for Human Health

Twenty-one manuscripts were studied.

- Antwerpes et al., studied regular coffee intake and neurocognitive performance in patients coinfected with HIV and hepatitis C virus, who experience an accelerated aging process and cognitive impairment. The authors showed a positive association between elevated coffee intake (three or more cups per day) and neurocognitive functioning, suggesting that coffee intake may be neuroprotective.
- Individuals consuming caffeine on a regular basis had a significantly lower risk of developing Parkinson's Disease (PD), and those that already had the disease showed a significantly decelerated PD progression. (Abalo, 2021)

Coffee intake, cardiovascular disease and all-cause mortality: observational and Mendelian randomization analyses in 95,000 to 230,000 individuals

Study consisted of observational associations in 95,366 Danish people.

- Coffee has been associated with lower risk of cardiovascular disease and all-cause mortality in meta-analyses.
- Lowest risks were observed in individuals with medium coffee intake. (Nordestgaard & Nordestgaard, 2016)

Mendelian randomization sounds like something from "*Star Wars.*" Did Darth Vader use Mendelian randomization? It actually means looking at genes to see whether a possible association or causal relationship exists. Darth Vader and Luke Skywalker share many genes since they are father and son. I would not like to share any genes with Jabba the Hutt (his full name is Jabba Desilijic Tiure). He was head of a crime empire.

A meta-analysis of prospective studies of coffee consumption and mortality for all causes, cancers and cardiovascular diseases

Literature search to January 2013 on the relation of coffee with mortality for all causes, all cancers, cardiovascular disease, coronary/ischemic heart disease and stroke. This meta-analysis provides quantitative evidence that coffee intake is inversely related to all reviewed causes and, probably, cardiovascular disease mortality also. (Malerba, et al., 2013)

The relationship of coffee consumption with mortality

We assessed the association between coffee consumption and mortality during 18 years of follow-up in men (41,736) and 24 years of follow up in women (86,214).

- Coffee consumption was assessed first in 1986 for men and in 1980 for women and then every two to four years through 2004.

The relative risks for all-cause mortality

- Less than one cup a month: 7% worse for men and 2% better for women
- One cup a month to four cups a week: 2% worse for men and 7% better for women
- Five to seven cups a week: 3% better for men and 18% better for women
- Two to three cups a day: 7% better for men and 16% better for women

- Four to five or more than six cups a day; 20% better for men and 17% better for women

The higher intake of coffee improved all-cause mortality the most. (Lopez-Garcia, van Dam, Li, Rodriguez-Artalejo, & Hu, 2008)

<u>Tea intake and cardiovascular disease: an umbrella review</u>

- Brewed tea (*Camellia sinensis*) is a major dietary source of flavonoids (polyphenols).
- Approximately one-fifth of Americans drink tea on a daily basis. Tea consumers have about 20 times the flavonoid intake of non-consumers.
- Several biological mechanisms support the beneficial relationship between tea intake and CVD risk. They include improving endothelial function, nitric oxide–dependent vasorelaxation, and blood pressure.

We conducted an umbrella review of 23 systematic studies from January 1, 2010 to February 22, 2020 evaluating tea in reducing CVD risk and severity.

- Each cup increase in daily black or green tea was associated with a 4% lower risk of stroke.
- No significant effects on HDL cholesterol and TG.
- **One to three cups of black or green tea improves CVD mortality by 2-27%.**
- **Tea flavonoids decrease LDL cholesterol, SBP, DBP in populations with and without underlying hypertension.**
- Green tea preparations when ingested in large bolus amounts in supplement form can lead to liver damage. This does not occur when consumed as beverages, or as a component of food.

- Typical caffeine side effects can also occur with tea (tea has much less caffeine than coffee.
- There are limited data in pregnant and lactating women.

(Keller & Wallace, 2021)

Chapter 4: Coffee, Tea and Diabetes

Coffee and doughnuts will not be studied in this chapter; they are discussed in the "yummy chapter." 11.3% of the US population have diabetes and 38% have prediabetes (National Diabetes Statistics Report). Diabetes has skyrocketed on the mothership "Obesity" with no safe landing in the near future.

Coffee and Lower Risk of Type 2 Diabetes: Arguments for a Causal Relationship

Prospective epidemiological studies concur an association between habitual coffee consumption and a lower risk of type 2 diabetes. Several aspects support a cause-effect relationship. Favorable factors include

- dependency on daily coffee dose
- similar outcomes in different regions of the world
- no differences between sexes, obese versus lean, young versus old, smokers versus nonsmokers, regardless of the number of confounders adjusted for. (Kolb, Martin, & Kempf, 2021)

Coffee does not lower glucose levels acutely. A major effect of coffee intake may be preservation of functional beta cell mass.

Long-term preservation of liver and beta cell function may account for the association of habitual coffee drinking with a lower risk of type 2 diabetes, rather than an acute improvement in lowering glucose.

I clearly concur with the favorable association between coffee and diabetes. If someone asks you if you concur, the correct answer is always yes (just ask Leonardo DiCaprio when he imitates a doctor in the 2002 movie "Catch Me If You Can").

Coffee consumption and risk of type 2 diabetes: a systematic review

A MEDLINE search through January 2005 yielded nine cohort studies including 193,473 participants.

- The risk was 35% lower for the highest coffee intake (more than six or seven cups a day).
- The risk was 28% lower for the second highest (four to six cups a day) compared with zero or less than two cups a day.
- These associations did not differ substantially by gender, obesity, or region (United States and Europe).

This systematic review supports the hypothesis that high habitual coffee consumption is associated with a 28%-35% lower risk of type 2 diabetes. (van Dam & Hu, 2005)

Caffeinated and decaffeinated coffee consumption and risk of type 2 diabetes: a systematic review and a dose-response meta-analysis

Twenty-eight prospective studies from 1966 to 2013 with 1,109,272 study participants and 45,335 cases of type 2 diabetes. The follow-up ranged from 10 months to 20 years.

- Compared with no or rare coffee consumption, the risk for diabetes was:

8% lower for one cup a day.

15% lower for two cups.

21% lower for three cups.

25% lower for four cups.
29% lower for five cups.
33% lower for 6 cups.

- The risk of diabetes for a one cup/day increase was 9% lower for caffeinated coffee consumption and 6% lower for decaffeinated coffee consumption.

Coffee consumption was inversely associated with the risk of type 2 diabetes in a dose-response manner. Both caffeinated and decaffeinated coffee were associated with reduced diabetes risk. (Ding, Bhupathiraju, Chen, van Dam, & Hu, 2014)

Regularly consuming a green/roasted coffee blend reduces the risk of metabolic syndrome

The effects of regularly consuming a green/roasted coffee blend (35/65) on metabolic syndrome were evaluated. Green beans are unroasted.

- A crossover, randomized, controlled study in 25 people with normal cholesterol and 27 people with elevated cholesterol aged 18-45 years. Three servings a day of the blend, providing 510.6 mg hydroxycinnamic acids (type of polyphenol) and 121.2 mg caffeine/day, were consumed versus a control drink for eight weeks.
- Systolic and diastolic blood pressure significantly decreased in both groups as well as percentage of body fat.
- Glucose concentration, insulin resistance, and triglyceride levels were reduced significantly.

Regular consumption of the green/roasted coffee blend may be recommended to healthy and hypercholesterolemic subjects to prevent metabolic syndrome as it produces positive effects on blood pressure, glucose and triglyceride levels. (Sarriá, et al., 2018)

Additive effects of green tea and coffee on all-cause mortality in patients with type 2 diabetes mellitus: the Fukuoka Diabetes Registry

We prospectively investigated the impact of green tea, coffee and their combination on mortality among Japanese patients with type 2 diabetes.

A total of 4,923 patients (2,790 men, 2,133 women) with type 2 diabetes (mean age 66 years) were followed (median, 5.3 years; follow-up rate, 99.5%).

Mortality rate for green tea:

15% better for one cup or less/day.

27% better for two to three cups/day.

40% better for four or more cups/day.

For coffee

12% better for less than cup/day.

19% better for one cup/day.

41% better for two or more cups/day.

With the combination

51% better for two to three cups/day of green tea with two or more cups/day of coffee.

58% better for four or more cups/day of green tea with one cup/day of coffee.

63% better for four or more cups/day of green tea with two or more cups/day of coffee. (Komorita, et al., 2020)

Higher consumption of green tea and coffee was associated with reduced all-cause mortality in patients with type 2 diabetes. Their combined effect appeared to be additive in patients with type 2 diabetes.

This makes me think that 2 fruits or vegetables (polyphenols) are better than one at promoting health.

Chapter 4: Coffee, Tea and Diabetes

Caffeinated coffee, decaffeinated coffee, and caffeine in relation to plasma C-peptide levels, a marker of insulin secretion, in U.S. women

We examined caffeinated, decaffeinated coffee and total caffeine in relation to C-peptide levels among 2,112 healthy women. Elevated C-peptide, a marker of insulin secretion, is linked to type 2 diabetes.

- Caffeinated, decaffeinated coffee, and caffeine were each inversely associated with C-peptide levels.
- C-peptide was 16% less in women who drank more than 4 cups/day of caffeinated or decaffeinated coffee compared with nondrinkers ($P < 0.005$ for each).
- We did not find any association between tea and C-peptide.

The inverse association between caffeinated coffee and C-peptide was considerably stronger in obese (27% reduction) and overweight women (20% reduction) than in normal-weight women (11% reduction) ($P = 0.005$).

Our findings suggest a potential reduction of insulin secretion by coffee in women. This may be related to other components in coffee rather than caffeine. (Wu, Willett, Hankinson, & Giovannucci, 2005)

Overweight and obese women are always going to be at higher risk of having an elevated C-peptide level compared to normal-weight women. Having extra weight is a risk factor for diabetes.

Tea consumption and long-term risk of type 2 diabetes and diabetic complications: a cohort study of 0.5 million Chinese adults

Investigate tea consumption with long-term risk of developing type 2 diabetes and risks of diabetic complications and death among patients with diabetes.

482,425 subjects without diabetes with a mean age of 51.2 years; 41% were male.
30,300 patients had diabetes with a mean age of 58.2 years; 39% were males.

- Of all daily tea consumers, 85.8% preferred green tea.
- In the diabetes-free population, 17,434 of 482,425 (3.6%) participants developed type 2 diabetes during 11.1 years of follow-up.

In Chinese adults, daily green tea consumption decreased risk of type 2 diabetes and decreased all-cause mortality in patients with diabetes. The associations for other types of tea were less clear. In addition, daily tea consumption was associated with a lower risk of diabetic microvascular complications (eye, nerve and kidney disease) but not macrovascular complications (heart disease, peripheral vascular disease and stroke). (Nie, et al., 2021)

The effect of green coffee extract supplementation on cardio metabolic risk factors: a systematic review and meta-analysis of randomized controlled trials

A literature search to October 2019 included 27 studies. Green coffee extract has the caffeine but not the coffee flavor.

- Pooled results revealed that green coffee supplementation significantly reduced fasting blood sugar, insulin, and triglyceride levels.
- Green coffee supplementation increased HDL (good cholesterol) levels. (Morvaridi, Rayyani, Jaafari, Khiabani, & Rahimlou, 2020)

Chapter 5: Coffee, Tea and Cancer

Cancer is a serious issue. Always listen to your oncologist (cancer specialist). Stick to conventional treatment and avoid treatments or advice based on anecdotal evidence and testimonial manure.

A Decade of Research on Coffee as an Anticarcinogenic Beverage

PubMed search to July 2021.

- Drinking coffee has often been discouraged, due to presumed negative effects, mainly attributed to caffeine. In 2019, only 25% of consumers think that coffee has beneficial effects on health. A 2014 survey performed by the World Cancer Research Fund (WCRF) revealed that as many as 36% of health professionals thought drinking coffee increases the risk of cancer.
- Studies published in recent years, including two large meta-analyzes in 2017, have shown that coffee consumption decreased the risk or development of 18 different types of cancer, including breast, prostate, oral, oral and pharyngeal, melanoma, skin and skin nonmelanoma, kidney, gastric, colorectal, endometrial, liver, leukemic and hepatocellular carcinoma, brain, and thyroid cancer, among others.
- 12 publications demonstrated an unfavorable association between coffee consumption and bladder, pancreatic, laryngeal, gastric and lung cancer.

Many epidemiological studies have shown benefit with decaffeinated coffee and that higher doses of coffee may provide more risk reduction. (Nigra, Teodoro, & Gil, 2021)

Coffee consumption and the risk of lung cancer: an updated meta-analysis of epidemiological studies

A meta-analysis looked at 17 studies involving 12,276 cases and 102,516 controls.

The summary risk of lung cancer was 17% higher for coffee drinkers compared with nondrinkers and 31% higher for the highest category of coffee consumption compared with the lowest category.

Lung cancer is one of the most prevalent malignancies in the world and is the leading cause of cancer death in the United States in both men and women. As reported by the World Health Organization, the steadily increasing proportion of elderly people in the world will result in ~50% increase in new cancer cases over the next 20 years. Particularly over the past five years, studies have consistently indicated that lung cancer risk is significantly increased by 47% in the overall population with the highest category intake of coffee compared with the lowest category intake. (remember, a risk increase of 200% means two people in 100 are affected instead of one.)

The present study suggested that coffee intake was associated with an increased risk of lung cancer. This study is informative because when you separate it between smokers and non-smokers, nonsmokers who drink more than three cups/day have a lower incidence of lung cancer by 15%. (Xie, et al., 2016)

Coffee and a cigarette in the morning is not a good start.

Chapter 5: Coffee, Tea and Cancer

Coffee Consumption and Lung Cancer Risk: A Prospective Cohort Study in Khon Kaen Thailand

To investigate the effect of coffee consumption on lung cancer between 1990 and 2001 in 24,528 Thai people.

- Coffee consumption was associated with 46% reduced risk for lung cancer.
- Cigarette smoking increased risk 276% and family history of lung cancer increased risk by 165%. (Kudwongsa, Promthet, Suwanrungruang, Phunmanee, & Vatanasapt, 2020)

Coffee consumption and the risk of cutaneous melanoma: a meta-analysis

Literature search to August 2015 comprising twelve studies with 832,956 participants for total coffee consumption.

- Five studies involved 717,151 participants for **caffeinated** coffee.
- Six studies involving 718,231 participants for **decaffeinated** coffee.

Pooled Risk for melanoma

- 20% lower risk for total coffee.
- 15% lower risk for caffeinated coffee.
- 8% lower risk for decaffeinated coffee.

Cutaneous melanoma risk decreased 3% for both decaf/caffeinated coffees and 4% for caffeinated coffee for one cup/day increments.

Coffee consumption may reduce the risk of cutaneous melanoma. (Wang, Li, & Zhang, 2016)

Caffeinated and decaffeinated coffee consumption and melanoma risk: a dose-response meta-analysis of prospective cohort studies

Literature search to March 2017 comprising seven studies with 1,418,779 participants and 9,211 melanoma cases.

- An increase in coffee consumption of one cup per day was associated with a 3% reduction in melanoma risk.

Coffee intake maybe protective against melanoma. (Micek, Godos, Lafranconi, Marranzano, & Pajak, 2018)

Coffee consumption and risk of colorectal cancer in the Cancer Prevention Study-II Nutrition Cohort

We examined associations of caffeinated and decaffeinated coffee intake with colorectal cancer risk overall and with colon and rectum separately. In 1999, 47,010 men and 60,051 women with no previous diagnosis of cancer, aged 47-96 years were surveyed for coffee intake. Consumption was updated in 2003. A total of 1829 (1.7%) colorectal cancer cases were verified through June 2015.

Consumption of ≥2 cups/day of decaffeinated coffee was associated with 18% lower risk of overall colorectal cancer, 18% lower risk of colon cancer and 37% lower risk of rectal cancer.

Consumption of ≥2 cups/day of caffeinated coffee was associated with 37% higher risk of rectal cancer but not with colorectal or colon cancer.

FYI rectum and colon make up colorectal area. (Um, et al., 2020)

Coffee consumption and colorectal cancer risk: a multicentre case-control study from Italy and Spain

Epidemiological evidence of coffee intake and colorectal cancer is inconsistent.

- We studied a total of 2,289 incident cases with colorectal cancer and 3,995 controls with information on coffee intake.

This large pooled analysis of two studies shows no association of coffee and decaffeinated coffee with colorectal cancer risk. (Rosato, et al., 2021)

Chapter 5: Coffee, Tea and Cancer

Coffee Consumption and Cancer Risk; An Assessment of the Health Implications Based on Recent Knowledge

A significant number of studies suggest that coffee consumption reduces cancer risk. We performed a search from January 2005 to December 2020.

The totality of eligible scientific papers supports the evidence that coffee intake is inversely associated with hepatocellular cancer risk and, to a slight extent, breast cancer risk among postmenopausal women. As to the association with other organs, including esophagus, pancreas, colorectum, kidneys, bladder, ovaries and prostate, the results are less clear as reports reveal conflicting results or statistically non-significant data. (Pauwels & Volterrani, 2021)

Post-diagnostic coffee and tea consumption and breast cancer survival

Coffee and tea consumption were studied after women were diagnosed with breast cancer.

8,900 women with stage I-stage III breast cancer from 1980-2010 in the Nurses' Health Study and from 1991-2011 in the Nurses' Health Study II. Post-diagnostic coffee and tea consumption was assessed every four years after diagnosis for up to 30 years.

- Higher post-diagnostic coffee consumption was associated with a lower breast cancer mortality compared with non-drinkers.
- Lower all-cause mortality with coffee compared with non-drinkers.
- More than two to three cups/day was associated with a 24% lower risk and more than three cups/day was associated with a 26% lower risk.

- Post-diagnostic tea consumption was associated with lower all-cause mortality compared with non-drinkers.

Among breast cancer survivors, higher post-diagnostic coffee consumption was associated with better breast cancer survival and overall survival. Higher post-diagnostic tea consumption may be related to better overall survival. (Farvid, et al., 2021)

<u>Coffee, including caffeinated and decaffeinated coffee, and the risk of hepatocellular carcinoma: a systematic review and dose-response meta-analysis</u>

Review of caffeinated and decaffeinated coffee and hepatocellular carcinoma.

- There were 18 cohort studies involving 2,272,642 participants and 2,905 cases, and eight case-control studies, involving 1,825 cases and 4,652 controls.

Drinking more than two cups per day of coffee was associated with a 35% reduction in the risk of hepatocellular carcinoma.

Increased consumption of caffeinated coffee and, to a lesser extent, decaffeinated coffee is associated with reduced risk of hepatocellular cancer, including pre-existing liver disease. (Kennedy, et al., 2017)

<u>Coffee consumption and prostate cancer risk: a meta-analysis of cohort studies</u>

An analysis of 13 cohort studies with 34,105 cases, 539,577 participants assessed for coffee consumption and prostate cancer risk.

- 10% benefit for the highest vs. lowest coffee intake.
- Cancer risk decreased 2.5% for every two cups/day increment in coffee consumption.
- Stratifying by geographic region, there was a statistically significant protective influence of coffee on prostate cancer risk among European populations.

Chapter 5: Coffee, Tea and Cancer

Coffee consumption may be associated with a reduced risk of prostate cancer. (Liu, et al., 2015)

The association between coffee consumption and bladder cancer in the bladder cancer epidemiology and nutritional determinants (BLEND) international pooled study

Evaluate the association between coffee consumption and bladder cancer.

- 13 case-control studies comprising 5,911 cases and 16,172 controls.
- **Coffee consumption increased the risk for bladder cancer in never smokers by 30% in low to moderate drinkers and 52% in consumers > 4 cups/day compared to non-coffee drinkers.**

Smokers already have increased risk of bladder cancer from tobacco and this is made worse after consumption of more than six cups/day. (Yu, et al., 2019)

Coffee Consumption and Its Inverse Relationship with Gastric Cancer: An Ecological Study

Explore the relationship between coffee consumption and stomach cancer in the 25 highest coffee-consuming countries.

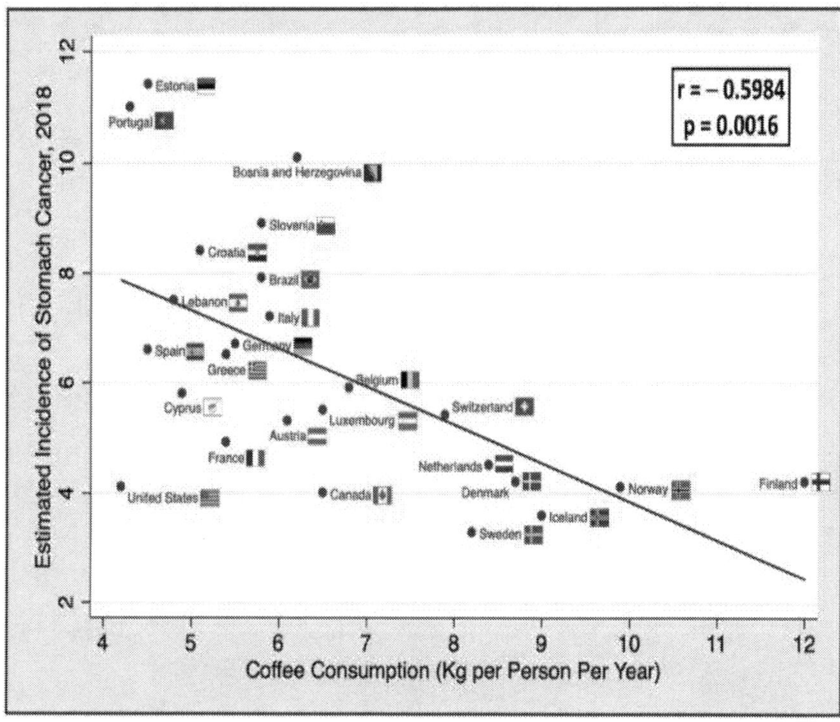

Figure 1

Coffee consumption and stomach cancer incidence. It shows the country correlation between annual coffee consumption and incidence of stomach cancer in 2018.

Figure 2

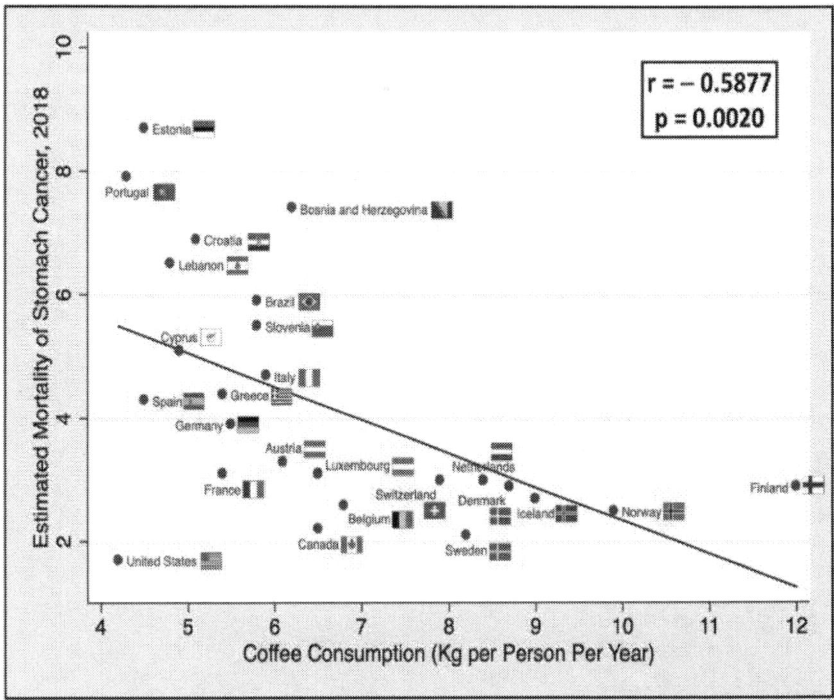

Coffee consumption and stomach cancer mortality. It shows the country correlation between annual coffee consumption and the estimated mortality of stomach cancer in 2018.

- A 2014 meta-analysis with 840,651 subjects found that coffee intake was not significantly associated with overall gastric cancer risk. Similar findings were reported in a 2015 meta-analysis involving 1,250,825 participants. Nevertheless, data about coffee consumption throughout life, type of coffee consumed, anatomical locations of gastric cancer, *Helicobacter pylori* infection, and precancerous lesions, were not considered in those studies.
- Certain confounding factors such as diet, lifestyle (consumption of fruits, vegetables, red meat, salt, cigarettes, and alcohol, and physical activity), socioeconomic status, place of residence, race, health

insurance, and *Helicobacter pylori* infection have been shown to play paramount roles in gastric cancer development.

Gastric cancer is one of the five most frequent malignancies. The relationship between coffee consumption and gastric cancer are conflicting. (Parra-Lara, Mendoza-Urbano, Bravo, Salamanca, & Zambrano, 2020)

Coffee consumption and risk of gastric cancer: an updated meta-analysis

Literature search of 22 studies involving 7,631 cases and 1,019,693 controls.

- The summary risk of gastric cancer was 6% lower for the highest category of coffee consumption compared with the lowest category, and 7% lower for coffee drinkers compared with nondrinkers.

Pooled risk for the population

- Less than one cup/day: 5% lower risk
- One to two cups/day: 8% lower risk
- Three to four cups/day: 12% lower risk

Coffee consumption might be associated with a decreased risk of gastric cancer. (Xie, Huang, He, & Su, 2016)

Caffeine, Type of Coffee, and Risk of Ovarian Cancer: A Dose-Response Meta-Analysis of Prospective Studies

- Meta-analysis of 14 prospective cohort studies till October 2018 on the association between dietary caffeine intake, different types of coffee consumption, and the risk of ovarian cancer.

We found no statistically significant association between caffeine intake or different types of coffee and

the risk of ovarian cancer. (Salari-Moghaddam, Milajerdi, Surkan, Larijani, & Esmaillzadeh, 2019)

Coffee, decaffeinated coffee, tea intake, and risk of renal cell cancer

- Case-control study conducted in Italy between 1992 and 2004.
- Coffee intake (mostly espresso and mocha – espresso with chocolate added) was not associated with renal cell cancer risk.

This study, based on a large dataset, provides further evidence that coffee, decaffeinated coffee, and tea consumption are not related to renal cell cancer risk. (Montella, et al., 2009)

Coffee consumption and risk of renal cell carcinoma in the NIH-AARP Diet and Health Study

We investigated the relationship between coffee and renal cell carcinoma (RCC) within a large cohort of 420,188 people over a 10 years follow-up.

- 38% lower risk among never-smokers drinking ≥4 cups/day and 15% lower risk with ever-smokers.
- 20% reduced risk for ≥2 cups/day vs non-drinkers.
- Associations were similar with caffeinated or decaffeinated coffee. (Rhee, et al., 2021)

Chapter 6: Coffee, Caffeine, Tea and Heart

Most people die of heart disease. Great advances in heart disease treatment have occurred in my lifetime and is a major reason our lifespan has improved over the last 50 years. Controlling blood pressure and cholesterol were milestone ideas. The first heart bypass (CABG) was in 1967 and the first coronary artery stent was in 1986.

<u>Caffeine and Arrhythmias: Time to Grind the Data</u>

It has been assumed that, because of the effects of caffeine on enhancing the mind and potentially increasing the heart rate, it may contribute to arrhythmias. This public perception is often based on anecdotal experience; however, the perception extends to the medical community, with more than 80% of U.S. physicians in 1988 recommending abstinence or reduction in caffeine intake for patients with palpitations or documented arrhythmias. Extensive research over the past decade suggests that many widely held beliefs regarding caffeine may not be evidence-based.

Caffeine pharmacology

- Caffeine increases the sinus rate by sympathomimetic effects. A dose of 250 mg of caffeine (3 cups of coffee) acutely increases norepinephrine and epinephrine by 75% and 207%, respectively.

Coffee and atrial arrhythmia

- In 2015, Lemery et al. administered 5 mg/kg caffeine before electrophysiology study in patients with supraventricular tachycardia (SVT) and were unable to demonstrate an effect on atrial or ventricular refractory periods or the inducibility of SVT.
- A community-based cohort of 1,388 participants undergoing 24-h Holter monitoring, Dixit et al. in 2016 failed to demonstrate higher caffeine intake and atrial or ventricular premature beats.
- To date, clinical studies have failed to show deleterious effects of caffeine on atrial and ventricular electrophysiologic properties.
- In 2016, population-based studies have consistently demonstrated a reduction in atrial fibrillation with increasing levels of caffeine ingestion. Incident atrial fibrillation (AF) events in 57,053 participants followed for 13.5 years were lower in habitual coffee drinkers at all levels of consumption.
- A 2014 meta-analysis of 6 prospective cohort studies with 228,465 participants showed AF incidence decreasing by 6% for every 300 mg/day increment in regular caffeine intake.
- A 2013 meta-analysis of 115,993 patients, demonstrated a significant 13% reduction in incident AF risk.
- In a 2011 population-based study of 130,054 people, 3,137 subjects (2.4%) were hospitalized for arrhythmia over 17.6 years' follow-up. Caffeine intake was again protective for arrhythmia risk.
- 11 major human studies reviewed in 2005 (360,980 patients, 15,198 AF cases) examining the relationship between caffeinated beverages and atrial arrhythmia. One small case-control study with no adjustments for other confounders reported coffee was detrimental, whereas 3 studies consistently demonstrated a benefit,

and the remaining studies showed no significant interaction.

- there may be individual differences in susceptibility to the effects of caffeine on electrophysiologic and autonomic factors that trigger arrhythmias in some people. Twenty-five percent of patients report coffee is an AF trigger, and those with a clear temporal association should accordingly be counseled to abstain.

Coffee and ventricular arrhythmia (VA)

- Caffeine does not appear to increase the likelihood of VA.
- A 1990 study of 22 patients with a history of VAs who underwent electrophysiological study before and 1 h post-coffee (275 mg caffeine) ingestion demonstrated no significant difference in inducibility of VAs.
- In 5 placebo-controlled 1991 trials, caffeine in doses of up to 500 mg daily (~6 cups of coffee) did not experience an increase or frequency of VAs.
- In 50 consecutive patients in 1989 with a history of malignant VAs receiving either coffee (containing 200 mg of caffeine) or a decaffeinated drink, there were no significant differences observed in ventricular ectopy or tachycardia, despite increases in serum catecholamine levels in the caffeinated group.
- A 2016 meta-analysis of 7 human studies found that caffeine consumption had no impact on incidence of ventricular ectopy.
- In a 2009 randomized study of 103 patients with post-myocardial infarction, regular caffeine (average: 353 mg/day) resulted in no significant arrhythmias compared with controls.
- Zuchinali et al. in 2016 performed a double-blinded crossover trial in 51 patients with moderate-to-severe left ventricle dysfunction at high risk of VAs,

consuming either 500 mg of caffeine or placebo. No significant differences were observed in arrhythmias at rest and with exercise.

- Large epidemiological studies compiled in 2013 suggest that regular caffeine drinkers have lower cardiovascular and all-cause mortality, with a potentially attenuated risk of coronary heart disease, heart failure, and stroke.
- Of 8 studies involving 232,717 patients, 6 studies demonstrated no association with VA.
- Only 2 older studies in 1999 and 1980 demonstrated an association between coffee consumption and VAs at very high levels of coffee intake only (>10 cups per day and >9 cups per day, respectively).

Tea

- In a 2016 case-control study of 801 subjects, green tea intake led to a significant reduction in paroxysmal and persistent AF.
- Benefits of tea may also extend to reducing VAs.
- Moderate tea consumption (up to 14 cups/week) was associated with a significant reduction in VAs in 3,882 patients following myocardial infarction.
- In a 2015 meta-analysis, consumption of 3 cups of tea per day significantly reduced the risk of cardiac death.

Energy drinks (ED)

- There have been increasing numbers of case reports between EDs and arrhythmias, including young patients without structural heart disease.
- EDs may be responsible for a prothrombotic state. Studies in healthy volunteers undergoing platelet function testing before and 60 min after ED consumption demonstrated a significant increase in platelet aggregation. (platelet aggregation increases clots).

- In 2013, The International Society of Sports Nutrition recommended that patients with pre-existing cardiovascular conditions refrain from use of EDs, and they warn that more than 1 ED/day, even in healthy individuals, may be harmful.

Conclusions

- **Many clinicians continue to counsel patients with atrial or VAs to avoid all caffeinated beverages, particularly coffee, despite an absence of evidence to support this approach.**
- **If, in individual cases where a clear temporal association between arrhythmia episodes and caffeine intake is apparent, then avoidance is sensible.**
- **Large-scale population-based studies and randomized controlled trials suggest coffee and tea are safe and may even reduce the incidence of arrhythmia.**
- **A regular intake of up to 300 mg/day appears to be safe and may even be protective against heart rhythm disorders** (Voskoboinik, Kalman, & Kistler, 2018)

Habitual coffee consumption and risk of heart failure: a dose-response meta-analysis

- Systematic review from January 1966 through December 2011. Five independent prospective studies included 6,522 heart failure events and 140,220 participants.
- The largest benefit was seen for 4 servings/day compared with no consumption.
- Elevated heart failure risk was present at higher levels of consumption.

- The relationship between coffee and heart failure risk did not vary by sex or by baseline history of myocardial infarction or diabetes

. (Mostofsky, Rice, Levitan, & Mittleman, 2012)

Coffee and tea consumption in the early adult lifespan and left ventricular function in middle age: the CARDIA study

We examined the association between coffee or tea consumption beginning in early adulthood (mean age 25.2) and cardiac function in midlife.

2,735 participants with long-term total caffeine intake, coffee, and tea consumption data from three visits over a 20 years interval and echocardiography. 57.4% were women, and 41.9% were African-American.

- There were no associations between either tea drinking or total caffeine intake and cardiac function ($P > 0.05$ for all).

Low-to-moderate daily coffee consumption from early adulthood to middle age was associated with better heart (LV) systolic and diastolic function in midlife. High daily coffee consumption (>4cups/day) was associated with worse LV function. (Nwabuo, et al., 2020)

This study was unique in that 41.9% were African-Americans. African-Americans are more likely to have hypertension than any other racial group with an incidence over 50%.

Coffee and Arterial Hypertension

Coffee is the most consumed drink next to water. Because 31.1% of adults in the world have hypertension, much controversy has been raised about the influence of coffee consumption on blood pressure.

- The results of numerous studies and meta-analyses indicate that moderate and habitual coffee consumption does not increase and may even reduce the risk of hypertension.
- Conversely, occasional coffee consumption can promote hypertension.

Moderate habitual coffee consumption in hypertensive persons does not appear to increase the risk of uncontrolled blood pressure and may even reduce the risk of death from any cause. (Surma & Oparil, 2021)

Coffee Consumption and Blood Pressure: Results of the Second Wave of the Cognition of Older People, Education, Recreational Activities, Nutrition, Comorbidities, and Functional Capacity Studies (COPERNICUS)

- Cohort study of 205 healthy older people examining the relationship between coffee consumption and blood pressure over a two years period. Coffee consumption was grouped into three categories: "never to a few times per month", "once a week to a few times per week", and "everyday".
- Adjustments were made for body composition, smoking status, age, sex, heart rate, and number of antihypertensive agents taken.

Participants who drank coffee everyday had a significant increase in systolic BP (mean increase of 8.63 mmHg) and mean BP (increase of 5.55 mmHg) after two years compared to "never or very rarely" (few times per month) drinkers.

DBP and PP were not affected by coffee consumption frequency in a statistically significant manner. (Kujawska, et al., 2021)

Pulse Pressure (PP) is systolic minus diastolic blood pressure and the higher the number, the stiffer a person's blood vessels are (risk factor for heart disease).

Green Tea and Coffee Consumption and All-Cause Mortality Among Persons With and Without Stroke or Myocardial Infarction

We examined green tea and coffee consumption and mortality in people with and without stroke or myocardial infarction.

- 46,213 Japanese participants (478 stroke survivors, 1,214 infarction survivors).
- 44,521 controls (no history of stroke or myocardial infarction) aged 40 to 79 years at baseline (1988-90)
- 18.5-year median follow-up period.

Risk for stroke, myocardial infarction survivors with green tea

27% lower risk for one to six cups/week.
35% lower risk for one to two cups/day.
44% lower risk for three to four cups/day.
48% lower risk for five to six cups/day.
62% lower risk for seven or more cups/day compared with nondrinkers.

- **Green tea consumption improves the prognosis for people with a stroke or heart attack in the past but does not provide any additional benefit to drinkers without history of either stroke or heart attack.**
- **Coffee did better.**
- **Coffee consumption was beneficial for decreasing mortality in everyone, except stroke survivors.** (Teramoto, Muraki, Yamagishi, Tamakoshi, & Iso, 2021)

Caffeine and coffee: effects on health and cardiovascular disease

Chapter 6: Coffee, Caffeine, Tea and Heart

Contrary to common belief, the published literature provides little evidence that coffee and/or caffeine in typical dosages increases the risk of myocardial infarction, sudden death or arrhythmia. (Chou & Benowitz, 1994)

This article was published in 1994 and is still true in 2022.

No association between coffee consumption and risk of atrial fibrillation: A Mendelian randomization study

- This study was based on summary-level data from the Atrial Fibrillation Consortium, including 588,190 individuals (65,446 cases and 522,744 non-cases).

This study does not support a causal association between habitual coffee consumption and risk of atrial fibrillation. (Yuan & Larsson, 2019)

Coffee consumption and risk of heart failure in the Physicians' Health Study

- We prospectively studied 20,433 middle-aged and older men. Coffee consumption and the incidence of heart failure was assessed based on annual questionnaires.

We found no association between either coffee consumption or dietary caffeine intake with heart failure risk among US male physicians. (Bodar, Chen, Sesso, Gaziano, & Djoussé, 2020)

Coffee Consumption and Cardiovascular Disease: A Condensed Review of Epidemiological Evidence and Mechanisms

In healthy people, habitual consumption of three to five cups of coffee per day is associated with a 15% reduction in the risk of a cardiovascular event, compared to non-drinkers and higher consumption was not linked to elevated cardiovascular risk.

- **In comparison to no coffee intake, usual consumption of one to five cups/day is associated with a lower risk of death.**
- **In people who have already suffered a cardiovascular event, habitual consumption does not increase the risk of a recurrent event or death.**
- **Hypertensive patients with uncontrolled blood pressure should avoid consuming large doses of caffeine.** (Rodríguez-Artalejo & López-García, 2018)

Two Coffees a Day Keep the Heart Doctor Away?

In this issue of *Circulation: Heart Failure*, Stevens et al report that 2 or ≥3 cups per day of caffeinated coffee is associated with lower long-term incident heart failure (HF) among 21,361 participants in 3 longitudinal cardiovascular cohort studies. This is consistent with prior studies.

- No risk of subsequent coronary heart disease or cardiovascular disease overall was observed with caffeinated coffee. Conversely, decaffeinated coffee was associated with an increased risk of incident HF, although this was only detected within one cohort study.
- Coffee, may be analogous to whole grains and vegetables as a dietary source of phenolic phytochemicals that could offer antioxidant protection from HF.

At a minimum, the current study appears to offer additional reassurance that coffee is unlikely to result in long-term cardiovascular harm. (Vest, 2021)

Coffee Consumption and Cardiovascular Health

A Medline search was conducted from 2010 to early 2015 with 25 pertinent reports on coffee drinking.

- These studies show a neutral or beneficial effect of coffee on cardiovascular health.

Chapter 6: Coffee, Caffeine, Tea and Heart

Coffee is safe to drink by both normal subjects and by those with preexisting CVDs and hypertension. (Chrysant, 2015)

<u>Short-term Effects of High-Dose Caffeine on Cardiac Arrhythmias in Patients with Heart Failure: A Randomized Clinical Trial</u>

Patients had chronic heart failure with moderate to severe systolic dysfunction (left ventricular ejection fraction less than 45%, normal is 65%).

- We studied the ingestion of caffeine (100 mg) or placebo, at one-hour intervals, for a total of 500 mg of caffeine or placebo during a five-hour protocol.
- We enrolled 51 patients (37 male; mean age, 60.6 years with mean left ventricular ejection fraction 29%, 31 had an implantable cardioverter-defibrillator device).

High doses of caffeine (500 mg) did not induce arrhythmias in patients at rest and during an exercise test in patients with decreased systolic heart function and high risk for ventricular arrhythmias. (Zuchinali, et al., 2016)

Five hundred mg of caffeine is a pretty large dose of caffeine in chronically ill patients. This provides evidence of caffeine safety in unhealthy patients.

<u>Does a single cup of caffeinated drink significantly increase blood pressure in young adults? A randomized controlled trial</u>

A total of 104 normotensive adults were randomized to receive either a cup of caffeinated or decaffeinated drink.

- The mean differences in systolic and diastolic blood pressure of the two groups were +2.77 mmHg and +2.11 mmHg respectively, and were not statistically significant. 5 mm Hg was used as the cutoff number.

Drinking a single cup of coffee (containing 80 mg of caffeine) does not have a significant effect on the blood pressure of healthy normotensive young adults one hour after the drink. (Teng, et al., 2016)

<u>Habitual coffee and caffeinated beverages consumption is inversely associated with arterial stiffness and central and peripheral blood pressure</u>

A sample of 1,095 subjects (mean age 53.2, female 56%) was stratified by daily coffee and caffeine consumption (i.e. non-drinkers, light drinkers, and moderate drinkers).

- Regular light and moderate coffee consumers showed decreased arterial stiffness values, as well as decreased blood pressure, compared to non-habitual coffee drinkers, even after adjusting for several cardiovascular risk factors.

The present results corroborate those in the literature that have highlighted the positive effect of habitual coffee consumption on arterial stiffness and blood pressure. (Del Giorno, et al., 2022)

<u>Coffee consumption and risk of hypertension: A prospective analysis in the cohort study</u>

Examine habitual coffee consumption with the risk of developing hypertension.

- 8,780 participants, aged 35-74 years, initially free of hypertension during a mean follow-up of 3.9 years.
- Most participants (90%) drank coffee, and the median intake was 150 mL/day.
- Compared to participants who never or almost never drink coffee, the risk of hypertension was 18% lower for individuals consuming 1-3 cups/day.
- The association between coffee consumption and incidence of hypertension was related to smoking status.

Chapter 6: Coffee, Caffeine, Tea and Heart

The beneficial effect of moderate coffee intake (1-3 cups/day) on risk of hypertension was observed only in never smokers. (Miranda, Goulart, Benseñor, Lotufo, & Marchioni, 2021)

<u>**The effect of coffee on blood pressure and cardiovascular disease in hypertensive individuals: a systematic review and meta-analysis**</u>

Summarize the evidence on the acute and longer-term effects of caffeine and coffee intake on blood pressure and between habitual coffee consumption and risk of cardiovascular disease in individuals with hypertension.

- A systematic review till April 2011.
- In five trials, the administration of 200-300 mg caffeine produced a mean increase of 8.1 mm Hg in systolic blood pressure and 5.7 mm Hg in diastolic pressure. The increase was observed in the first hour after caffeine intake and lasted three hours or less.
- In three studies of the longer-term effect of coffee (two weeks), no increase in blood pressure was observed with coffee, caffeine-free diet drink or decaffeinated coffee.
- Seven cohort studies found no evidence of an association between habitual coffee consumption and a higher risk of cardiovascular disease.

In hypertensive individuals, caffeine intake produces an acute increase in blood pressure for up to three hours. However, current evidence does not support an association between longer-term coffee consumption and increased blood pressure or between habitual coffee consumption and an increased risk of cardiovascular disease in hypertensive subjects. (Mesas, Leon-Muñoz, Rodriguez-Artalejo, & Lopez-Garcia, 2011)

Impact of Coffee Consumption on Physiological Markers of Cardiovascular Risk: A Systematic Review

A substantial number of observational studies suggest a beneficial relationship between coffee consumption and the risk for cardiovascular disease. The basis for this association is not clear.

- In this review, we specifically study the impact of coffee on inflammatory biomarkers as one potential mechanism for this observation.

Based on our systematic review of randomized controlled studies, we cannot confidently conclude that an anti-inflammatory effect of coffee is a major contributing factor to the lower all-cause mortality reported in observational studies. (Daneschvar, Smetana, Brindamour, Bain, & Mukamal, 2021)

Chapter 7: Coffee and Kidneys

My wife thinks drinking coffee before a race is a bad idea since it makes her urinate. I'm the kidney specialist and she's a gynecologist. I guess I must be wrong again. Happy wife, happy life.

Coffee Consumption is Associated with a Decreased Risk of Incident Chronic Kidney Disease: A Systematic Review and Meta-analysis of Cohort Studies

- A review to November 2019 comprising 25,849 participants comparing the risk of developing CKD (chronic kidney disease) among coffee-drinkers versus non-drinkers.

The meta-analysis found a significant 13% decreased risk of incident CKD among coffee-drinkers compared with non-drinkers. (Srithongkul & Ungprasert, 2020)

Caffeine and diuresis during rest and exercise: A meta-analysis

- Acute caffeine ingestion may increase urine volume, prompting concerns about fluid balance during exercise and sporting events.
- 16 studies were reviewed.

- The median caffeine dosage was 300 mg (about three cups). Urine volume increased 109 ± 195 mL for caffeine ingestion and 16.0 ± 19.2% for non-caffeine conditions. Females were more susceptible to diuretic effect than males.

Caffeine exerted a minor diuretic effect which was negated by exercise. Concerns regarding unwanted fluid loss associated with caffeine consumption are unwarranted particularly when ingestion precedes exercise. (Zhang, et al., 2015)

Effect of Coffee Consumption on Renal Outcome: A Systematic Review and Meta-Analysis of Clinical Studies

We investigated the relationship between coffee intake and chronic kidney disease-related outcomes.

- Literature search covered 1960 to 2020, analyzing 12 studies involving 505,841 subjects.
- There was a significantly lower risk of incident end stage kidney disease (18%), albuminuria (19%), and death (28%) in coffee users (i.e. albuminuria is associated with kidney disease) in individuals taking two or more cups a day compared to those who drank one cup or less a day. (Kanbay, et al., 2021)

Chapter 8: Coffee/Caffeine and the Digestive Tract

Coffee does an extraordinary job at reducing the risk of chronic liver disease and liver cancer. On the lighter side, coffee should not be used as an enema.

The safety and effectiveness of self-administered coffee enema: A systematic review of case reports
This review of 9 case reports does not recommend coffee enemas for self-care given the unsolved issues on its safety and insufficient evidence with regard to the effectiveness. (Son, et al., 2020)

"I'll take my enema extra hot with extra whip please".

Effects of Coffee on the Gastro-Intestinal Tract: A Narrative Review and Literature Update

- About 25% of the population suffers from functional dyspepsia worldwide. Functional dyspepsia applies to recurring signs and symptoms of indigestion that have no obvious cause. This syndrome is often associated with smoking, taking aspirin or NSAIDs, eating spicy food, and infection by *Helicobacter pylori*. No clear research answer is present between coffee and functional dyspepsia.

- GERD (gastro-esophageal reflux disease) is the unpleasant return of stomach acid contents into the esophagus. The most common cause is obesity, especially in women.
- GERD is linked to spicy and high-fat foods, alcohol, high-salt diet, carbonated beverages, citrus, coffee, and chocolate.
- Low-level coffee consumption does not seem to aggravate GERD, while higher levels may increase the risk. Surprisingly, there is no clear consensus in the literature between coffee consumption and the risk of GERD.
- In most studies, there was no association between coffee drinking and the risk of peptic ulcers. A large meta-analysis of risk factors of peptic ulcers reported that about 90% of peptic ulcer-related symptoms may relate to NSAID use, infection by *H. pylori*, and tobacco smoking.
- Coffee consumption has been linked to a reduction in pancreatitis, an inflammation of the pancreas mainly induced by alcohol.
- In prospective cohort studies, coffee intake was significantly associated with a 17% risk reduction of gallbladder stones, but only in women, not in men. Gallstones occur more frequently in women.
- Coffee does not influence the rapidity of stomach emptying.
- Distal colonic motility increases as rapidly as 4 minutes after coffee ingestion.
- Regular coffee stimulates the motility of the colon as much as cereals, 23% more than decaffeinated coffee or 60% more than a glass of water. However, this effect varies with individuals. Coffee consumption is inversely associated with chronic constipation.

Chapter 8: Coffee/Caffeine and the Digestive Tract

- Coffee is a low-cost strategy to accelerate postoperative recovery of intestinal function/motility after colorectal and gynecological surgery. The most recent review and meta-analysis on postoperative ileus was published at the end of 2021 and included 13 trials concerning colorectal surgeries, cesarean sections, and gynecologic surgeries on a total of 1,246 patients.
- coffee consumption promotes beneficial bacterial populations. The composition of the microbiota seems to play a much more important role in disease processes than expected in the past.

Coffee and Cancer of the Gastrointestinal Tract

- In 2016, the International Agency for Research on Cancer (IARC) found the evidence between coffee consumption and digestive cancers to be inconsistent, with the exception of the liver.
- Coffee intake reduces the risk of oral cavity cancer at all doses as reported by a 2020 meta-analysis of 15 studies.
- No association between coffee consumption and esophageal cancer was reported in a recent meta-analysis of 11 studies.
- Stomach cancers are classified as cardia and non-cardia type depending on their anatomical location. Cardia subtypes behave as esophageal cancers, while non-cardia types most often relate to the presence of *Helicobacter pylori* in addition to risk factors common to both types.
- A 2016 meta-analysis of 22 studies involving 7,631 cases, reported that coffee intake, at any level, significantly decreases the risk of developing stomach cancer by 7% compared to no consumption. The risk reduction reached 12% in high consumers (3–4

cups/day) and 5–8% in consumers of less than one or 1–2 cups/day.

- A pooled analysis including 18 studies, 8,198 cases, and 21,419 controls reported no risk change in stomach cancer for coffee drinkers compared to rare or non-drinkers.
- A high consumption of ≥7 cups of coffee daily increased the risk of stomach cancer by 20%. A positive association was found for the intake of ≥5 cups of coffee daily and gastric cardia cancer.
- Additional studies are still needed to clarify the relationship between coffee consumption and pancreatic cancer.
- In a 2017 cohort of 72,680 Swedish adults (45–83 years), the risk of developing gallbladder cancer was decreased by 24%, 50%, or 59% for the consumption of 2 cups, 3 cups, or ≥4 cups per day respectively.
- Coffee consumption reduced the risk of disease progression and death in patients suffering from advanced or metastatic colorectal cancer.

Cancer of the Liver

- Chronic liver disease is the fifth most frequent cause of death. Likewise, liver cancer is the fifth most common cancer in men and the ninth most frequent in women worldwide. A 2017 meta-analysis reported that each additional cup of coffee reduces the risk of liver cancer by 15%. Several other meta-analyses reached similar conclusions.
- A 2020 meta-analysis concluded a significant protection against liver cancer at 2 cups/day. In all these studies, the degree of protection increased with larger amounts of coffee consumed.

Chapter 8: Coffee/Caffeine and the Digestive Tract

- Coffee reduced risk of liver cancer recurrence and improved survival in patients that underwent liver transplantation.
- Coffee reduces the risk of chronic liver disease including viral hepatitis B and C, alcohol-induced liver disease or cirrhosis, and non-alcoholic fatty liver disease (NAFLD).
- Coffee consumption is associated with reduced risk of liver fibrosis, even in HIV-HCV co-infected patients with elevated alcohol consumption (2018).
- Protective effect of coffee against liver fibrosis.
- Coffee consumption was inversely related to elevated levels of ALT and AST (liver enzymes).
- Coffee consumption has not been reported to generate any deleterious effects on the various organs of the digestive tract. (Nehlig, Effects of Coffee on the Gastro-Intestinal Tract: A Narrative Review and Literature Update, 2022)

<u>No Association of Coffee Consumption with Gastric Ulcer, Duodenal Ulcer, Reflux Esophagitis, and Non-Erosive Reflux Disease: A Cross-Sectional Study of 8,013 Healthy Subjects in Japan</u>

Because caffeine increases gastric acid secretion, negative effects of coffee on upper-gastrointestinal diseases have been precariously accepted, despite inadequate epidemiological evidence.

- 8,013 study subjects comprised of 5,451 coffee drinkers and 2,562 non-coffee drinkers
- Gastric ulcer (GU), duodenal ulcer (DU), reflux esophagitis (RE), and non-erosive reflux disease (NERD) were diagnosed by endoscopy, and NERD

was diagnosed by the symptoms of heartburn and regurgitation.

- Associations between coffee, age, gender, BMI, *Helicobacter pylori (HP)* infection, pepsinogen I/II ratio, smoking, and alcohol were studied.

There was no significant relationship between coffee consumption and the four major acid-related upper gastrointestinal disorders. Coffee consumption was defined as one or more cups of coffee per day and non-drinkers were less than a cup of coffee per day. (Shimamoto, et al., 2013)

The key to accepting the research is the major role confounders like smoking, obesity and Helicobacter infection play.

<u>Coffee or Tea, Hot or Cold, are not Associated with Risk of Barrett's Esophagus</u>

Barrett's esophagus (BE) is the precursor lesion for esophageal adenocarcinoma (EAC). BE affects up to 15% of persons with frequent symptoms of gastroesophageal reflux disease (GERD) and 1%-2% of the adult population.

- This study examined the association between consumption of tea or coffee with risk of BE in 310 United States veterans with histologically confirmed BE with 1,728 individuals as controls.
- These data do not support an association between consumption of coffee or tea and risk of BE. It is unlikely that avoidance of coffee or tea will protect against BE.
- A 2014 prospective study of >400,000 participants reported no association between coffee and tea consumption and EAC. A 2010 prospective study also found an inverse association with coffee consumption. (Sajja, El-Serag, & Thrift, 2016)

Chapter 8: Coffee/Caffeine and the Digestive Tract

<u>Significance of various factors in patients with functional dyspepsia and peptic ulcer disease in Greece. A comparative prospective study</u>

The study group (295 patients) were chosen among consecutive outpatients who had undergone an upper gastro-intestinal (GI) endoscopy because of dyspepsia. As controls, 54 previously studied, healthy non-dyspeptic people, well matched for age and sex, were used.

- Significantly more patients with PUD were smokers and alcohol drinkers.
- H pylori antral colonization was found in 61% of patients with FD (functional dyspepsia) as compared with 74% (Gastric ulcer) and 85% (Duodenal ulcer) of patients.
- Factors such as educational level, area of residence, and coffee/cola drink consumption did not differ in the studied groups of patients. (Archimandritis, Sipsas, Tryphonos, Tsirantonaki, & Tjivras, 1995)

<u>The effect of coffee consumption on the non-alcoholic fatty liver disease and liver fibrosis: A meta-analysis of 11 epidemiological studies</u>

- This study comprises two literature meta-analyses.
- Coffee decreased the risk of NAFLD by 23%.
- Coffee also significantly decreased the risk of progressing from NAFLD to liver fibrosis by 32% compared to non-drinkers. (Hayat, et al., 2021)

<u>Co-Medication and Nutrition in Hepatocellular Carcinoma: Potentially Preventative Strategies in Hepatocellular Carcinoma</u>

In the USA, HCC is the most rapidly increasing cancer cause of death, and the rate increased by 43% between 2000 and 2016.

- Cirrhosis is the strongest predictor of HCC incidence and mortality, as 80–90% of all HCC patients have an underlying chronic liver disease.

Statins in the Prevention of HCC (Hepatocellular Carcinoma)

- Statins are widely used for treatment of hyperlipidemia. They are essential for primary and secondary prevention of cardiovascular diseases. (primary prevents disease and secondary reduces impact of disease).
- Several studies have demonstrated the protective effects of statins in patients with chronic liver disease, especially related to hepatitis B and C infections.
- Five recent meta-analyses support the protective effects of statins in primary liver cancer risk, especially in high-risk individuals.
- Zhong et al. evaluated 25 studies including >2 million individuals and indicated a dose-dependent benefit between statin intake and primary liver cancer risk.
- Facciorusso et al. included 1,925,964 patients showing that lipophilic statins (most are lipophilic except Crestor and Pravachol) were associated with 51% HCC prevention. The underlying effects seem to be dose-dependent.
- Islam et al. identified 24 studies with 59,073 patients showing statin medication reduced risk 46% of HCC.
- Li et al. in a 2020 meta-analysis of 519,707 on statin medication showed a 46% reduced risk of HCC.
- Besides contributing to greater survival in patients with cirrhosis, multiple randomized controlled trials also indicate a benefit in advanced stages of HCC.
- A 2013 case-control study by Lai et al. further confirmed a 28% decreased risk of HCC with statins.

Caffeine and Tea

Chapter 8: Coffee/Caffeine and the Digestive Tract

- Coffee consumption was repeatedly associated with a dose-dependent reduced risk of HCC.
- A 2017 meta-analysis involving more than 2 million participants observed that increasing coffee consumption by 2 cups per day reduced the risk of HCC by 35%. In addition to coffee consumption, benefits were also seen for the regular use of tea. However, data concerning the use of decaffeinated coffee were rather conflicting.

Omega-3 Polyunsaturated Fatty Acids (PUFAs)

- A prospective study in Japan with >90,000 subjects indicated that consumption of fish with high PUFAs decreased risk of HCC.
- A 2015 meta-analysis of 10 studies found that fish consumption decreased the risk of HCC by 35% and that dietary intake of PUFAs was associated with a decreased risk of HCC.

Fruits, Vegetables, and Plants

- Dietary factors are likely to play an important role in the prevention of HCC. Obesity is considered a major driver of hepatocellular cancer.
- Yang et al. indicated that increased whole grain intake correlated significantly with lower HCC risk. (Kusnik, et al., 2021)

Chapter 9: Alzheimer's Disease and Parkinson's Disease

Alzheimer's disease and Parkinson's disease are the two most common neurodegenerative disorders. They develop in millions of people and decrease both the quality of life and the number of years of life. Almost all families are affected by one or the other.

Neuroprotective Effects of Coffee Bioactive Compounds: A Review

Below are multiple studies with most, but not all, expressing protective effects of coffee on Alzheimer's disease, Parkinson's disease and stroke.

- The 2002 Canadian Study of Health and Aging on a group of 1,023 individuals aged 65 years or older showed that coffee reduced the risk of Alzheimer's disease by 31%.
- On the contrary, a 2015 meta-analysis showed no significant relationship between caffeine intake and cognitive disorders.
- The risk of Parkinson's disease was reduced by 30-38% in a systematic review and meta-analysis in caffeine drinkers.
- A 2014 analysis by Qi and Li suggested a decreased risk of Parkinson's disease with coffee consumption.

- Ross et al. in 2000, based on 27 years of follow-up in American Japanese, noted a five-time lower risk of developing Parkinson's disease in 45-68 years-old people drinking coffee containing about 421 mg of caffeine per day (about 3 cups).
- Hu et al. in 2007, in a nearly 13-year control study involving about 14,500 people (about 62 years old), showed that the risk decreased by 45% and 59% for Parkinson's disease for subjects drinking one to four, and five or more cups of coffee per day, respectively, and did not differ between sexes.
- Several studies showed that decaffeinated coffee was not associated with neurodegenerative disorders risk, promoting caffeine as the key ingredient.

Other ingredients in coffee

- Chlorogenic acid is found in fruit, vegetables, spices, olive oil, wine, tea, and especially coffee. Both caffeinated and decaffeinated coffee contain a large amount of chlorogenic acid. The clinical data on chlorogenic acid is limited.
- Caffeic acid is produced by many plants, not only by coffee plants. Like many other polyphenols, caffeic acid exerts potent antioxidant and free radical scavenging properties. No specific clinical studies have been done.
- Trigonelline is another coffee component that has antioxidant features that is important in aroma but has not been extensively studied.
- Kahweol and cafestol are present in unfiltered coffees such as Scandinavian-style boiled coffee, Turkish-style coffee, French press coffee, and espresso. These two compounds increase cholesterol and have limited clinical studies. (Socała, Szopa, Serefko, Poleszak, & Wlaź, 2020)

Chapter 9: Alzheimer's Disease and Parkinson's Disease

Dose-response meta-analysis on coffee, tea and caffeine consumption with risk of Parkinson's disease

- A total of 13 articles involving 901,764 participants for coffee, eight articles involving 344,895 participants for tea and seven articles involving 492,724 participants for caffeine were included.

Tea and caffeine consumption decreased Parkinson's disease risk with increasing doses. The maximum benefit with coffee was at about three cups a day. (Qi & Li, 2014)

Non-genetic risk and protective factors and biomarkers for neurological disorders: a meta-umbrella systematic review of umbrella reviews

Analysis of umbrella reviews until Sept. 20, 2018.

In Parkinson's disease and Alzheimer's disease, coffee consumption and physical activity were protective factors. (Mentis, Dardiotis, Efthymiou, & Chrousos, 2021)

Association of Coffee, Decaffeinated Coffee and Caffeine Intake from Coffee with Cognitive Performance in Older Adults: National Health and Nutrition Examination Survey (NHANES) 2011-2014

Association of coffee and caffeine with cognitive performance in 2,513 participants aged 60 years or older.

Caffeinated coffee and caffeine from coffee were associated with improved cognitive performance, while decaffeinated coffee was not associated with cognitive performance. (Dong, Li, Sun, Li, & Zhang, 2020)

Association of coffee, green tea, and caffeine with the risk of dementia in older Japanese people

Examine the consumption of coffee, green tea, caffeine and dementia risk of 13,757 community-dwelling individuals aged 40-74 years with 8 years follow-up.

High levels of coffee and caffeine consumption were significantly associated with a reduced dementia risk in a dose-dependent manner, especially in men. Moreover, coffee consumption of ≥3 cups/day was associated with a 50% reduction in dementia risk. (Matsushita, et al., 2021)

Caffeine as a protective factor in dementia and Alzheimer's disease

- Most studies (three of five) support coffee's favorable effects against cognitive decline, dementia or Alzheimer's disease.
- Two studies had combined coffee and tea drinking and indicated some positive effects on cognitive functioning.
- For tea drinking, protective effects against cognitive decline/dementia are less evident. (Eskelinen & Kivipelto, 2010)

Midlife coffee and tea drinking and the risk of late-life dementia: a population-based CAIDE study

We aimed to study the association between coffee and/or tea consumption at midlife and dementia/Alzheimer's disease risk in later life.

- After an average follow-up of 21 years, 1,409 individuals (71%) aged 65 to 79 completed the re-examination in 1998.
- Coffee drinkers at midlife had lower risk of dementia and Alzheimer's compared with those drinking little or no coffee.

- The lowest risk (65% decreased risk) was found in people who drank three to five cups per day.
- Tea drinking was relatively uncommon and not related to risk.

Coffee drinking at midlife is associated with a decreased risk of dementia/Alzheimer's disease later in life. (Eskelinen, Ngandu, Tuomilehto, Soininen, & Kivipelto, 2009)

Association between coffee consumption and total dietary caffeine intake with cognitive functioning: cross-sectional assessment in an elderly Mediterranean population

Evaluation of coffee, caffeine intake with cognitive testing in 6,427 participants with mean age 65 ± 5 years who were overweight/obese with metabolic syndrome.

- Participants in the top third of total caffeine intake had lower odds of poor cognitive functioning than those in the lowest third.
- Coffee consumption and total caffeine intake were associated with better cognitive functioning as measured by neuropsychological tests.
- These associations were not observed for decaffeinated coffee consumption. (Paz-Graniel, et al., 2021)

Neuroprotective Effects and Mechanisms of Tea Bioactive Components in Neurodegenerative Diseases

More than 80% of dementias in the world are caused by Alzheimer's disease.

Parkinson's disease is the second most common neurodegenerative disease in elderly people.

- A 2016 study with follow-up for 5.7 years involving 13,645 Japanese, 65 years-old or older, showed green tea consumption significantly reduced the risk of dementia.

- A 2009 study among 278 Parkinson's disease patients revealed onset was delayed by 7.7 years when tea consumption was more than three cups a day.
- A 2014 study of 34,4895 participants showed that caffeine (200 mg/day) and tea (two cups a day) decreased Parkinson's disease risk by 17% and 26%, respectively.
- Although there are many epidemiological studies showing that tea has neuroprotective effects, several inconsistent results are also reported. For instance, a 2009 survey including 1,409 participants (71% ages 65-79 years) showed that drinking coffee was related to the prevention of Alzheimer's disease, while drinking tea was not.
- Tea is divided into unfermented (green, white), semi-fermented (oolong), fully fermented (black), and post-fermented (dark).
- Unfermented teas contain more polyphenols (think of fruits/vegetables).

Polyphenols and other products in tea have more preclinical evidence then human studies so no firm conclusions can be made about the various isolated components. (Chen, et al., 2018)

The neuroprotective effects of caffeine: a prospective population study (the Three City Study)

This study examined the association between caffeine intake, cognitive decline, and dementia in 4,197 women and 2,820 men older than 65 years from three French cities. Evaluations were done at baseline, two years and four years.

- Women who drank more than three cups of coffee per day showed 33% less decline in verbal retrieval, 18%

less decline in visuospatial memory over four years than women consuming one cup or less.
- The protective effect of caffeine was observed to increase with age with women.
- No relation was found between caffeine intake and cognitive decline in men.
- Caffeine consumption did not reduce dementia risk over four years.

Caffeine may be of potential use in prolonging the period of mild cognitive impairment in women prior to a diagnosis of dementia. (Ritchie, et al., 2007)

Alcohol, coffee and tea intake and the risk of cognitive deficits: a dose–response meta-analysis

With high morbidity and lack of effective treatments, dementia is a devastating problem. Identifying any modifiable factors could have a great impact.
Four databases and 29 studies were included up to 4th June 2020.

- Light consumption of alcohol (<11 g/day (one drink is 14 g) and coffee (<2.8 cups/day) might be independently associated with reduced risk for developing cognitive deficits compared to abstinence.
- Drinking one cup of tea per day brings a 6% reduction in cognitive deficits, whereas two cups per day brought an 11% decrease. (Ran, et al., 2021)

Relationships Between Caffeine Intake and Risk for Probable Dementia or Global Cognitive Impairment: The Women's Health Initiative Memory Study

We investigated the relationship between caffeine intake and cognitive impairment or probable dementia in 6,467

women aged 65 and older with 10 years or fewer of annual cognitive assessments.
Our findings suggest a 26% lower risk of probable dementia or cognitive impairment in older women whose caffeine consumption was above median (261 mg or two to three cups per day). (Driscoll, et al., 2016)

Associations Between Caffeine Consumption, Cognitive Decline, and Dementia: A Systematic Review

Dementia is a progressive deterioration of cognitive functions and loss of independence in activities of daily living.

- Cho et al. (2018) found better cognitive scores for individuals with Parkinson's disease who consumed coffee compared to non-coffee drinkers.
- More beneficial associations for green tea (39%) and other/non-specified tea (37%), compared to black/oolong tea (29%).
- Only black/oolong tea doesn't have a protective effect (less polyphenols).
- The number of studies showing positive associations was 46 of 57 (81%) including 111,926 of 153,070 (73%) subjects, indicating that caffeine has a beneficial effect on the risk of dementia/cognitive decline.
- More than 70% of studies showed that caffeine has a favorable effect.
- Across all studies, only two studies had a negative effect.

Caffeine improves cognitive function and risk of dementia and this is most effective with moderate amounts of coffee and green tea in females more than males. (Chen, Scheltens, Groot, & Ossenkoppele, 2020)

Chapter 9: Alzheimer's Disease and Parkinson's Disease

Effect of Caffeine Consumption on the Risk for Neurological and Psychiatric Disorders: Sex Differences in Human

- In the USA, adults consume an average of 179 mg of caffeine daily, which is equivalent to 2 cups (100 mg/240 mL) of ground coffee.
- Some studies have shown that by drinking more than three cups of coffee a day, caffeine reduces the risk of developing AD and PD.
- caffeine consumption has a positive effect of reducing the risk of stroke, dementia, and depression in women and reducing the risk of PD in men, but also has a negative effect of increasing sleep disorders and anxiety disorders in adolescence in both men and women. (Jee, Lee, Bormate, & Jung, 2020)

Chapter 10: Caffeine and Depression/Suicide

Suicide was the 10th leading cause of death in 2019 and is usually the second most common reason for death in the age group 10-34 years-old (CDC).

Coffee, tea, caffeine and risk of depression: A systematic review and dose-response meta-analysis of observational studies

A literature search was conducted till June 2015, analyzing 12 studies for a total of 346,913 individuals and 8,146 cases of depression.

- Those with higher coffee consumption had a 24% reduction of depression.
- A peak of protective effect was 400 ml/day (about four cups).
- A borderline nonsignificant association between tea consumption and risk of depression was found.

This study suggests a protective effect of coffee on risk of depression. (Grosso, Micek, Castellano, Pajak, & Galvano, 2016)

Coffee and caffeine consumption and depression: A meta-analysis of observational studies

Literature search from Jan. 1, 1980 to May 1, 2015. 330,677 participants from seven studies in the coffee-depression analysis,

38,223 participants from eight studies in the caffeine-depression analysis.

- Compared with lowest-level consumption, coffee consumption decreased risk for depression by 24% and caffeine consumption decreased risk by 28%.
- The risk of depression decreased by 8% for each cup/day increment in coffee intake.
- The association between caffeine consumption and depression became significant when the caffeine consumption was higher than 68 mg/day and lower than 509 mg/day.

Coffee and caffeine consumption were significantly associated with decreased risk of depression. Essentially, a cup of coffee daily decreases risk of depression. (Wang, Shen, Wu, & Zhang, 2016)

Coffee, caffeine, and risk of completed suicide: results from three prospective cohorts of American adults

To evaluate the association between coffee/caffeine consumption and suicide risk.

1. 43,599 men in the Health Professionals Follow-up Study (1988-2008).
2. 73,820 women in the Nurses' Health Study (1992-2008).
3. 91,005 women in the NHS II (1993-2007).

Consumption of caffeine, coffee, and decaffeinated coffee, was assessed every 4 years.

- 45% lower risk of suicide for those consuming 2-3 cups/day compared to ≤ 1 cup/week of caffeinated coffee (< 8 oz/237 ml).
- 53% lower risk of suicide for those consuming ≥ 4 cups/day (P trend < 0.001).

These results involving 208,424 (43,599 men, 164,825 women) support an association between caffeine consumption and lower risk of suicide. (Lucas, et al., 2014)

A prospective study of coffee drinking and suicide in women

Among the many reported central nervous system effects of long-term caffeine use is improvement in mood.

- To examine the relationship of coffee and caffeine intake to risk of death from suicide.
- We conducted a 10-year follow-up study (1980 to 1990) of 86,626 US female registered nurses aged 34 to 59 years in 1980.
- Compared with non-drinkers of coffee, the risk of suicide in women was 66% lower in women who consumed two to three cups per day and 58% lower in women who consumed four or more cups per day. These findings remained essentially unchanged after adjusting for potential confounding factors. A strong inverse relationship was similarly found for caffeine intake from all sources and risk of suicide. (Kawachi, Willett, Colditz, Stampfer, & Speizer, 1996)

Chapter 11: Caffeine and Genetics

Before we discuss how caffeine interacts with people differently, a few basic genetic explanations may be helpful. Humans have 46 chromosomes. We get a set of 23 chromosomes from each biological parent. There are about 25,000 genes located on our chromosomes. A gene is a long sequence of DNA. DNA is made up of a long sequence of combinations of 4 nucleotides (adenine, guanine, cytosine and thymine). The four nucleotides encode a message that gives the formula to make things such as proteins. Proteins allow us to have chemical reactions and perform other duties. Some proteins are enzymes. Enzymes promote chemical reactions. A very important enzyme system is called cytochrome P450. The P450 enzymes are responsible for 95% of the body's caffeine metabolism. I find words are easier to understand if we define them.

The name "cytochrome P450" is a description of its characteristics. The enzymes are bound to the membrane of cells (cyto), contain heme pigment (chrome and P). When bound to carbon monoxide, these proteins produce a spectrum with a wavelength at approximately 450 nm. Hence "cytochrome P450". Caffeine is broken down in the liver by an enzyme called CYP1A2. CYP1A2 activity is variable in humans due to a combination of genetic

polymorphisms (different versions) and environmental factors including foods and drugs that can induce or inhibit enzyme activity. To date, 16 defined variations (alleles) are known and many others have not been fully defined yet. At least 30 small variations have been identified in coding and non-coding regions of the CYP1A2 gene. Human CYtochrome P450 enzyme 1A2 (CYP1A2) accounts for 13% to 15% of hepatic CYP enzymes. The gene called ADORA2A (ADenOsine Receptor A2A) has the blueprints for making one of the receptors that caffeine interacts with. Different versions (genetic polymorphisms) of the gene ADORA2A and enzyme CYP1A2 will influence caffeine's ability as a health promoting agent. Further research into the influence of genetics on caffeine metabolism is needed.

The following article gives a taste of how unique each individual is. All of the possible genetic combinations require the use of supercomputers to help decipher the material. Millions of years of evolution has been advantageous for organisms. Usually getting information from the horse's mouth is reliable.

> **Rare and common variant discovery by whole-genome sequencing of 101 Thoroughbred racehorses**
> The Thoroughbred breed was formed by crossing Oriental horse breeds and British native horses. In this study, we constructed a database from 101 Thoroughbred racehorses. Whole genome sequencing revealed a total of 12,173,068 SNVs (single-nucleotide variants). The number of SNVs detected in individual horses ranged from 4.8 to 5.3 million. Individual horses had a maximum of 25,554 rare variants. Therefore, these rare variants may affect differences in traits and phenotypes among individuals. (Tozaki, et al., 2021)

Chapter 11: Caffeine and Genetics

Humans and most organisms have lots and lots of variations and also many similarities. This article gives a taste of that principle.

Caffeine, exercise physiology, and time-trial performance: no effect of *ADORA2A* or *CYP1A2* genotypes

Investigate the influence of *ADORA2A* and *CYP1A2* genotypes on effects of caffeine.

- 40 male cyclists were screened for *ADORA2A* and *CYP1A2* genotypes in a randomized, double-blind, placebo-controlled study. Participants ingested 5 mg/kg of caffeine or placebo one hour before test.
- Caffeine significantly reduced perceived exertion, and increased blood lactate, respiratory exchange ratio, and minute ventilation (all performance measures)
- Variability in the effect of caffeine on performance is not explained by *ADORA2A* or *CYP1A2* genotypes. (Glaister, et al., 2021)

The Role of Genetics in Moderating the Inter-Individual Differences in the Ergogenicity of Caffeine

Since the removal of caffeine from the WADA banned list, its use amongst athletes has become widespread with one study reporting approximately 73.8% of athletes consuming caffeine shortly before or during an event, especially endurance athletes. CYP1A2 is responsible for the majority of the metabolism of caffeine, and ADORA2A has been linked to caffeine-induced anxiety.

- Individuals with enhanced caffeine metabolism have been classified as *"fast metabolizers"* (about 40% of the general population), whereas *"slow metabolizers"* have a reduced caffeine metabolism (about 60% of the population). The majority of people are either fast or slow metabolizers.

- Slow metabolizers are likely to have a prolonged caffeine effect which can be beneficial for performance or harmful for anxiety and insomnia.
- The investigations into the effects of CYP1A2 genotypes on caffeine remain equivocal.

It should be noted that the half-life of caffeine is 4-6 h but can vary between 2–12 h in most adults; and it is not yet known with confidence the interaction that results from the altered caffeine metabolism with fast and slow metabolizers. (Southward K. , Rutherfurd-Markwick, Badenhorst, & Ali, 2018)

Coffee effectively attenuates impaired attention in *ADORA2A* C/C-allele carriers during chronic sleep restriction

- National surveys indicate that more than 30% of the adult population in Western societies report sleeping less than the recommended 7–8 hours on weekday nights, and roughly 15% regularly sleep less than 6 hours.

We investigated if coffee consumption counteracts chronically restricted sleep in genetically caffeine sensitive men and women with the C/C genotype of *ADORA2A*. Participants slept only 5 hours in bed for five nights followed by regular coffee (*n* = 12; 200 mg caffeine at breakfast and 100 mg caffeine after lunch) and decaffeinated coffee (*n* = 14). At regular intervals four times each day, participants rated their sleepiness and performed several tasks.

- In caffeine-sensitive subjects *ADORA2A C/*C-homozygotes (caffeine-sensitive) regular coffee (300 mg caffeine/day) transiently improved all aspects of reduced attention.
- Paraxanthine is an ergogenic product of caffeine. Roughly 10 hours after coffee intake, the paraxanthine

concentration reaches levels comparable to or even higher than those of caffeine. Both caffeine and paraxanthine should be considered when interpreting the effects of coffee consumption. (Baur, et al., 2021)

The effect of caffeine on cognitive performance is influenced by CYP1A2 but not ADORA2A genotype, yet neither genotype affects exercise performance in healthy adults

Determine the influence of ADORA2A and CYP1A2 SNPs on exercise and cognitive performance after caffeine ingestion. Knowing how different genotypes react is important since 90% of individuals are CYP1A2 "*fast*" or "*slow*" metabolizers. Eighteen young, healthy, adults using a double-blind, placebo-controlled crossover design.

- **ADORA2A genotypes have "high" or "low" sensitivity to caffeine**
- **CYP1A2 genotypes are "fast" metabolizers or "slow" metabolizers of caffeine**

Results

- The beneficial effect of caffeine on cognitive performance was greater in CYP1A2 '*fast*' metabolizers compared with '*slow*'.
- There were no differences in cognitive performance between individuals with ADORA2A '*high*' or '*low*' sensitivity to caffeine.

No differences in exercise performance or caffeine metabolism emerged between ADORA2A or CYP1A2 genotypes. (Carswell, Howland, Martinez-Gonzalez, Baron, & Davison, 2020)

Chapter 12: A Few Tea Studies

People were drinking tea for thousands of years before coffee was discovered. It surprises me that coffee seems to have more scientific literature than tea despite tea being around for a lot longer. Many people add milk to tea, but butter was added for thousands of years to add more flavor. Tea has much less caffeine compared to coffee (an 8-ounces cup of coffee provides about 145 mg of caffeine; tea beverages contain 20–80 mg of caffeine per 8-ounces). The benefits of tea seem to relate to polyphenols (remember fruits and vegetables) and not caffeine.

Short-Term Tea Consumption Is Not Associated with a Reduction in Blood Lipids or Pressure: A Systematic Review and Meta-Analysis of Randomized Controlled Trials

A review investigated the effects of green and/or black tea (≥4 weeks) on systolic blood pressure, diastolic blood pressure, and cholesterol in healthy populations and adults with metabolic syndrome, prediabetes, and hypercholesterolemia.

•A total of 14 randomized, controlled trials assigned 798 participants to either green tea, black tea, or placebo. Study ranged from four to 24 weeks (mean: 7.4 weeks). **Short-term (4-24 weeks) tea consumption does not appear to significantly affect blood pressure or lipids in healthy or at-risk adults.** (Igho-Osagie, et al., 2020)

Effect of Decaffeinated Green Tea Polyphenols on Body Fat and Precocious Puberty in Obese Girls: A Randomized Controlled Trial

- Obesity is an important contributing factor for precocious puberty, especially in girls. Female precocious puberty is defined as the development of secondary sexual characteristics before the age of 8 or menstruation before the age of 10. Early sexual development in children can lead to rapid bone maturation with decreased adult height, psychological problems, and increased reproductive tract cancers in adulthoods.
  This is a double-blinded randomized controlled trial. 62 girls with obesity aged 6-10 years old were randomly assigned to receive 400 mg/day DGTP (decaffeinated Green Tea Polyphenols) or placebo for 12 weeks.
- Body mass index, waist circumference, and waist-to-hip ratio significantly decreased in both groups, but the percentage of body fat (PBF), serum uric acid (UA), and the volumes of ovaries decreased significantly only within the DGTP group.

DGTP (decaf green tea) have shown beneficial effects on obesity and postponed early sexual development in girls with obesity. (Xie, et al., 2021)

Chapter 12: A Few Tea Studies

Tea Consumption and Health Outcomes: Umbrella Review of Meta-Analyses of Observational Studies in Humans

Review of 96 meta-analyses studied tea consumption and 40 health outcomes.

- Tea consumption shows greater benefits than harm to health in this review.
- **Tea consumption decreased the risks of total mortality, cardiac death, coronary artery disease, stroke, and type 2 diabetes mellitus with two to three cups per day.**
- Beneficial associations are also found for several cancers, as well as skeletal, cognitive, and maternal outcomes.
  Harmful associations are found for esophageal and gastric cancer when the temperature of intake is more than 131-140 degrees F. (Yi, et al., 2019)

A comprehensive insight into effects of green tea extract in polycystic ovary syndrome: a systematic review

Polycystic ovarian syndrome (PCOS) affects about 5-20% of women of reproductive ages. This condition involves irregular menstruation, increased androgens, hirsutism, severe acne, obesity, insulin resistance, type 2 diabetes, cardiovascular disease (CVD), non-ovulation, and infertility. This review examines current knowledge about GTE (green tea extract) in PCOS.

- Allahdadian et al. in 2015, demonstrated statistically significant weight loss, decreased insulin levels, FBS, and free testosterone levels in overweight and obese PCOS women after prescribing two capsules of GTE 500 mg/day for 12 weeks.
- Mombaini et al. in 2017, reported that body weight, BMI, waist circumstance, and body fat percentage

decreased significantly after GTE 500 mg/day for 45 days in women with PCOS.

- Tehrani et al. found that 500 mg GTE supplementation for 12 weeks led to statistically significant weight reduction, decreased FBS, insulin, and free testosterone among patients with PCOS.
- In contrast, Chan et al. in 2006, reported no statistically significant effects of consuming 540 mg of EGCG (common polyphenol in green tea) for 3 months on weight reduction, FBS, insulin, and other hormones in obese PCOS women compared to a control group.
- In four studies, three reported that 500 mg/day extract of GTE caused improvements in women with PCOS.
- Regarding the mechanism, GTE is a thermogenic agent that reduces body weight by increasing energy expenditure and fat oxidation.

Current evidence indicates that green tea extract (GTE) supplementation has potential beneficial effects on PCOS. (Maleki, et al., 2021)

Health Benefits and Chemical Composition of Matcha Green Tea: A Review

- The Japanese powdered green tea, matcha, contains high amounts of antioxidants and anti-inflammatory agents. It has promising potential health benefits, mainly through a high concentration of polyphenols (anti-oxidants)

  Many substances have been shown in the laboratory or in preclinical testing to have beneficial effects, but without human studies, everything is potential or speculation. (Kochman, Jakubczyk, Antoniewicz, Mruk, & Janda, 2021)

Chapter 13: Caffeine, Insomnia and Withdrawal

Sleep is something we take for granted. Good quality sleep turns on many desirable hormones and poor-quality sleep aggravates heart disease, lung disease and diminishes quality of life.

"I'm so good at sleep that I can do it with my eyes closed"

<u>The impact of daily caffeine intake on nighttime sleep in young adult men</u>

Acute caffeine intake can delay sleep initiation and reduce sleep quality.

- We investigated the sleep of 20 male young habitual caffeine consumers during a double-blind, randomized, crossover study including three 10-day conditions: caffeine (3 × 150 mg caffeine daily for 10 days), withdrawal (3 × 150 mg caffeine for 8 days, then switch to placebo), and placebo (3 × placebo daily for 10 days).

Daily caffeine intake in the morning and afternoon hours does not strongly impair nighttime sleep structure nor subjective sleep quality in healthy good

sleepers who regularly consume caffeine. (Weibel, et al., 2021)

Multiple caffeine doses maintain vigilance, attention, complex motor sequence expression, and manual dexterity during 77 hours of total sleep deprivation

We investigated the efficacy of multiple repeated doses of caffeine during 77 hours of total sleep deprivation (3.2 days).

- Twenty-three males and females, 18-35 years of age, moderate caffeine consumers, completed the Psychomotor Vigilance Task 141 times during the test period.
- Caffeine was given over three nights without sleep. Participants received either caffeine (200 mg every 2 hours x 4) or placebo at the beginning of each two-hour test block from 0100-0900 (800 mg total per night).
- While Psychomotor Vigilance Task speed declined for both groups across all three nights, the caffeine group consistently outperformed the placebo group.
- While clearly superior to placebo, caffeine failed to sustain performance compared to normal baseline levels beyond the first few hours of sleep deprivation. Declining performance and attentional lapses continued to worsen with decrements exceeding more than 50% within the first 24 hours.

Caffeine is an effective countermeasure to total sleep deprivation.

Caffeine is more effective than placebo but does not replace sleep. (Killgore & Kamimori, 2020)

This is a badass study. I don't know what the fee was for volunteering for this study, but I hope it was more than just a gift card. In my opinion, sleep deprivation is a form of torture. I never did all-nighters in college, and I don't think they help test scores.

Chapter 13: Caffeine, Insomnia and Withdrawal

Being up all-night as an intern does not make a better doctor. It makes a better coffee-drinker.

Sleeping hours: what is the ideal number and how does age impact this?

Habitual short sleep duration can promote obesity, type 2 diabetes, hypertension, cardiovascular disease, depression, and all-cause mortality.

Older adults tend to have a harder time falling asleep and staying asleep. This decreased ability to sleep in older adults is often secondary to comorbidities and medications (polypharmacy).

- Optimal sleep is the amount of sleep needed to optimize outcomes (performance, cognitive function, mental/physical health, quality of life, etc.). Each health outcome should fall somewhere within the recommended sleep duration range, for example, nine hours of sleep for athletic performance, seven hours for academics. High-performance athletes need more sleep to recover from intense training.

Napping is increasingly seen as a public health tool and countermeasure for sleep deprivation in terms of reducing accidents and cardiovascular events and improving working performance. (Chaput, Dutil, & Sampasa-Kanyinga, 2018)

Caffeine Effects on Sleep Taken 0, 3, or 6 Hours before Going to Bed

- One recent population-based study of 18-58 years-old (mean age = 28.5) estimated that 90% of individuals consume caffeine in the afternoon (12 p.m.-6 p.m.), and 68.5% of people consume caffeine in the evening (6 p.m.-midnight).
- The average person consumes 319 ± 181 mg of caffeine per day.

- The study group comprised 12 healthy normal sleepers.

The results suggest that 400 mg of caffeine (about 3-4 cups) taken 0, 3, or even 6 hours prior to bedtime significantly disrupts sleep. Even at 6 hours, caffeine reduced sleep by more than an hour. (Drake, Roehrs, Shambroom, & Roth, 2015)

That is a decent amount of coffee later in the day or at night.

<u>Caffeine supplementation in the hospital: Potential role for the treatment of caffeine withdrawal</u>

- Patients placed NPO (nothing by mouth) in the hospital are susceptible to caffeine withdrawal.
- Caffeine has shown a role in prophylaxis and treatment of postoperative headache.
- Caffeine needs further study as a modality to prevent in-hospital caffeine withdrawal.

Caffeine withdrawal in the hospital setting is an underappreciated syndrome. Withdrawal may occur upon abstinence from chronic daily exposure at doses as low as 100 mg/day and following only 3–7 days of consumption at higher doses. Some studies suggest caffeine withdrawal may contribute to intensive care delirium and that caffeine may promote wakefulness post-anesthesia. (Agritelley & Goldberger, 2021)

<u>Withdrawal syndrome after the double-blind cessation of caffeine consumption</u>

We studied 62 normal adults whose intake of caffeine was low to moderate (mean amount, 235 mg-about 2.5 cups of coffee/day). They were then caffeine free for two days followed by either placebo or caffeine capsules equal to their usual daily amount.

Chapter 13: Caffeine, Insomnia and Withdrawal

- More subjects had scores exhibiting unfavorable symptoms than adults who resumed usual caffeine intake.

Those who consume low or moderate amounts of caffeine (235 mg or about 2.5 cups/day) can exhibit withdrawal symptoms within 48 hours without caffeine exposure. (Silverman, Evans, Strain, & Griffiths, 1992)

<u>Use of therapeutic caffeine in acute care postoperative and critical care settings: a scoping review</u>

- Caffeine withdrawal in the postoperative period increases the incidence of headache, which can be effectively treated with perioperative caffeine.
- Administration of caffeine results in faster emergence from sedation and anesthesia, particularly in individuals who are at high risk for complications. Caffeine seems to be safe in moderate doses in the perioperative period and in the intensive care setting.
- The use of caffeine after elective colorectal surgery has been recommended to reduce the incidence of postoperative ileus (slow return of gut function).
- Caffeine has been used in neonatal intensive care units to treat apnea-related syndromes with no long-term adverse effects. In infants, caffeine stimulates the respiratory center.
- The effects on the cardiovascular system are seen by mild changes to heart rate and blood pressure, with no consensus in the literature that increased caffeine consumption will increase risk of arrhythmias.
- Abrupt cessation of caffeine in chronic users, such as with fasted patients postoperatively, will affect 10% to 55% of individuals and may have symptoms including headache, drowsiness, decreased alertness, flu-like symptoms, nausea/vomiting, and muscle-aches.

Caffeine use in the intensive care unit

- Sadat et al. in 2017 randomized 80 mechanically ventilated ICU patients to either receive 3.5 g of coffee in 100 mL of water or placebo. There was a significant improvement in respiratory status compared to placebo.

Caffeine in the perioperative period

- There were two prospective randomized controlled trials which found prophylactic caffeine decreased the incidence of postoperative headache.
- Five studies found the administration of intravenous caffeine enhanced emergence from anesthesia.
- Gouda et al. in 2010 randomized 60 patients with obstructive sleep apnea either to receive 500 mg IV caffeine or saline. Individuals who received caffeine had significantly faster extubation times and fewer respiratory complications.
- Similar results were demonstrated in 2018 by Fong et al., who randomized eight patients to receive IV caffeine at 7.5 mg/kg or saline and had significantly faster emergence from anesthesia. Caffeine caused no adverse outcomes.
- Warner et al. in 2018 published a retrospective audit of caffeine administration (median dose of 150 mg) in the post-anesthetic recovery area to increase alertness in 151 heavily sedated patients. There was a significant improvement in sedation scores and no reported adverse events.
- Intraoperative or postoperative caffeine may increase the incidence of postoperative nausea/vomiting. Intraoperative caffeine was found not to affect the incidence of postoperative atrial fibrillation and reduced the time to void after indwelling bladder catheter removal.

Chapter 13: Caffeine, Insomnia and Withdrawal

- A 1996 national survey of 882 nurses found that 85% still practiced caffeine restriction in patients after an acute myocardial infarction.

Discussion

- Onset of caffeine withdrawal occurs as early as 12-24 hours post abstinence, with symptoms lasting between two to nine days. It is not surprising that when chronic caffeine users are required to fast for surgery, they develop a caffeine withdrawal headache. Caffeine perioperatively can reduce the incidence of postoperative headache.
- While there is routine screening and management for alcohol or smoking, caffeine consumption or withdrawal is not routinely documented before surgery.
- Caffeine can facilitate emergence from sedation or anesthesia. As caffeine is a central nervous system stimulant, there is a risk that early administration of caffeine could increase awareness during anesthesia. The use of caffeine in the ICU setting may decrease fatigue and improve participation in daytime physical therapy.
- Caffeine has been shown in a 2020 study to effectively improve gastrointestinal motility with no significant side effects. Historically, caffeine intake has been limited in the perioperative period because of the risk of vasospasm and cardiac events. However, caffeine use after an acute myocardial infarction may reduce the risk of cardiovascular mortality and does not increase the risk of atrial fibrillation after cardiac surgery in a 2018 study. (Bright, Raman, & Laupland, 2021)

Chapter 14: Coffee and Other Issues

This is not the reason why coffee is the most popular drug in the world.

The effect of on-demand caffeine consumption on treating patients with premature ejaculation: a double-blind randomized clinical trial

Premature ejaculation is a common sexual issue in male adults.

In a double-blind, random-controlled trial, 40 healthy individuals with premature ejaculation were allocated into two groups: caffeine and placebo.

- The caffeine group received 100 mg encapsulated caffeine for three weeks, two hours before intercourse.
- Intravaginal ejaculation latency time (IELT) and index of sexual satisfaction (ISS) were measured before and after treatment in both groups.
- Mean age of the participants was 39.9 ±8.72 years.
- A significant difference was seen in the caffeine group (IELT: 312 seconds vs 144 seconds, and ISS: 97 vs 77, respectively).

Our study demonstrates that 100mg on-demand caffeine can significantly improve premature ejaculation and satisfaction. (Saadat, Ahmadi, & Panahi, 2015)

Now, I know why my wife bought me a new coffeemaker! I knew there was something to Joe DiMaggio being called Mr. Coffee and being married to Marilyn Monroe (this lame joke shows my age and people under 50 won't understand it).

Coffee consumption and risk of hearing impairment in men and women

Hearing loss is the fifth leading cause of disability in the world.

- Assess coffee consumption and risk of disabling hearing impairment over a 10 years period.
- 36,923 participants (16,142 men and 20,781 women) [mean age 56.6 years, 1.6 cups/d].
- Men who consumed 1, and ≥2 cups/d had a 28% lower risk of hearing impairment compared with those who consumed <1 cup/d of coffee. This association was similar for caffeinated and decaffeinated coffee.
- Men with obesity had a 61% lower risk of hearing impairment for consumption of ≥2 vs. <1 cups/d.
- No association was found between coffee and hearing function among women. (Machado-Fragua, et al., 2021)

It would be interesting if they separated the men into married, never married, or ever married along with coffee consumption and hearing impairment. Loud noises like yelling and broken dishes can damage fragile hair cells!

The Use of Caffeine by People with Epilepsy: The Myths and the Evidence

Until clinical studies suggest otherwise, caffeine intake is safe in people with epilepsy (seizures). (Bauer & Sander, 2019)

Chapter 14: Coffee and Other Issues

<u>Consumption of a dark roast coffee decreases the level of spontaneous DNA strand breaks: a randomized controlled trial</u>

Spontaneous DNA strand breaks are a well-established marker of health risk and aging. We analyzed the effect of consuming a dark-roast coffee blend on the level of spontaneous DNA strand breaks.

Eighty-four healthy men were randomized to consume daily for four weeks either 750 ml of fresh coffee (about two cups) or 750 ml of water.

- At baseline, both groups exhibited a similar level of spontaneous DNA strand breaks. In the intervention phase, spontaneous DNA strand breaks significantly decreased in the coffee group, leading to a 27% difference.

We conclude that regular coffee consumption contributes to DNA integrity. (Bakuradze, et al., 2015)

<u>The calming effect of roasted coffee aroma in patients undergoing dental procedures</u>

- Aromatherapy is an alternative medicine treatment for stress, anxiety, depression, and insomnia. It uses a diffuser.
- Dental anxiety is present in over 11% of the population with moderate anxiety in about 25% of the population. This study investigated the calming effect of coffee aroma while the patients underwent dental procedures (probing and scaling).
- Salivary α-amylase (sAA), cortisol (sCort) levels, blood pressure, and pulse rates were measured as objective evidence to support stress relief along with subjective assessments.
- The patients inhaling coffee aroma had significantly decreased sAA and sCort levels (40% and 25%

differences, respectively) along with lower pulse rates and favorable subjective assessments.

- The liking for coffee aroma or coffee drinking had no effect on the sAA and sCort responses. (Pachimsawat, Tangprasert, & Jantaratnotai, 2021)

Because coffee aroma is noticeable over no coffee aroma, this study makes me think of the placebo effect. My conclusion is the positive feelings about coffee aroma turned on the hormone responses that promoted objective chemical findings.

Can coffee consumption be used to accelerate the recovery of bowel function after cesarean section? Randomized prospective trial

Group 1 (n = 51) drank three cups of coffee (one cup at two, six, and 18 hours after cesarean), whereas group 2 (n = 52) was not given any treatment.

- The mean time to passage of first flatus (mean 8.6 vs. 11.3 hours), defecation (20.7 vs. 29.1 hours), and toleration of solid food (8.78 vs. 12.88 hours) were all significantly shorter in the coffee group. The control group required more pain medications and anti-emetics.

Coffee enhances the recovery of gastrointestinal function after elective cesarean section. Usually patients have no difficulty after C-section and meals are routinely ordered without delay. (Bozkurt Koseoglu, Korkmaz Toker, Gokbel, Celikkol, & Gungorduk, 2020)

The association between coffee consumption and periodontitis: a cross-sectional study of a northern German population

6,209 participants. Standardized periodontal examination were done.

There was a 151% increased risk between strong coffee consumption (≥ 7or more cups/day) and periodontitis compared with low coffee consumption.

Low and moderate coffee consumption was not associated with periodontitis.

High caffeine intake could inhibit bone metabolism as a possible mechanism. Moderate coffee consumption was not associated with periodontitis, compared with low coffee consumption. (Struppek, et al., 2022)

Chapter 15: Coffee/Caffeine and Naysayers

It's always important to be tolerant of other people and their opinions, even if they are certifiably crazy and make your "blood boil". I have never personally seen blood boil in 30 years of practice, and it is not on my bucket list. I will give the naysayers the same font and size as the other articles because I believe in fair play. I don't have the killer instinct like Tiger Woods or Michael Jordan. Some studies are neutral or do not show benefits of coffee/caffeine and it is important to show equal balance.

<u>Coffee consumption and risk of fractures: a systematic review and dose-response meta-analysis</u>

We performed a review on coffee consumption and the risk of fractures.

- 253,514 participants with 12,939 fracture cases from 15 studies.
- The risk of fractures at the highest level of coffee consumption was 14% higher in women and 26% lower in men.
- The risk of fractures in women who consumed 2 cups per day was 2% higher and 46% higher with 8 cups.

Daily consumption of coffee is associated with an increased risk of fractures in women and a decreased risk in men. (Lee, et al., 2014)

Effect of coffee consumption on dyslipidemia: A meta-analysis of randomized controlled trials

The association between coffee consumption and blood lipids has inconsistent results. Literature search until April 2020 with 12 studies.

- Coffee consumption significantly increased total cholesterol, triglyceride, LDL cholesterol with no significant effect on HDL cholesterol.

Coffee consumption may be associated with an elevated risk for dyslipidemia. (Du, Lv, Zha, Hong, & Luo, 2020)

Coffee consumption and mortality in Japan with 18 years of follow-up: the Jichi Medical School Cohort Study

9,946 (men/women: 3,870/6,076) subjects evaluated the association between coffee intake and all-cause mortality and mortality due to cancer, coronary heart disease, or stroke over 18.4 years.

- **No significant association was shown between coffee consumption and all-cause mortality.**
- **Stroke mortality was 37% lower with 1-2 cups of coffee daily than in those who do not consume coffee, and this association occurred only in men.** (Sakamaki, et al., 2021)

Habitual coffee intake and plasma lipid profile: Evidence from UK Biobank

- Association between habitual coffee intake and lipid profiles from 362,571 participants.

- Long-term heavy coffee consumption may lead to an unfavorable lipid profile. (Zhou & Hyppönen, 2021)

Maternal coffee intake and the risk of bleeding in early pregnancy: a cross-sectional analysis

Examine the association between pre-pregnancy coffee consumption and risk of bleeding in early pregnancy.

- A cross-sectional analysis of 3,510 pregnant women from Korea. Bleeding was defined as the occurrence of vaginal bleeding in the first 20 weeks of pregnancy.
- Heavy coffee drinkers (≥2 cups/day) showed a significantly higher risk of bleeding in early pregnancy, even in women with low risk for pregnancy-related complications.

The results suggest that caffeine intake before conception and during pregnancy should be reduced. (Choi, Koo, & Park, 2020)

Caffeine added to coffee does not alter the acute testosterone response to exercise in resistance trained males

- This study investigated the effects of coffee ingestion with supplemental caffeine (CAF) on serum testosterone (T) responses to exercise in recreationally strength-trained males.
- Subjects ingested 6 mg/kg body weight of caffeine via 12 ounces of coffee prior to exercise in a randomized, within-subject, crossover design. The exercise session consisted of 21 minutes of high-intensity interval cycling followed by resistance exercise.
- T was elevated immediately and 30-minutes post-exercise by 20.5% and 14.3% respectively with or without caffeine.

While past literature suggests caffeine may additionally enhance testosterone post-exercise, data from the current study does not. (Landry, Saunders, Akers, & Womack, 2019)

The Effects of High Doses of Caffeine on Maximal Strength and Muscular Endurance in Athletes Habituated to Caffeine

This study assessed the intake of 9 and 11 mg/kg of caffeine on maximal strength and muscle endurance in habitual caffeine users (~411 mg/day).

- Randomized, crossover, double-blind design with 16 healthy strength-trained male athletes (age=24.2 years, weight=175 lbs., BMI=24.5, bench press 1RM=260 lbs. Each participant performed three sessions.

High acute doses of caffeine (9 and 11 mg/kg) did not improve muscle strength nor muscle endurance in athletes who were habitual caffeine users. (Wilk, Krzysztofik, Filip, Zajac, & Del Coso, 2019)

Physiological responses to caffeine during endurance running in habitual caffeine users

Six varsity-level runners were studied over 90 minutes of treadmill running to determine the effects of caffeine (6 mg/kg) in a randomized, crossover, double-blind manner. Subjects were habitual caffeine consumers (200 mg/day). Caffeine administration (6 mg/kg) in athletic, habitual caffeine drinkers did not improve performance in endurance running. (Tarnopolsky, Atkinson, MacDougall, Sale, & Sutton, 1989)

Coffee, CYP1A2 genotype, and risk of myocardial infarction

Coffee is metabolized by P450 1A2 (CYP1A2) liver enzyme. Individuals who have CYP1A2*1A allele are "*rapid*" caffeine metabolizers, whereas CYP1A2*1F are "*slow*" caffeine metabolizers.

- Determine whether CYP1A2 genotypes modify coffee consumption and risk of acute nonfatal myocardial infarction.
- 2,014 people with a first acute nonfatal myocardial infarction and controls were genotyped for enzyme variety.

Intake of coffee was associated with an increased risk of nonfatal myocardial infarction only among individuals with slow caffeine metabolism, suggesting that caffeine plays a role in this association. (Cornelis, El-Sohemy, Kabagambe, & Campos, 2006)

<u>The influence of CYP1A2 genotype in the blood pressure response to caffeine ingestion is affected by physical activity status and caffeine consumption level</u>

This study aimed to investigate blood pressure response to caffeine ingestion looking at CYP1A2 genotype, physical activity status and habitual caffeine consumption.

- Thirty-seven participants (19-50 years old) were categorized according to:
    - genotype: CYP1A2 (AA) "*fast metabolizer*" or CYP1A2 (AC) "*slow metabolizer.*"
    - physical activity level: sedentary or physically active.
    - caffeine consumption: non-habitual and habitual heavy consumer.
- All groups had BP assessed before and one hour after caffeine ingestion (6 mg/kg).
- Physical activity only modulated the blood pressure responses to acute caffeine ingestion in "*slow*" individuals.
- Caffeine ingestion in slow caffeine metabolizers is more likely to have an increased blood pressure response

independent of past consumption levels. (Soares, Schneider, Valle, & Schenkel, 2018)

This seems reasonable since caffeine sticks around longer in slow metabolizers.

Coffee, caffeine and blood pressure: a critical review

A literature search from 1966 to 1999 on the blood pressure effects of coffee or caffeine.

- Acute intake of coffee and caffeine increases blood pressure. The pressor response is strongest in hypertensive subjects. Some studies with repeated administration of caffeine showed a persistent pressor effect, whereas in others chronic caffeine ingestion did not increase blood pressure.

Epidemiologic studies have produced contradictory findings regarding the association between blood pressure and coffee consumption. During regular use, tolerance to the cardiovascular responses develops in some people, and therefore no systematic elevation of blood pressure in long-term and in population studies can be shown.

We conclude that regular coffee may be harmful to some hypertension-prone subjects. (Nurminen, Niittynen, Korpela, & Vapaatalo, 1999)

Effects of Caffeine Supplementation on Physical Performance of Soccer Players: Systematic Review and Meta-Analysis

Investigate the effects of caffeine to improve performance in soccer players. Literature search for randomized clinical trials till March 28, 2020.

We found no significant improvement in soccer-related performance with caffeine compared with placebo or no intervention. However, caffeine appears to be safe. (Ferreira, et al., 2021)

Chapter 15: Coffee/Caffeine and Naysayers

Trigger Factors for Spontaneous Intracerebral Hemorrhage: A Case-Crossover Study

We included consecutive patients diagnosed with ICH (intracerebral hemorrhage-head bleed) between July 1, 2013, and December 31, 2019. We interviewed 149 patients (mean age 64, 66% male) on their exposure to 12 potential trigger factors in the (hazard) period before onset of ICH compared to their normal exposure to these trigger factors in the year before the ICH (remember a 200% increase means 2 people in 100 instead of 1).

Hazard period is an hour before symptoms.

Results:

- 250% increased risk after caffeine consumption.
- 200-350% after Valsalva (bear down) maneuvers
- 480% after coffee consumption alone.
- 660% after lifting >25 kg. (55 lbs.).
- 1010% after minor head trauma.
- 3040% after sexual activity.
- 3760% after straining for defecation.
- 2189% after vigorous exercise.
- 5070% after flu-like disease or fever.

(van Etten ES, et al., 2022)

Chapter 16: Caffeine and Energy Drinks

Energy drinks were not popular in my generation. I am surprised they are so popular in the military. Here are two quotes about energy drinks: "I didn't sleep well last night so I made my coffee this morning with Red Bull instead of water. I got halfway to work before I realized I forgot my car"
"To me, drinking responsibly means don't spill it".
"Energy drinks are like duct tape, it fixes everything".

Energy Drinks: A Contemporary Issues Paper

Since their introduction in 1987, energy drinks have become increasingly popular.

- Energy drinks typically contain caffeine, taurine, glucuronolactone, vitamins, herbal extracts, proprietary blends, and/or amino acids. They are available with or without sugar and may or may not be carbonated, thus the range of products is broad.
- They often contain high concentrations of caffeine.
- According to the U.S. Food and Drug Administration, 400 mg/day, or about four or five cups of coffee, is the amount of caffeine generally considered safe for healthy adults.
- The amount of caffeine in over-the-counter products is limited to a maximum of 200 mg per dose, whereas

there is no limit for energy drinks. Energy drinks get around the 200-mg dose limit by saying the container has more than one serving.

Adverse effects associated with energy drink consumption

- Based on 2012 Australian poison control center data over seven years, the most commonly reported symptoms were palpitations, agitation, tremor, and gastrointestinal upset.
- Between 2000 and 2012, the U.S. Poison Control Center reported 5,103 exposures to energy products with 552 adverse events: one fatal, 24 serious, and 527 moderate adverse events. Importantly, 44.7% were in children younger than 6.
- According to the FDA's adverse event reporting system, between 2004 and 2012, 166 reports were received describing adverse events, including 18 deaths. Together, the FDA and Poison Control logged more than 700 adverse events.
- The FDA's reporting system is estimated to capture only about 1% of the true adverse events associated with energy drinks; thus, the number of adverse events and deaths is likely much higher.
- Sudden cardiac death, coronary artery spasm, coronary artery thrombosis, coronary artery dissection, aortic dissection, ST-segment elevation myocardial infarction, stress cardiomyopathy (Takotsubo cardiomyopathy), seizures, and intracerebral hemorrhage have been noted in case reports. It is important to note that in many of these cases, confounding variables such as co-ingestions (*e.g.*, drugs, alcohol), genetic predispositions, underlying cardiovascular abnormalities, and strenuous exercise were discovered, so specific causality cannot be attributed to energy drink consumption alone.
- About 6% of patients experience gastrointestinal upset.

- Acute renal failure, rhabdomyolysis (muscle damage), and metabolic acidosis have been described with energy drinks.
- Obesity is associated with energy drinks, with a usual can containing 216-248 calories.
- Adolescents and young adults who consumed energy drinks were more likely to report mind racing, restlessness, jitteriness, and trouble sleeping. They were more likely to indulge in risk-taking behaviors. Energy drinks are often combined with alcohol, potentially increasing alcohol consumption and potential harm.
- The American Academy of Pediatrics and the National Federation of State High School Associations each recommended that energy drinks never be consumed by children or adolescents.
- The American Beverage Association in 2017 recommended that energy drinks 1) be marketed separately from sports drinks, 2) not be sold or marketed in schools, and 3) not be marketed to children. (Higgins, Babu, Deuster, & Shearer, 2018)

The effect of energy drinks on the urge to drink alcohol in young adults

Marczinski and colleagues (2013) showed that energy drinks combined with alcohol augment a person's desire to drink more alcohol relative to drinking alcohol alone. The current study replicates these findings using a robust measure of alcohol craving.

We studied 75 participants aged 18 to 30 years. Participants received a cocktail containing either 60 ml (1.37 shots) of vodka and a Red Bull or 60 ml of vodka with soda water; both cocktails contained 200 ml of fruit drink.

- The primary outcome measures were multiple pretest and posttest alcohol/drug questionnaires and breath alcohol concentration.

- The vodka/Red Bull drink showed a significant increase in urge to drink alcohol compared with the alcohol-only condition.

Combining energy drinks with alcohol significantly increased the urge to drink alcohol relative to drinking alcohol alone. (McKetin & Coen, 2014)

<u>Adverse Events Reported to the United States Food and Drug Administration Related to Caffeine-Containing Products</u>

Examine differences in federally reported adverse events between caffeine-containing and non-caffeine-containing products.

- All adverse event reports between Jan. 1, 2014, and June 29, 2018.

Caffeine-containing products have a greater association with severe adverse events compared with non-caffeine-containing products. Exposure to pre-workout and weight-loss products had greater odds of being associated with a more serious adverse event relative to non-caffeinated products. (Jagim, Harty, Fischer, Kerksick, & Erickson, 2020)

<u>Caffeine increases sugar-sweetened beverage consumption in a free-living population: a randomized controlled trial</u>

Sugar-sweetened beverage consumption has been associated with overweight and obesity. The objective was to assess the influence that caffeine has on the consumption of such beverages.

- Participants (n=99) were blindly assigned to either a caffeinated sugar-sweetened beverage or a non-caffeinated sugar-sweetened beverage group.
- They then tracked consumption of either product over a 28-day period.

Chapter 16: Caffeine and Energy Drinks

The addition of low concentrations of caffeine to sugar-sweetened beverages significantly increased their consumption. Regulating caffeine as a food additive may be an effective strategy to decrease the consumption of nutrient-poor high-energy foods and beverages and potentially limit unhealthy weight gain. (Keast, Swinburn, Sayompark, Whitelock, & Riddell, 2015)

<u>Safety issues associated with commercially available energy drinks</u>

- A multiple-source search was conducted from 1980 to September 2007.
- Most energy drinks contain products such as guarana, ginseng, and taurine. As much as 80 to 300 mg of caffeine and 35 grams of sugar (140 calories) per eight-ounce serving are commonly present in energy drinks such as Cocaine, Pimp Juice, Red Bull, and Spike Shooter.
- **No negative reports or therapeutic benefits were identified with taurine, ginseng, and guarana used in the amounts found in most energy drinks.**
- Four documented case reports of caffeine-associated deaths were found, as well as four separate cases of seizures.
- **Caffeine and sugar are present in amounts known to cause a variety of adverse health effects.** (Clauson, Shields, McQueen, & Persad, 2008)

The names are clearly invented to attract impressionable youth. To keep your pimp hand strong, why wouldn't you drink Pimp Juice? Do teenagers really need to be jacked-up more than normal? I don't think so.

<u>Effect of a thermogenic beverage on 24-hour energy metabolism in humans</u>

Does consumption of an energy beverage increase 24-hour metabolism in healthy, young, lean individuals.

- Thirty-one male and female subjects consumed 3×250-mL servings of a beverage containing green tea polyphenols, caffeine, and calcium for three days in a single-center, double-blind, placebo-controlled, crossover design study. On the third day, energy metabolism was measured in a calorimeter chamber.
- Twenty-four-hour energy expenditure was significantly lower in women than in men.
- Treatment increased 24-hour energy expenditure by 106 kcal.
- No significant differences were observed in blood pressure and heart rate.
- **The study provides evidence that consumption of a beverage containing green tea polyphenols, caffeine, and calcium increases 24-hour energy expenditure by 4.6%** (Rudelle, et al., 2007)

The metabolism of women is lower than men as a result of less muscle mass, which essentially determines metabolism. This is one reason why exercise is so important, to maintain muscle mass. If you take 106 kcals per day and multiply by a year (365 days), that results in 38,690 kcals. Since one pound is 3,500 kcals, this translates to 11 pounds a year. Eleven pounds is more than a typical person gains in a year. My impression is the calories in many of the drinks are more than 106 calories so the net result is a gain in calories rather than a loss.

There is no easy way to lose weight except "*put the fork down and move more.*"

Chapter 16: Caffeine and Energy Drinks

Exploring the Role of Caffeine Use in Adult-ADHD Symptom Severity of US Army Soldiers

- Adult-ADHD (attention deficit hyperactivity disorder) prevalence in the U.S. Army has been estimated to be around 7.6-9.0%.
- Substance use disorder is among the most common comorbid psychiatric conditions in adult ADHD and is nearly twice as common compared to the general population. The main abuse drugs are alcohol, nicotine, cannabis, amphetamines, cocaine and opiates with a duration more than five years for amphetamine (39.5%) and alcohol (56.6%), respectively.

The aim of the present study was to explore the use of caffeine, caffeinated drinks and alcohol among soldiers with ADHD.

- The study involved 1,239 soldiers with ADHD and 17,674 peers without evidence of psychiatric disorders. ADHD subjects were diagnosed in childhood, prior to any deployment.
- Individuals with ADHD had higher substance use disorder and consumed more caffeinated beverages compared to their non-ADHD colleagues.
- In the military population, a high rate of energy drink intake is common.

Our data may suggest the use of caffeine as an adjuvant and a promising treatment tool to implement the efficacy of currently prescribed stimulants. (Cipollone, et al., 2020)

The military does not allow prescription treatment of ADHD. My limited experience with VA systems and a few military patients has given me the continued impression that military health care is substandard compared to the private sector. I do believe the VA does an exceptional job with vaccines, colorectal screening and paying for some drugs. The people that serve our country deserve better care.

A young kid self-medicating for ADHD with energy drinks is not acceptable.

Cardiovascular and Autonomic Responses to Energy Drinks—Clinical Implications

- In the United States, 51% of college students consume at least one energy drink per month and almost a third of students between grades 8 and 12 drink them.
- Some 45% of deployed military personnel are reported to consume a minimum of one energy drink daily, with 14% having three or more.
- In a 2015 randomized study of three different caffeine preparations (5-Hour Energy, Starbucks Double-Shot, and 3 mg/kg of caffeine powder) versus placebo, Paulus et al. reported that all caffeine groups showed elevations in mood, faster reaction times, and improved cognition.
- In a 2009 study of Red Bull, Ragsdale et al. showed no significant increases in blood pressure after intake of energy drinks, neither at rest nor during exercise or cold stress. In fact, Red Bull attenuated the blood pressure response to the cold pressor test (immersing hand in ice water to cause pain/stress). Red Bull elicited a significant increase in pain tolerance in all subjects.
- In a 2014 randomized crossover study of Red Bull (114 mg of caffeine) versus tap water, Grasser et al. noted a significant increase in systolic pressure (5.2 mmHg) and diastolic pressure (6.1 mmHg) as well as increases in heart rate of about 3.7 beats/min. In a subsequent randomized crossover study of Red Bull versus tap water, these investigators again noted increases in systolic pressure (7 mmHg), diastolic pressure (4 mmHg) and heart rate (7 beats/min).
- The concept of increased sympathetic outflow mediating an increase in blood pressure after

consuming energy drinks is supported by a randomized, double-blind, placebo-controlled 2015 study by Svatikova et al.
- Despite their widespread consumption, there are no systematic prospective studies of clinical cardiovascular outcomes in response to energy drinks. (Somers & Svatikova, 2020)

Pharmacokinetic analysis and comparison of caffeine administered rapidly or slowly in coffee chilled or hot versus chilled energy drink in healthy young adults

There is concern that inordinately high levels of caffeine may result from the rapid consumption of cold energy drinks.

- This study compares the pharmacokinetics of caffeine under various drink temperatures, rate of consumption and vehicles (coffee versus energy drink).
- Five caffeine (dose=160 mg) conditions were evaluated in an open-label, group-randomized, crossover fashion with 24 healthy subjects ranging in age from 18 to 30.
- The overall impact of these variables is small. (White, et al., 2016)

This study suggests that caffeine absorption and exposure from coffee and energy drinks are similar irrespective of beverage temperature or rate of consumption.

Chapter 17: Caffeine and Chocolate

The amount of caffeine in chocolate varies by the percentage of cocoa it contains. The higher the cocoa content, the higher the caffeine content and other health promoting compounds (polyphenols) and the more bitter it tastes. For example, dark chocolate has close to 3 times the caffeine content compared to milk chocolate. The sugar and extra calories with chocolate complicate the potential benefits. Similar to cinnamon tablets helping type 2 diabetes, cacao (cocoa) tablets can be bought for the caffeine and other polyphenols.

Chocolate is a very common source of caffeine for both children and adults. The discovery is attributed to the Aztec civilization and for most of its history, chocolate was a drink. It was a bitter drink till Europeans added honey or cane sugar. By 1868, a small company called "Cadbury" was selling small boxes of chocolate candies in England. A few years later, milk chocolate was sold by another familiar name, "Nestle." There are many quotes about chocolate. Here are a few by anonymous sources:

"A balanced diet is chocolate in both hands."

"Chocolate comes from cocoa, which is a tree; that makes it a plant. Chocolate is salad."

"Dear Diamond, we all know who is really a girl's best friend. Sincerely yours, Chocolate."

The survival time of chocolates on hospital wards: covert observational study

To quantify the consumption of chocolates in a hospital ward, we observed four wards at three hospitals in the United Kingdom.

- Observers covertly placed two 350-gram boxes of Quality Street (Nestlé) and Roses (Cadbury) chocolates on each ward (eight boxes containing 258 individual chocolates). These boxes were kept under continuous covert surveillance.

Results: 191 out of 258 (74%) chocolates were eaten.

- Median survival time of a chocolate was 51 minutes.
- Mean time to open a box was 12 minutes.
- Chocolates were consumed by health care assistants (28%), nurses (28%), followed by doctors (15%). (Gajendragadkar, et al., 2013)

Medicine is a very competitive field, but there are no rules when it comes to free chocolate. I am not surprised that it took 12 minutes to open a box of chocolate but somewhat disappointed that the median survival time was as long as 51 minutes.

Patterns of chocolate consumption

Cacao (Theobroma cacao) was not used in making sweets until the 1800s, when the cocoa press was invented. The 1994 Per capita consumption of chocolate per person in the United States was moderate (about 10 lbs./year) compared to many northern European countries (about 15-20 lbs./year). The Western United States contained the highest proportion of chocolate consumers. Chocolate was consumed by more people in the winter and as snacks. The mean amount of chocolate consumed was about 30-90 grams/day (1/2 to two chocolate bars) depending on gender and age group.

In 2020, the USA consumed about 10 lbs./ year per person with Switzerland leading at about 20 lbs. Unfortunately, chocolate is an affluent product and many poor countries have very low consumption rates. (Seligson, Krummel, & Apgar, 1994)

Chocolate consumption and all-cause and cause-specific mortality in a US population: a post hoc analysis of the PLCO cancer screening trial

- Several meta-analyses (2017, 2019) found that chocolate consumption was inversely associated with risks of stroke, coronary heart disease, and heart failure.
- A 2009 cohort study of 1,169 acute myocardial infarction survivors observed that higher chocolate consumption conferred lower mortality from CVD.
- A 2020 prospective study of 84,709 postmenopausal women revealed that chocolate consumption decreased mortality from all causes, CVD, and Alzheimer's disease.
- A 2015 prospective study of healthy men and women found that increasing chocolate consumption was significantly associated with decreased cardiovascular mortality.
- Several prospective studies found that low to moderate but not high chocolate consumption was favorably associated with risks of atrial fibrillation and heart failure.
- Several randomized controlled trials have found that dark chocolate consumption efficiently decreases blood pressure, increases insulin sensitivity, improves cholesterol profile and endothelial function, and inhibits platelet aggregation.

We conducted a post hoc analysis of the Prostate, Lung, Colorectal, and Ovarian (PLCO) Cancer Screening Trial to examine if chocolate consumption confers reduced risks of all-cause and cause-specific mortality in a US population. The mean age was 65.3 years, males were 46.3% and the average chocolate consumption was 1.5 servings/week. Mean follow-up of 13.5 years.

- Chocolate consumption was inversely associated with cardiovascular mortality, while no significant association was observed for cancer mortality.
- Chocolate consumption decreased the death rate from Alzheimer's disease.
- **Smoking removed any favorable associations.**
- **The most benefit was with 0.6-0.7 servings/week. Individuals consuming low amounts of chocolate could benefit without excess calories.**

In conclusion, in this US population aged 55 to 74 years, chocolate consumption is associated with lower risks of death from all causes, cardiovascular disease, and Alzheimer's disease. (Zhong, et al., 2021)

<u>Intake of Cocoa Products and Risk of Type 2 Diabetes: The Multiethnic Cohort</u>

Association of chocolate consumption with type 2 diabetes (T2D) incidence.

- 151,691 participants of Native Hawaiian, Japanese American, Latino, African American, and white ancestry with 7.8±3.5 years of follow-up.
- highest vs. lowest (≥10 vs. <1 g/day) consumption had 10% lower rate of T2D.
- frequency (≥4/week vs. <1/month) of intake had 19% lower rate of T2D.
- The estimated polyphenol intake from cocoa products (≥3 vs. <1 mg/day) showed a 7% lower rate of T2D.

- Significant interactions were only found in Japanese Americans, normal weight individuals, and those without co-morbidities. (Maskarinec G, 2019)
- The benefits of cocoa are limited to certain groups probably due to the negative benefits of the added calories associated with chocolate.

Chocolate consumption in relation to blood pressure and risk of cardiovascular disease in German adults

Investigate the association of chocolate with blood pressure and incidence of cardiovascular disease with a mean follow-up of about eight years.

- Dietary intake, including chocolate, and blood pressure were assessed at baseline (1994–98) in 19,357 healthy participants (aged 35–65 years).
- 57% consumed milk chocolate, 24% consumed dark chocolate, 2% consumed white chocolate and 17% unspecified.
- Chocolate consumption was related to a lower systolic and diastolic blood pressure in a linear fashion.
- Consumption of six grams per day (Hershey Kiss is 4.5 grams) was associated with a 39% lower risk of the combined outcome of myocardial infarction and stroke.
- The inverse relations were observed despite lower intakes of fruit and vegetables (i.e. health promoting foods) in people consuming more chocolate.
- The blood pressure-lowering effect of chocolate has been assessed in a number of intervention studies.
- The preference of milk chocolate over dark chocolate may have contributed to the weaker blood pressure estimates; milk chocolate contains less cocoa than dark chocolate. (Buijsse, Weikert, Drogan, Bergmann, & Boeing, 2010)

Chocolate Consumption is Inversely Associated with Calcified Atherosclerotic Plaque in the Coronary Arteries: The NHLBI Family Heart Study

It has been shown that the extent of calcified atherosclerotic plaque in the coronary arteries can be measured by cardiac CT.

A diet rich in fruit and vegetables, dark chocolate, or red wine – all good sources of flavonoids (polyphenols) – has been associated with a lower risk of coronary artery disease, cardiovascular mortality, lower blood pressure, and inhibition of platelet aggregation.

We collected data on 2,217 participants, mean age 50.7 years and 44% were men.

Chocolate consumption was inversely associated with prevalent coronary artery calcium in a dose-response manner. (Djoussé, et al., 2011)

Chocolate consumption and risk of heart failure in the Physicians' Health Study

We prospectively studied 20,278 men with a mean age of 66.4 years.

- Five or more servings/week of chocolate (5+ oz per week equals 3.2 Hershey chocolate bars) led to a 41% lower risk of heart failure in men with a BMI (body mass index) less than 25 but not in those with BMI greater than 25 (BMI greater than 25 indicates overweight) (Petrone, Gaziano, & Djoussé, 2014)

I think a person's weight is a big factor. A person who has extra weight does not need the extra calories from chocolate; this extra weight may offset any benefit from chocolate. Cacao tablets would be better.

Chapter 17: Caffeine and Chocolate

Habitual chocolate consumption and risk of cardiovascular disease among healthy men and women

Evaluate habitual chocolate consumption and the risk of cardiovascular events.

- Nine studies with 157,809 participants (99.6% European white), mean age 49-79 years old, follow-up 8-16 years.

We observed evidence that higher intake of chocolate may be associated with less cardiovascular disease and mortality. (Kwok, et al., 2015)

Chocolate consumption and risk of cardiovascular diseases: a meta-analysis of prospective studies

A systematic review and meta-analysis up to June 6, 2018 assessing the risk of cardiovascular disease with chocolate consumption.

- 23 studies including 405,304 participants.

Chocolate consumption may be associated with reduced risk of cardiovascular disease at <100 g/week consumption (about 500 calories) Higher levels may negate the health benefits and induce adverse effects associated with high sugar consumption. (Ren, et al., 2019)
(A typical Hershey chocolate bar is 220 calories)

Dark chocolate supplementation reduces the oxygen cost of moderate intensity cycling

Examine whether dark chocolate (DC) will improve performance in comparison to white chocolate (WC).
Using a randomized, crossover design nine moderately trained males (mean age 21.1 years) performed two cycling trials, two weeks apart, with either 40 g of DC or WC consumed daily. The DC and WC were equal caloric content.

- Blood lactate, heart rate was not different between conditions.
- The main finding was that regular consumption of DC daily (40 g) for fourteen days resulted in significantly higher performance measures compared to both baseline and WC conditions. Consumption of DC significantly increased VO2max compared to baseline ($P = 0.037$).

Ingestion of DC (more cocoa = caffeine) for 14 days reduced the oxygen cost of moderate intensity exercise and may be an effective ergogenic aid. (Patel, Brouner, & Spendiff, 2015)

Chapter 18: Coffee and Pregnancy

Most obstetricians do not object to pregnant patients having 1-2 cups of coffee per day during pregnancy. My wife is an Obstetrician.

Association Between Maternal Caffeine Consumption and Metabolism and Neonatal Anthropometry: A Secondary Analysis of the NICHD Fetal Growth Studies-Singletons

Evaluate the association between maternal caffeine intake and neonatal size in fast or slow caffeine metabolizers.

A longitudinal cohort study enrolled 2,055 nonsmoking low risk women between 2009 and 2013. Secondary analysis was completed in 2020.

Small reductions in neonatal measurements with increasing caffeine consumption were observed. Findings suggest that caffeine consumption during pregnancy, even at levels much lower than the recommended 200 mg per day of caffeine, are associated with decreased fetal growth. Results did not differ due to fast or slow caffeine metabolism genotypes. (Gleason, et al., 2021)

Assessment of Caffeine Consumption and Maternal Cardiometabolic Pregnancy Complications

Women are recommended to limit caffeine consumption to less than 200 mg per day based on risks to fetal health.

- Determine whether caffeinated-beverage intake and plasma caffeine and paraxanthine (breakdown product of caffeine) are associated with complications in pregnancy (i.e., gestational diabetes [GDM], preeclampsia, and gestational hypertension [GH]).
- 422 (16.3%) were Asian/Pacific Islander women, 741 (28.9%) were Hispanic women, 717 (27.8%) were non-Hispanic Black women, and 703 (27.2%) were non-Hispanic White women.
- Intake at 16 to 22 weeks was associated with 47% lower GDM risk.

Second trimester caffeinated beverage intake within current recommendations was not associated with higher GDM, preeclampsia or GH. These findings may be reassuring for women with moderate caffeine intake. (Hinkle, et al., 2021)

This study is even more reassuring since the majority of women were minorities with an elevated risk of pregnancy complications.

Chapter 19: Old School

Here are some interesting comments or stories about coffee and exercise. They range from 1862 to 1942. People spoke and wrote differently then. In many instances, the written word would be considered inappropriate now. Medical knowledge was limited, and many ideas we take for granted had yet to be articulated. Life was simpler and harder; a person's lifespan was much shorter. I included some silly rebuttals for humor.

1862

Utility of Coffee in Soldier's Diet

M. Larrey, having been called upon by the council of Health for his opinion as to the desirableness of extensive employment of coffee in the soldier's diet, speaks in his reply in the warmest terms concerning its use. He states that upon his father's recommendation it was employed freely in Algeria, with the best effects upon the soldier's health, as a substitute for brandy. It has also seemed to act in some measure as a prophylactic to intermittent fever. (Utility of Coffee in Soldiers' Diet, 1862)

War is so much more civilized after a good coffee break or cup of Joe.

1877

Medical Degrees for Women.

–On March 2nd, 1877, the Senate of the University of London, England, decided by a vote of fourteen to eight, to admit women to medical degrees in that institution. From every section of the civilized world, we almost daily learn of such privileges being granted to the sex. (Medical Degrees for Women., 1877)

I guess, the eight that did not vote in favor must have come from the uncivilized world?

1890

Science June 20, 1890

Coffee Inebriety

Dr. Mendel of Berlin has lately published a clinical study of this neurosis, his observations being made upon the women of the working population. He found large numbers of women who consumed over a pound of coffee in a week; and some men drank considerably more, besides beer and wine. The leading symptoms were profound depression of spirits, and frequent headaches, with insomnia. A strong dose of coffee would relieve this for a time, then it would return. The muscles would become weak and trembling, and the hands would tremble even at rest. An increasing aversion to labor and any steady work was noticeable. The heart's action was rapid and irregular, and palpitations and a heavy feeling in the precordial region were present. Dyspepsia of an extreme nervous type was also present. These symptoms constantly grow worse, and are only relieved by large quantities of coffee, generally of the infusion. In some cases, the tincture was used (opium). The victims suffer so seriously that they dare not abandon it, for fear of death. Where brandy is taken, only temporary relief follows. The face becomes sallow, and the hands and feet cold; and an expression of dread and agony settles over the countenance, only relieved by using strong doses of coffee. In all these cases, acute inflammation is likely to appear any time. An injury of any part of the body is the starting-point for inflammations of an erysipelatous character. Melancholy and hysteria are present in all cases. Coffee inebriates are more common among the neurasthenics, and are more concealed because the effects of excessive doses of coffee are obscure and largely unknown. Many opium and alcoholic cases have an early history of excessive use of coffee, and are always more degenerate and difficult to treat. A ... field for future study opens up in this direction. (Coffee Inebriety, 1890)

Wow, I guess that's some pretty strong coffee! Clearly the takeaway message is that coffee must be a gateway drug leading to much more dangerous drugs such as opium and alcohol! Everyone knows that illegal and dangerous drugs are usually sold on street corners. Is it a coincidence or conspiracy that many street corners have Starbucks?

1891

COFFEE POISONING.

Although "*coffee when well-prepared is beyond question one of the ambrosial luxuries of modern life,*" yet there is danger in the cup unless taken with somewhat more of judgment than is usually expended upon it. While to the majority its taste and action are agreeable, for others it is really a poison? A matter which is all the more important in consequence of the price having undergone a material and progressive decrease during the past eight or nine years, which, among other things, has led to a rapid increase in its consumption.

> The people of the United States consume, it is said, about one-third of the total coffee production, and this we are told "*may account in great measure for the prevailing nervous characteristics of many of our population, their increasing mental activity, and the actual accomplishment of work that might otherwise be impossible.*" Dr. Love, writing some years ago on the use and abuse of coffee, went so far as to say that "*in excess it is even more dangerous than alcohol, for it is not, like the latter, a nutrient, nor is the effect of its excessive use so apparent or unrespectable.*" The intellectual faculties excited to the greatest degree by the use of coffee are, we are told, the imagination and the memory. It produces an augmentation in the power of attention, a vivacity of thought and conception, increased capacity for mental and physical work, and transitory ambitions often beyond the physical or mental capability of the individual. Hence many dangers. It is not merely that the taking of coffee enables some people to wear themselves out more quickly than they would have done without it. Besides this it may produce directly deleterious effects, among which may be noted a feeling of apprehension and general tremulousness; disturbance of digestion; paroxysmal sneezing and coryza, or itching of the skin; wakefulness, and corresponding exhaustion of the nervous centers, neurasthenia, palpitation and rapid pulse; while in acute coffee poisoning there may be excitability to the extent of delirium. We do not think that coffee is often taken in this country to the extent mentioned by Dr. Leszynsky, but one cannot but observe that many of the symptoms which he describes are similar to those which we commonly associate with excessive tea drinking.
> (Leszynsky, 1891)

I need to drink extra coffee just to read through this descriptive odyssey! My parents never warned me about "excessive tea drinking." By bringing tea into the picture, he

is indirectly talking about the common ingredient in both coffee and tea — caffeine and other polyphenols.

1891

<u>Coffee</u>

After years of extended observation and pronounced personal experience, I feel justified in announcing:

1. The world has in the infusion of coffee one of its most valuable beverages.
2. As a prompt diffusible stimulant, either by the stomach or by injection into the rectum, it is in all cases of shock preferable to alcohol.
3. It is antagonistic to malaria, and especially destructive to the typhoid bacillus and cholera germ, and for this reason it is an admirable remedial agent in these conditions both as a direct stimulant, an antiseptic and an encourager of elimination.
4. One of its chief advantages in health and disease is in the fact that it aids in the securement of that psychical satisfaction which is conducive to hope, comfort, good digestion, great power of resistance and rapid recuperation.
5. In season, it supports, tides over dangers, helps the appropriative powers of the system, whips up the flagging energies, enhances the endurance, but is in no sense a food, and for these reasons and many others, it should be used temperately, as should all of nature's benign gifts.
6. In excess it is even more dangerous than alcohol for it is not like the latter, a nutrient, nor is the effect of its excessive use so apparent or unrespectable.

I. N. Love, M.D., St. Louis (Love, 1891)

Sounds like someone is using too much of his own product! I love the coffee endorsement as an encourager of elimination.

1892

RESTORATIVES. COFFEE-COCOA-CHOCOLATE.

Coffee is a valuable restorative, which though it closely resembles tea in constitution, has its own special characteristics and properties. The first coffee-house was opened in London in 1652, and since that date the use of coffee has constantly increased. Coffee has been called in France "*an intellectual drink*" owing to the fact that it has a decided stimulating influence on the nervous centers, lessens the need for sleep, and increases the capacity for mental work. It also seems to have the power of augmenting the functional activity of the muscles. Like tea, coffee lessens the sense of hunger, and will banish fatigue. To the soldier on the march it has proved the most valuable restorative, and for the explorer in the Arctic regions a warm cup of coffee has been declared to be a far better nightcap than rum and water.

The benefits of coffee are strongly expressed by Germain See, the French physician. In comparing alcohol and coffee, he says, "*The muscular system and muscular energy are marvelously roused by coffee, and a man fatigued or overworked can find no more wholesome support, whereas alcohol produces in the muscles a dubious passing excitement, and in the end, a degeneration of all the organs of human activity.*"

Cocoa is derived from the seed of a plant called the Theobroma cacao. The name was given by the botanist Linnaeus who expressed his high opinion of cocoa by the name *"Theobroma" "food for the gods."* A small amount of solid chocolate will be found a most valuable preventive against hunger when circumstances oblige one to go long without food. (Hart, 1892)

1894

The Hospital March 24, 1894
New Drugs and Preparations
Caffeine

Dr Falsans has been struck by the number of cases in which he has seen much cerebral excitement, violent delirium, and insomnia following the use of caffeine. In one case there were hallucinations, and he suggests that sometimes the hallucination and delirium which are set down as due to some specific disease are really caused by the caffeine which has been administered as a stimulant. This, he thinks, is especially likely when the patients are alcoholic or neurotic. Czarkowski calls attention to the contrary indications against the employment of caffeine in cases of alcoholism. He reports three cases in which intense excitement followed its use, and therefore he thinks that in such patients we should always begin with a small dose and gradually increase it if necessary. (New Drugs and Preparations- Carreine, 1894)

This confirms an old idea that probably predates 1894: Giving coffee to someone intoxicated simply makes the individual a wide-awake drunk.

1900

The Hospital June 23, 1900.
The Abuse of Exercise.
Thomas D. Lister M.D.

As a result of what is possibly an enforced neglect of personal muscular activity for a large portion of the year, there is a considerable class to whom exercise is a disagreeable sort of medicine which is taken in holiday doses only. Unfortunately, the simple direction, "*Don't overdo it."* is usually all that the patient hears, and exercise is taken very much at the patient's discretion, or indiscretion, as the case may be.

Few would now be found to dispute the assertion that exercise of the right kind and amount is as important to the attainment of perfect bodily health as food of the right quality and quantity. More people die of overfeeding than over-fasting. (Lister, 1900)

The reluctance to exercise has not changed for more than 120 years.

1905

The Canadian Medical Association Journal April 8, 1905

Heart-Strain and School Athletics.

The common field sports of public school are not without their opponents both from the "*flannelled fool, muddied oaf*" point of view, and also on the score of the physical damage likely to accrue from over-exertion. Dr. Arthur Lambert "*I am led to doubt whether the heart of the truly healthy boy ever breaks down as the result of exertion, not because the strain is too severe for the hearts of that age or physical development, but because the individual boy possess some cardiac insufficiency, either primary or dependent upon some condition such as anemia or recent influenza".* (Heart-Strain and School Athletics., 1905)

His impression is pretty correct today. If a young person does not have asthma, and develops a severe problem with activity, they usually have a primary cardiac issue. I want to go to the medical school Dr. Lambert went to!

1909

The British Medical Journal Sept 25, 1909.
<u>School Athletics and Boys' Races.</u>

Drs. Blake and Larrabee, between 1900 and 1903, carried out a set of observations on Marathon runners in Boston, and reported that: The Marathon races of the past five years prove that it is entirely possible to train considerable numbers of picked young men to develop speed far beyond anything obtained in modern armies. If we consider the speed at which the winners ran, the character of the roads, the frequency of hills, and the oppressive atmospheric conditions, it seems marvelous that the human body can be trained to withstand so much with so comparatively little depression. The unpleasant results of longest duration seem to have been blisters on the soles of the feet. In the entire three years we neither saw nor heard of any serious persistent after effects, and it has yet to be proven that even strenuous contests leave behind them a permanent injury. (School Athletics and Boys' Races., 1905)

The first Boston Marathon had

- **18 starters in 1897**
- **126 starters in 1907**
- **197 starters in 1960**
- **5,417 starters in 1980**
- **17,813 starters in 2000 and is presently capped-off at 30,000.**

1912

The Hospital March 30, 1912. (England).
<u>Competitive Athletics.</u>

The Bureau of Medicine and Surgery has come to the conclusion that it is not so much the games and competitions themselves that do the harm, as the overtraining and too prolonged periods of preparation that the crack athletes indulge in. Long-distance racing is held to be the most injurious of all sports; and Marathon racing is regarded as the worst of all. With these conclusions it is easy to sympathize: they contain a lesson which this country may well take to heart. Yet it is doubtful whether the mischief thus done is anything like so great in this country as in the States. It is an old observation that the American takes his sports much more seriously than we do, and thereby can often defeat his English competitor. To win is the great ambition over there, whereas to have a good game is the chief motive here. (Competitive Athletics., 1912)

We must beat those weak English every time and steal their Grey Poupon, biscuits and tea and drive away in their Aston Martins. Please, Be Calm and Carry On.

1912

The Psychological Clinic April 15, 1912.

Effects of Coffee-Drinking Upon Children

Charles Keen Taylor, M.A.

Statistics were obtained from 464 children. It was found that about 29% drank no coffee, 46% drank a cup per day, 12% drank two cups, 8 % three cups and 5% drank four or more cups. The children who drank coffee regularly averaged from one and a half to more than four pounds less in weight, from a half-inch to more than an inch less in height, and all the way to three pounds less in hand-strength than those who never drank coffee. As a conclusion, the writer would say that it seems likely that the regular drinking of coffee by children has an effect which is certainly not beneficial, that indeed it seems to make children less "*fit*" physically as well as mentally than those who do not use coffee. If this is true, then some support is given to the modern movement which advocates the substituting of cocoa or chocolate for coffee as a beverage for children. (Taylor, 1912)

When I was growing up, I did not know any friend or even any kid who ever drank coffee. Drinking coffee may have helped me 55 years ago when I was walking 20 miles in the freezing cold to first grade in my hand-me-down shoes and clothes.

1912

The Hospital November 30, 1912.

Athletics and Motherhood: An American View.

Moderate athletic exercise, all are agreed, is beneficial to the general health of girls. Most schools, colleges, and gymnasiums excuse their girls from such exercise for one to three days at the onset of menstruation. Some authorities would vigorously interdict all exercise during menstruation; others, on the other hand, allow moderate exercise to normal healthy girls during, as well as between, the periods. Those who follow the latter plan point to the case of circus riders and other acrobatic performers who cannot be thus excused and seem to suffer extraordinarily few ill effects in consequence. (Athletics and Motherhood: An American View, 1912)

Apparently, the show must go on! I always knew circus performers were special, but not that special. I would guess that "The bearded lady" probably did not have periods.

1919

The Hospital May 31, 1919 "The Poison in the Cup"
Dangers of Middle-Class Restaurants, Coffee Stalls and some Public Houses.

Whilst eating a hasty meal in a very busy middle-class restaurant near one of our large London railway stations, we chanced to witness certain cleansing rites being performed upon the establishment's eating utensils. The technique of the operation was of quite spartan simplicity. Knives, forks, and spoons were put into a species of large jam pot and the plates into a tub. No steam rose from either receptacle. When necessary a knife or fork was taken out of the pot, hastily wiped on a cloth, and duly presented to a customer. To see is to believe, and we must say that this little experience surprised us. Thirsting for further knowledge, we sought a coffee stall at midnight, an hour of busy custom, and were again amazed to find that the only cleansing process observed was a hasty dip of the soiled article into an enameled bowl of water, followed by a hasty rub with a damp towel, which was common to all the utensils wiped. Now a very eager crowd clamored round this stall, the attendants working at high pressure to supply their needs. The supply of crockery was scanty and frequent washings required everything being performed at break-neck speed.

On another occasion we visited a public-house in a densely populated area near London Bridge at the busy time of the day, the bar being packed to the doors with a thirsty motley crowd all eager to be served. In this instance the glasses were used over and over again, the cleansing process being a mere dip into a bowl of cold water and a hasty wipe with a cloth.

We protest vigorously against such proceedings, for if the authorities give licenses or rights to publicans and suchlike

> to serve the public, they should also protect the public weal. For reasons of common decency and cleanliness alone, we would insist upon the proper washing of eating and drinking utensils, but in addition there is allowed to exist a grave risk in spread of communicable disease.
> A proportion of our population suffer from syphilis and a proportion of these have the disease in its communicable stage. Such people are free to use our public eating and drinking places and to spread infection if defective hygiene is allowed to flourish in the manner we have indicated. To give a case in point: after a visit to a venereal clinic we visited a restaurant nearby, and there also refreshing herself was a young woman whom we had seen at the clinic half an hour previously. She was suffering from severe secondary syphilis, and had been given a dated card of admission to hospital for doses of intravenous salvarsan. This question of hygiene we refer to our Ministry of Health or other constituted authority, and suggest that a proper supervision be exercised over the cleanliness of our public eating and drinking places. Knives, forks, and the like should be thoroughly washed in boiling water, preferably containing a dilute innocuous antiseptic, and afterwards wiped on a clean cloth. The imposition of inspection and supervision would be quite an easy matter, and of definite public service, both in preventing spread of contagious disease and in impressing the moral effect of cleanliness upon the poorer classes of our population. (Dangers of Middle-Class Restaurants, Coffee Stalls and some Public Houses., 1919)

I'm pretty sure that this scenario prompted Starbucks, McDonald's and other businesses such as banks and restaurants to develop drive-throughs. Clearly, that is the obvious solution to avoid any motley crews from spreading syphilis. Most people died of infection or trauma during our

existence as a species. As an aside, plastic silverware was introduced in the 1940s.

1920

The British Medical Journal May 15, 1920
Weight, Height, and longevity.
Lewis Orr, manager of the Scottish Life Assurance Company

Among the proposers for life assurance, he said, were some who, though they had no adverse points in their family or personal history, and showed no signs of disease, were light in weight and poor in chest development; their chance of living long depended upon their consenting to take a course of physical exercises and recreation in the open air.
Mr. Orr, after quoting Hippocrates to the effect that "*corpulence is not only a disease in itself, but the harbinger of other diseases,*" went on to say that in life insurance heavy weights showed a heavy mortality and that among heavy weights those with a protuberant abdomen were the least desirable. (Orr, 1920)

Exercise separates healthy people from unhealthy people and obesity promotes many diseases as so eloquently noted by Hippocrates over a thousand years ago. Hippocrates was right on many issues. Out of respect, I need to give a shout-out to him; "TOGA! TOGA!".

1921

The Hospital May 21, 1921.
The Public Well-Being. Athletics for Girls.

The usual kind of newspaper controversy has been started by the violent and sweeping condemnation of girls' games made at a conference of headmistresses and women "*who have made a study of physical culture.*" A resolution was passed protesting against the present system of physical education for girls as being injurious to future generations. But the mistake made by these educationists and their friends was so to overstate their case as to play directly into the hands of opponents of their theories. To assert, for instance, that the modern physically trained girl is a degenerate, that feet are the only part of a woman's body that needs development is to reduce the discussion to the level of the ridiculous. (The Public Well-Being. Athletics for Girls., 1921)

Now I know why women collect shoes, to help develop their feet and prevent them from being labeled as "degenerate."

1922

THE CAUSE OF EXPLOSION IN CHOCOLATE CANDIES

JOHN WEINZIRL University of Washington, Seattle.

During the past three years, a number of instances of explosion of chocolate candies have been brought to the writer's attention. It appears that explosion in chocolates is rather a common occurrence, that it affects a considerable percentage of certain lots, and that few if any chocolate candy-makers escape the difficulty.

An extended search of the literature has been made, but no reference dealing directly with this problem has been found. A number of investigators, notably Prescott, Stiles, and Cummins, have dealt with the sanitary aspects of the candy industry, but explosion of chocolates was not noted.

The trade journal, Western Confectioner, July, 1920, contains a two-page article by J.P. Booker, in which he says: "*After working on the problem for fourteen years, I am convinced that the bursting of chocolates is caused by the germ "coli."*" The

conclusion is said to be based upon the work of several chemists. The germ is supposed to come from water and from starch.
The explosion of the chocolates occurs sometime after their manufacture, usually ten days to two weeks or longer. At times the chocolate coating is merely cracked while at others it is broken into a number of fragments. Under any circumstances the centers of the candies are exposed, the product presents an untidy appearance and deterioration occurs. As a rule, the flavor is impaired, owing to the development of rancidity and off flavors. Apparently, the candy maker is unable to foretell the trouble, which does not seem to be limited to any particular type of chocolate. However, the chocolate must have a fondant center. A fondant is composed of egg white, sugar, flour, flavoring and perhaps other ingredients such as cream, butter, nuts, fruits, etc. (Weinzirl, 1922)

This is very insightful for several reasons. When someone has surgery, an abscess will usually present itself in 10-14 days, exactly as is described here with chocolates. The egg, butter and cream in the fondant center were the source of the bacteria. If someone looks good 14 days after surgery, most likely they will not have an infection. This chocolate story may make readers more knowledgeable about the timeline for infection after surgery. Remember, this was 1922; penicillin was not discovered until 1928 and not used until 1940.
I love the dedication of working on the question for fourteen years. It's like the expression, "It took me 20 years to become an overnight sensation."

1932

An Apparent Epidemic of Left-Handedness.
Norma Y. Scheidemann

Chapter 19: Old School

This has absolutely nothing to do with the book's topic, but I love this story. Everyone needs heroes.

The writer recently was consulted in regard to what seemed to be a veritable epidemic of left-handedness. Practically all the boys of a Los Angeles junior high school homeroom group were found to be left-handed. When questioned by the homeroom teacher each boy staunchly insisted that he had been left-handed *"ever since he was born."* Observations showed that the left hand consistently was given preference for most manual activities. When the homeroom teacher suggested these boys use the right hand for writing, each claimed he just couldn't do a thing with the right hand. Samples of their right-handed writing seemed to verify these statements. Careful investigation, however, disclosed the fact that these boys were baseball enthusiasts. To them, left-handedness seemed to contribute materially to Babe Ruth's success and they considered it imperative that they too be left-handed if they were to attain Babe Ruth's eminence. (Scheidemann, 1932)

1942

The Canadian Medical Association Journal June 1942
Farewell Chocolate Soldier

The American Army has exchanged the chocolate ration of the soldier in the field for five pieces of hard candy, individually wrapped and in assorted flavors. Recent fatigue tests at Minnesota University have shown that men have a greater energy output if they take sugar periodically through the day rather than in large quantities at mealtimes.

Sugar for the Services,
Candy for the troops-
A soldier shorn of sugar
Invariably droops.
If you want your soldiers

Stiffened at the waist
Give them sugar candy,
Flavoring to taste.
Forget Papa's instructions,
Forget Mamma's appeal-
The energetic soldier
Must eat between his meals. (Farewell Chocolate Soldier, 1942)

I may be mistaken, but I think this is the groundbreaking research behind not giving little kids candy in the morning at child-care centers.

1914

Nascher's *Geriatrics* at 100

In 1914, the first American medical textbook on aging was published. Its author was Ignatz Nascher, a physician and pharmacist in New York City. For the title, *Geriatrics*, Nascher used the word he himself had proposed nearly five years earlier.

This is not a book that is nice about old age, and it is not generous to the elderly. It begins with a description of their appearance, often *"repellent": flabby, slouching, with excessive hair and blue lips, a "tout ensemble" of decay that arouses "repugnance."* The aged, Nascher writes, are "*generally careless, apathetic, and gloomy*". Their lives "*for all practical purposes ... are useless*". Their helplessness instills "*a spirit of irritability if not positive enmity*" in the young. Most noxious is their self-interest, a theme to which Nascher returns repeatedly. An old man "*demands constant attention and complains of the slightest neglect*", he becomes indignant and suspicious, he develops an "*overwhelming interest in self ... which gradually subordinates every other interest in life*".

Chapter 19: Old School

Certain passages make the modern reader cringe. Nascher has a particular interest in what he calls "*brain fog*," the diminishing cognitive speed and attention of the elderly, and uses the term to explain a range of phenomena, including why old men fall asleep in sermons.

He recognizes the "*uncertainty of the action of drugs upon the senile organism*", issues warnings against using medications to treat the side effects of other medications, and weighs in with particular vigor against the use of sedative hypnotics. He discusses what we now call multimorbidity, the coexistence of multiple chronic conditions in a single patient?

In the introduction to *Geriatrics*, Abraham Jacobi – one of the founders of pediatrics in the United States – frames this issue.

The recovery from every new disease contracted at any period of life is handicapped by the tissue changes left behind from the previous accidents or ailments. There are few persons of advanced years without a permanent blemish – one or many – which make the diagnosis of any additional illness or comorbid condition more difficult, treatment more uncertain, and complete recovery more doubtful. (xviii) (Cohen, 2014)

Dr. Naschers descriptions are not very nice about older people but I like Dr. Jacobi's description.

Chapter 20: Longevity

Coffee/caffeine may improve longevity and quality of life. Everyone's goal is to have many good years and limit the number of bad years. Bad years can be defined as having a chronic illness or illnesses that affect your daily life and decrease your ability to do enjoyable things.

I heard that the secret to longevity is not arguing and my wife thought that was ridiculous. You know, she's probably right.

> **Demography of longevity: past, present, and future trends**
> Life expectancy at birth has roughly tripled over the course of human history. Early gains were due to a general improvement in living standards and the control of infectious diseases. Reductions in infant and child mortality led to a rapid increase in life expectancy. Since 1970, the main factor improving longevity is a reduction in death rates among the elderly. In particular, death rates due to cardiovascular disease and cancer have declined in recent decades thanks to a variety of factors, including successful medical intervention. Based on available evidence, the human lifespan shows no sign of approaching a fixed limit. Both the average and the maximum life span have increased steadily over time for more than a century. By extrapolating past trends, life expectancy at birth in industrialized countries may be about 85-87 years at the middle of the 21st century. (Wilmoth, 2000)

Life expectancy in the United States, 1860-2020

Over the past 160 years, life expectancy in the United States has risen from 39.4 years in 1860 to 78.9 years in 2020. One of the major reasons is that infant and child mortality rates have decreased significantly. Medical advancements, fewer wars and improved living standards have also occurred. Despite this overall increase, life expectancy has dropped three times since 1860; from 1865 to 1870 as a result of the Civil War, from 1915 to 1920 during the First World War and following the 2018 flu epidemic (61,000 died); it has dropped again between 2015 and now. The most recent drop is not a result of any specific event but has been attributed to negative societal trends, such as poor diets, sedentary lifestyles, high medical costs, and increasing rates of suicide and drug use.

Today in the United States, about half of all adults have some form of cardiovascular disease. Thus, physical activity and exercise training have become the best remedy for the prevention and treatment of illness. At least half of Americans are not meeting the physical activity guidelines of more than 150 minutes/week of moderate exercise. Significant longevity benefits are conferred by even just 15 minutes/day of light or moderate physical activity. (O'Neill, 2021)

The Covid 19 pandemic has decreased life expectancy (over 1 million deaths so far).

Closure of 'Third Places'? Exploring Potential Consequences for Collective Health and Wellbeing

- In every community, there are places outside the home and workplace that people go to hang-out, relax or just feel safe. They could be a coffee shop, hair salon, barber shop, restaurant, corner store, etc. They are not exclusive, fancy or expensive. People go there for social interaction, friendship, and sense of belonging. These "third places" decrease stress, loneliness, isolation and fear. They provide cohesiveness and sense of community. Unfortunately, these "third places" are closing across the United States.

- Defined by Oldenburg (1999) as 'the great, good places', third places are an essential component of an area's *social infrastructure.*
- Third places are part of a trilogy. First places are home. Second places are workplace. (Finlay, Esposito, Kim, Gomez-Lopez, & Clarke, 2019)

Major cardiovascular disease (CVD) risk factors in midlife and extreme longevity

- Earlier studies have revealed the multitude of factors associated with longevity: genetic factors may explain about 25% of the variation of lifespan, while healthy lifestyle habits in midlife also play an important role.
- Yates et al. studied the association of factors at age 70 with survival to 90; they revealed that the probability of reaching 90 years is 54% for those men who did not have any risk factors, and 4% for those who had five risk factors (smoking, diabetes, obesity, hypertension, sedentary lifestyle) at mean age of 72.

In the present study, healthy Finnish businessmen and executives with a mean age of 50 years (range 46-55 years) were followed.

Risk factors at 70 years of age (smoking, BMI, blood pressure, lipids, fasting glucose).

- **No major risk factors: 51% reached 90 years of age**
- **One major risk factor: 33%**
- **Two risk factors: 30%**

- **Three risk factors: 20%**
- **Four risk factors: 18%.**
- **Five risk factors: 7%**

- There was a linear relationship between the number of risk factors and reaching 90 years of age.

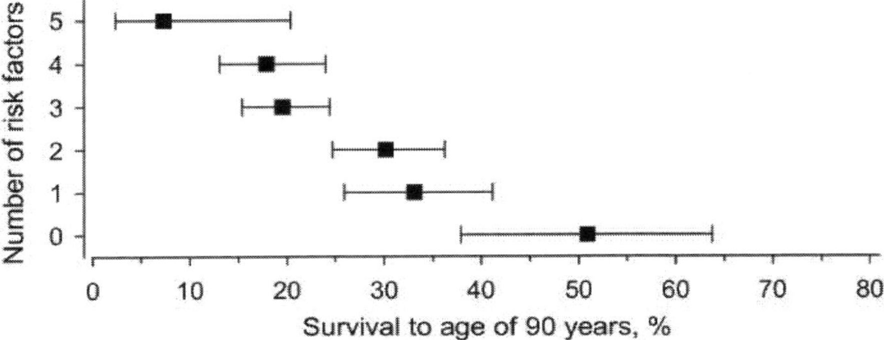

- Smoking, higher BMI, and higher levels of glucose and cholesterol were significant predictors for mortality.
- **"*Compression of morbidity*" decrease disabilities and illnesses into a minimum period in later years.**
- **Prevention and advanced treatment of chronic diseases enable an individual to maintain functionality and age "*successfully*".**
- The obesity epidemic continues to lack effective treatments. (Urtamo, Jyväkorpi, Kautiainen, Pitkälä, & Strandberg, 2020)

<u>Why did life expectancy decline in the United States in 2015? A gender-specific analysis</u>

- Men and women born in 1900 lived on average 48.3 and 51.1 years, and by 1950 life expectancy rose to 66 years for men and 71.7 years for women.
- In 2015, life expectancy at birth in the United States was lower by 0.17 year (62 days) than in 2014 (Xu et al., 2015).

- Previous reductions were in 1993 as a result of the HIV/AIDS epidemic and in 1980 from a deadly influenza epidemic.
- The prevalence of obesity continues to negatively affect life expectancy.
- The mean age at death decreased for most causes of death (14 of 20 causes for men, and 15 of 20 causes for women), especially for white women.
- For men, increased death was fueled by rising rates of accidental poisoning (drug abuse) among whites and Hispanics, and homicide among blacks.
- Men and women experienced a decline in life expectancy of similar magnitude.

Women's decline was driven mostly by an increase in old-age mortality.
Men's decline was driven mostly by an increase in accidental poisoning (drug abuse), mental illnesses, and homicide. (Acciai & Firebaugh, 2017)

Why has Japan become the world's most long-lived country: insights from a food and nutrition perspective

Japan has the longest average life expectancy (84.79 years 2021). The low mortality rates from heart disease and cancer (particularly breast and prostate) are thought to reflect the low prevalence of obesity in Japan; low intake of red meat, high intake of fish, plant foods such as soybeans, and non-sugar-sweetened beverages such as green tea. Japan is in the top ten countries for tea drinking but not in the top 25 for coffee use. (Tsugane, 2021)

Decline in Cardiovascular Mortality: Possible Causes and Implications

- The first 60 years of the 20th century saw a remarkable transformation in health and longevity. In 1900, life expectancy in the U.S. was only 47.3 years (46.3 for men, 48.3 for women and only 33 for Blacks). Infectious diseases such as pneumonia, influenza, tuberculosis, and gastroenteritis were the leading causes of death. By 1960, improvements in sanitation and the development of vaccines and antibiotics increased life expectancy to 69.7 years. Heart disease, cancer, and stroke replaced infectious diseases as the leading causes of death.

- Heart disease mortality per 100,000 fell from 307 in 1950 to 135 in 1996, while the stroke rate per 100,000 fell from 89 to 27.
- The cardiovascular mortality (heart disease and stroke) rate fell from 376 to 274 per 100,000 from 1990 to 2013.
- The continuing global epidemic of obesity remains one of the greatest public health challenges.
- In spite of the steady decline in smoking since the publication of the first Surgeon General's Report on Smoking and Health in 1964, smoking still continues to appear at just above 18% in the U.S. population.
- Lack of influenza vaccination in 18% of the population contributes significantly to disparities in cardiovascular mortality among major population subgroups.

Examples of major advances in the prevention and treatment of coronary heart disease:

Advance	Year or Period	Impact on the Prevention and Treatment of Coronary Heart Disease and Risk Factors
Framingham Heart Study	1960s	New targets for atherosclerotic

identified smoking, high blood pressure, and high blood cholesterol as major cardiovascular risk factors		coronary heart disease prevention and treatment
First coronary artery bypass surgery	1960	Surgical procedure to bypass clogged arteries
Surgeon General's Report on Smoking and Health	1964	Publicized dangers of cigarette smoking
Hypertension Detection and Follow-up Program	Early 1970s	Demonstrated benefit of treating even moderate hypertension
First percutaneous coronary angioplasty	1977	Successful restoration of perfusion in occluded coronary arteries via percutaneous catheter
Discovery of the low-density lipoprotein receptor	1970s	Michael Brown and Joseph Goldstein laid the groundwork for statins
Lipid Research Clinics Coronary Primary Prevention Trial	1984	Established benefit of cholesterol lowering
National clinical practice guidelines for high BP and	1987	Established standards and targets for blood pressure and cholesterol

high blood cholesterol		
Development of statins, angiotensin-converting enzyme inhibitors and calcium channel blockers	1987–8	New powerful drugs for managing cholesterol and blood pressure
Thrombolysis in Myocardial Infarction Trial	1987	Thrombolysis in acute myocardial infarction
First coronary stent	1988	Made angioplasty more durable
Scandinavian Simvastatin Survival Study	1994	First statin endpoint trial showed reduction in mortality. Many other statin trials followed.
Systolic Hypertension in the Elderly	1996	Established the benefit of treating isolated systolic hypertension in elderly. Many other blood pressure trials followed.
Systolic Blood Pressure Intervention Trial	2015	Established the benefit of intensive BP control (to target systolic pressure less than 120 mmHg) in high-risk patients without diabetes

(Mensah, et al., 2017)

Chapter 21: Centenarians

When researchers look at people over 100 years old, verification and documentation are very important due to mistakes and intentional false records. The number of centenarians has dropped well over 50% since accurate record-keeping developed. I truly believe going from 99 to 100 is as difficult as going from birth to 18; it's a long, dangerous year.

Becoming Centenarians: Disease and Functioning Trajectories of Older U.S. Adults as They Survive to 100

- Although centenarians are still rare in the U.S. population, the number of U.S. centenarians has grown rapidly in the past 30 years.
- Centenarians are more likely to be female, widowed, and living alone.
- More than half of centenarians aged with disease, about 20% with disability and 10% with cognitive impairment.
- Although centenarians are living longer than most of their group, they are doing so with poor health and functioning.
- Women's aging trajectories are characterized by more disability and disease than their male counterparts.

- About 55% remained cognitively intact over the study period, confirming that dementia is not an inevitable condition of living longer lives.
- Those with higher levels of education were more likely to remain cognitively intact, confirming the importance and persistence of social interaction even among centenarians. (Ailshire, Beltrán-Sánchez, & Crimmins, 2015)

Are We Approaching a Biological Limit to Human Longevity?

A 2016 *Nature* publication suggested the limit to human lifespan is 115 years.

- The International Database on Longevity contains information on four living supercentenarians and age at death of 668 supercentenarians (110 and older)
- The mortality of supercentenarians increases rapidly after age 113.

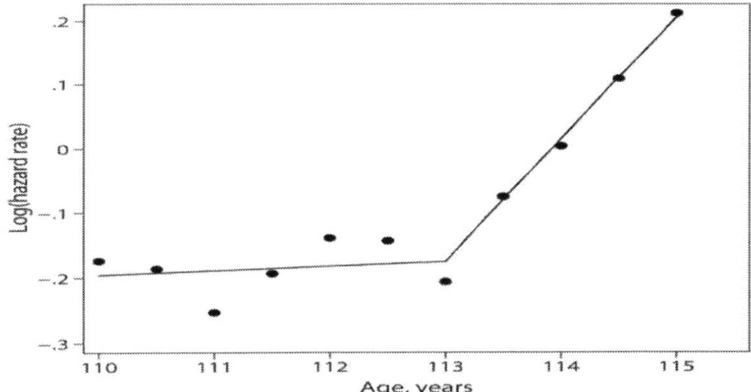

Maximum reported age at death, by year of birth in the International Database on Longevity.

- According to researchers and estimated calculations, the maximum life span is equal to 117 years for a population size of 1 billion. Further calculations for a population of 10 billion resulted in maximum life span estimation of 120 years for women and 113 years for men. These estimates are in agreement with existing longevity records if we exclude one outlier (Jeanne Calment lived to 122).

- Many gerontologists are more conservative now regarding the future growth of longevity, citing environmental problems, climate change, social inequality, and evolutionary reasoning. (Gavrilova & Gavrilov, 2020)

"Centenarians—A Model to Study the Molecular Basis of Lifespan and Health-span"

- The number of people age 80 years or older is projected to increase more than threefold between 2017 and 2050.
- **The increase in lifespan does not coincide with an increase in the duration of good health free from serious chronic diseases.**
- Exceptional longevity should be classified as those older than 90 if we look at it from a statistical point of view. The normal range for a given test is based on results seen in 95% of the population. People in their 90s are in the 5th percentile of the survival curve and are considered outside the normal range. Nevertheless, it is often the canonical age of 100 that is regarded as the threshold of exceptional longevity. Worldwide, the number of centenarians fluctuates between half a million and a million with five women to one man. (Caruso & Puca, 2021)

Five women for one man. Finally, a statistic that makes sense in this book!

New Developments in Biodemography of Aging and Longevity

- **The prevalence of centenarians is very low, about one per 10,000.**
- Parental longevity is a strong independent predictor of survival to age 100.
- Birth in the northeast region of the United States and birth in the second half of the year are significant predictors of exceptional longevity (for men but not women).
- There is a strong positive effect of farming on longevity for men.
- Factors for women included parental longevity and, surprisingly, the availability of radio in the household in 1930. Having a radio indicated household wealth, which may explain the finding. A 2011 study found that radio listening increased quality of life and decreased depression.
- **Numerous studies demonstrate that biological relatives of centenarians have a substantial survival advantage.**
- **There is a survival advantage for brothers and sisters of centenarians: brothers lived 2.6 years longer; sisters lived 2.9 years.**
- We hypothesize that male centenarians and their brothers share living conditions and lifestyles favorable for men, such as farming.
- A maternal age of 20-24 years increases the chances of children having longevity.
- A 2011 study of Canadian centenarians and a 2008 Swedish study demonstrated beneficial effects of young maternal age on lifespan of offspring.
- Adult siblings born in September, October, or November have significantly higher odds of becoming centenarians. (Gavrilov & Gavrilova, 2015)

Chapter 21: Centenarians

Biodemography is the statistical study of human populations (new word for me).

An oral health study of centenarians and children of centenarians

Centenarians and their offspring have better oral health than their respective birth cohorts. Oral health is a helpful marker for systemic health and healthy aging. (Kaufman, et al., 2014)

If one does not take care of his teeth, he does not take care of his overall health, either.

Female Fertility Has a Negative Relationship With Longevity in Chinese Oldest-Old Population: A Cross-Sectional Study

The China Hainan Centenarian Cohort Study included 1,226 females with 758 centenarian women (100 years or older) and 468 women aged 80-99 years.

- Chinese women who lived to 100 had fewer children and waited longer to have children compared to women who did not live to 100.
- Estradiol (estrogen) levels were positively associated and testosterone levels were negatively associated with longevity. (Zhu, et al., 2021)

Chapter 22: Middle Ages

The Middle Ages are not much different than middle age in people. It can be a time of future reflection and enjoyment turning into the Renaissance or a decline in quality of life filled with stagnation - the Dark Ages.

A person who has made good choices in life is now able to enjoy things with less pressure. Similarly, people who have been afflicted with certain diseases or maladaptive behaviors start to exhibit the damage associated with them. Middle age leads to a fork in the road that everyone has to choose. Luck and genetics are very important when we get to the fork. Many good people have bad luck and they are not given a choice and that is unfortunate.

<u>Cardiorespiratory Fitness in Middle Age and Health Care Costs in Later Life</u>

- Having few cardiovascular risk factors in middle age is associated with lower health care costs in later life.
- This study sought to evaluate the association of health care costs in later life with fitness in midlife after adjustment for cardiovascular risk factors.
- We studied 19,571 healthy individuals who underwent fitness assessment by treadmill testing at a mean age of 49.

- Over 126,388 person-years of follow-up, average annual health care costs were significantly lower for participants aged 65 years or older with high midlife fitness than with low midlife fitness in both men ($7,569 vs. $12,811) and women ($6,065 vs. $10,029).

Greater fitness in middle age (49 years) is strongly associated with lower health care costs 22 years later in life. (Bachmann, et al., 2015)

Saving $4,000 to $5,000 dollars in health care costs is a great incentive for exercise.

Exercise Attenuates the Major Hallmarks of Aging

- A growing challenge is to help elderly people maintain independence until the end of life.
- Physical inactivity is a major health problem worldwide. Exercise certainly cannot reverse the aging process, but it does attenuate many of its effects.
- The benefits of regular exercise have a dose–response effect. Higher levels of moderate-to-vigorous exercise (450 minutes or more/week, clearly above the minimum recommendations of 150 min/week) are associated with longer life expectancy.
- Elite athletes -- those sustaining the highest possible exercise levels (*e.g.*, Tour de France or former Olympic marathoners) -- usually live considerably longer than the general population. (Garatachea, et al., 2015)

Lack of exercise is a major cause of chronic diseases

Overwhelming evidence proves that reduction in daily physical activity is a primary cause of chronic diseases/conditions and physical activity/exercise is effective treatment. Physical activity promotes optimal health and prevents premature death.

- The energy level necessary to do daily activities and chores around the house can be standardized to a scientific measure called metabolic equivalents. One metabolic equivalent is the energy exerted at rest. It takes four metabolic equivalents to do normal activities. If a person has endurance of less than four metabolic equivalents, research studies have shown an increased risk for cardiac events, and an increased length of hospitalizations and recovery from surgeries.

In a 2006 study, patients were grouped by metabolic equivalent capacity in relationship to complications after open abdominal nonvascular surgery.

- Those from the group with less than four metabolic equivalents had cardiac complications in 64% of cases.
- 4–7 metabolic equivalents had 29% complications.
- 7–10 metabolic equivalents had 8%.
- The gold standard of cardiorespiratory fitness is VO_2max, or maximum aerobic fitness. An acceptable substitute for VO_2max is the length of time running or cycling in a standardized test.
- In the Dallas Bed Rest study, healthy young males' VO_2max (fitness level) decreased 27% after 20 days of continuous bed rest.
- A 2008 study in Denmark showed a 7% decrease in VO_2max simply by reducing daily step number from 10,501 to 1,344.
- **Estimated daily step numbers have declined ~50% to ~70% since the introduction of powered machinery to our society.**
- Quotations attributed to Hippocrates foster the benefits of physical activity.

"If we could give every individual the right amount of nourishment and exercise, not too little and not too much, we would have found the safest way to health".

"Walking is man's best medicine"

Researcher Jerry Morris wrote a paper in 1949 showing that drivers of London's double-decker buses and government clerks are more likely to die from heart disease than conductors and postmen. He made the connection between the more physically active conductors and postmen and the more sedentary bus drivers and clerks that physical activity protects against heart disease and sedentary activity promotes heart disease. Physically active conductors had a 30% lower rate of coronary heart disease than physically inactive bus drivers. Morris' 1953 report was a milestone; documenting that daily physical inactivity was associated with increased morbidity and mortality. In his 90s, he wrote, "*We in the West are the first generation in human history in which the mass of the population has to deliberately exercise to be healthy*".

- Bone loss occurs 10 times faster in space than with aging. The lack of gravity causes rapid deterioration of strength and muscle mass. Being sedentary or being in bed from illness is analogous to being in space, resulting in dramatic losses of muscle and bone strength.
- Using untrained pairs of identical twins reveals that about 40–50% of VO_2max is a result of genetics.
- Publications on 80 identical twins unequivocally show that if one twin has lower physical activity, he exhibits increased risk for chronic diseases.
- **Weightlifting causes hypertrophy of muscles and prolonged daily running increases mitochondria, but each activity does not result in both. Both types of exercise (endurance and strength) are needed to prevent physical frailty.**
- All-cause mortality increased 46% and cardiovascular mortality rose 80% for TV viewing time of more than four hours a day compared to less than two hours a day.

- Erikssen et al. in 1998 concluded that even small improvements in physical fitness are associated with a significantly lowered risk of death.
- Low muscle strength increases all-cause-mortality in thirteen studies using subjects > 65 years of age. Sedentary lifestyle accelerates aging of skeletal muscle by 24 years.

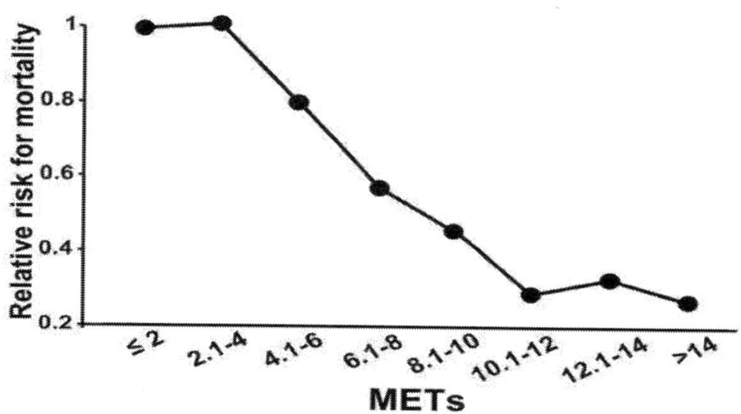

- Risk of mortality decreases as the level of conditioning increases.
- **The average U.S. sedentary adult needs to burn at least 600 kcal more each day for appropriate physical activity.**
- Energy expenditure was significantly greater when daily domestic tasks were performed without the aid of machines or equipment. An estimated 110 kcal/d was estimated to be expended by the combined impact of machines. The annualization of 110 kcal/day is the caloric equivalent of 11.5 pounds/yr.
- **A threshold of ~60 minutes a day of moderate-intensity activity throughout a 13-year study was needed to gain <5 lbs. in 34,079 healthy US women consuming a usual diet.**

- Physical inactivity strongly increases prediabetes in those younger than 60.
- Type 2 diabetes is estimated to cost men 11.6 life-years and women 14.3 life-years when diagnosed at age 40.
- Physical inactivity is a cause of at least one in three deaths from coronary heart disease.
- In a 2004 prospective study of 18,000 women aged 71-80, higher levels of long-term regular physical activity were strongly associated with higher levels of cognitive function and a 20% lower risk of cognitive impairment.
- Moderate and high levels of physical activity were associated with significantly lower risks for Alzheimer's disease and dementia.
- Studies have found 10 days of walking for 30 minutes a day resulted in a decrease in the Hamilton Rating Scale for Depression.
- A literature review through March 1997 found that those in the highest physical activity category had ~40%-50% reduction in risk of colon cancer.
- A 2009 meta-analysis found that physical activity was clearly associated with a 30% lower risk of endometrial cancer.
- **Physical inactivity increases risk factors for more than 30 chronic diseases/conditions.**
- **Models of extreme physical inactivity are so dramatic in the magnitude of health detriment that Human Institutional Research Boards would likely be hesitant, for ethical reasons, to approve random controlled trials lasting years if irreversible overt chronic disease were to occur because of physical inactivity.**
- **Exercise provides a higher therapeutic index (benefits/side effects) than any drug therapy could provide. It requires the integration of almost every organ system.**

- Physical activity diminishes mortality by 30% in the U.S. Stated alternatively, physical inactivity increases mortality by 30%, or by 720,000 annual deaths (one death every 44 seconds).
- **Modern humans have been able to engineer most physical activity out of daily life. Humans now have a choice not to be physically active**. (Booth, Roberts, & Laye, 2012)

Public health impact of daily life triggers of sudden cardiac death: A systematic review and comparative risk assessment

Sudden cardiac death (SCD) may be triggered by daily circumstances and activities such as stressful events, physical exertion or substance abuse. Meta-analysis of 8 studies.

Triggers from the highest to the lowest risk: (risk varied from almost 500% to 10% higher risk)

- physical exertion
- recent cocaine use
- episodic alcohol consumption
- recent amphetamine use
- episodic coffee consumption
- psycho-emotional stress within the previous month
- influenza infection
- recent cannabis use.

Potential triggers for SCD.

- 14.5% episodic alcohol consumption
- 9.4% physical exertion
- 6.9% cocaine
- 6% episodic coffee consumption
- 3% psycho-emotional stress in the previous month
- 1.7% amphetamines

- 0.9% cannabis
- 0.3% influenza infections.

To appreciate this article, think of how the above triggers influence the risk of a bad outcome. For example, an obese older sedentary man shoveling snow who suddenly drops dead from a heart attack. (Čulić, AlTurki, & Proietti, 2021)

Chapter 23: Aging Performance

Athletes train longer and harder than ever before. In the past, athletes needed regular jobs to support themselves during the off-season. Johnny Unitas (1979 Hall of Fame NFL quarterback) was a pile-driver on construction jobs during his early years. Many career-ending injuries are no longer career-ending. Older athletes break records routinely now.

Improved Race Times in Marathoners Older than 75 Years in the Last 25 Years in the World's Largest Marathons

We examined race data of 1,691 marathon finishers (218 women and 1,473 men) between 1990 and 2014 in four races (Berlin, New York, Chicago and Boston).

- The number of female and male finishers increased significantly across years.
- The number of women and men in age groups 75-79 and 80-84 increased.
- Across years, women and men reduced their race times.
- Women and men aged 75-79 improved race times. (Ahmadyar, Rosemann, Rüst, & Knechtle, 2016)

At the age when most people are dying, there are people finishing marathons. Men and women can achieve great things through lifelong exercise.

Master Athletes Are Extending the Limits of Human Endurance

- Over the past three decades, there has been a continual increase in the number of master athletes (i.e., older than 40) in endurance and ultra-endurance (longer than six hours) events.
- The percentage of male finishers older than 40 is frequently higher than those younger than 40 years.
- At the New York Marathon, male master runners represent more than 50% of total male finishers, while female master athletes represent 40% of total female finishers.
- For 100-km (45 miles) and 161-km (73 miles) ultramarathon running, master runners represent the greatest part of the finishers; up to 73% for 100-km.
- Master triathletes now represent more than 55% of the total field for males and more than 45% for females at the world championship Ironman in Hawaii.

Elite ultra-endurance athletes get older

- The current age of elite marathoners is around 30 years for both males and females, and the age of peak performance generally increases as race distance increases.
- At the Hawaii Ironman, the age of the top 10 finishers increased over time from 26 to 35 years for females and from 27 to 34 years for males.
- The upper age limit of elite ultra-endurance athletes has increased during the past decades, bringing into question the age limit of peak performance.
- **Gender differences in endurance performance for elite athletes are generally close to 10%.**

Chapter 23: Aging Performance

- **Men have a greater V02max than women because they have larger hearts, higher hemoglobin levels, less body fat, and greater muscle mass.**
- Gender differences are of biological origin, and the gap between elite males and females is unlikely to narrow naturally.
- **Decrease in maximal oxygen consumption (i.e., V02max) is the predominant contributor to the decline in performance with advancing age.**
- **V02max declines by ~10% per decade after 30 years.**
- **Reduction in maximal heart rate seems to be the predominant mechanism for decreased performance.**
- The rate of maximal heart rate decrease (~0.7 beat/min/year) is irrespective of conditioning with advancing age.
- The age-related decline in endurance performance is closely related with reductions in exercise training volume and intensity.
- Increasing injuries, reductions in time to train, and decreased motivation are increasing factors for master athletes. (Lepers & Stapley, 2016)

<u>Performance Differences Between the Sexes in the Boston Marathon from 1972 to 2017</u>

Of 553,890 race starters, 98% completed the race with 64% men and 34% women.

- Female participation started at 2.81% in 1972 and reached 45.68% in 2016. (Knechtle, Di Gangi, Rüst, & Nikolaidis, 2020)

What is impressive is that 98% of more than a half million runners completed the race over a 45-year span. Even when the weather was challenging, people still persevered.

The first time I ran the Boston Marathon, plantar fasciitis started bothering me at about mile 8. I thought I could live with myself if I ran to the halfway point, then get a ride to the finish. I went to a local ambulance on the course and said I did not feel I could finish. They looked at me funny. This irritated me enough to start running again until I finished the race, although I felt like crying. My time was slow at 3 hours 35 minutes 36 seconds (8:14 pace). I clearly am glad I was not part of the 2% who did not finish.

<u>Declining performance of master athletes: silhouettes of the trajectory of healthy human aging?</u>

An objective of aging research is not to increase lifespan *per se*, but to increase the "*health-span*" (number of years with good health) and to compress morbidity in later life.

- Aging has long been associated with an increase in sedentary behavior.
- The falloff in performance is generally similar for both men and women.
- Tanaka & Seals suggested that declines in performance appear to be mediated in large part by a reduction in the absolute intensity and total volume of training undertaken. If the older athletes simply increased their training load, then performance would increase. It could be argued that older athletes, particularly at the elite level, are already training at the maximum capability their age allows.
- Power-based activities such as 100-meter sprint running are not limited by cardiorespiratory fitness, but essentially by neuromuscular/muscular–tendinous function. Importantly, while these two examples are from running, the decline in performance with age is essentially the same among many athletic disciplines.

- **It is clear that exercise does not halt the aging process.**
- **The diminution in athletic performance is the result of the inherent aging process.** (Lazarus & Harridge, 2017)

Gender difference of aging performance decay rate in normalized Masters World Records of Athletics: much less than expected

- Master athletes compete within age groups divided into five-year periods, from 35-39 years-old, 40-44, and so on. This study compared the declining trends of performance.
- The decline of all the disciplines is very similar for females and males and it is very gentle from 30 to 50 years. It is almost linear from 50 to 70 years and then the decay is progressively steeper.

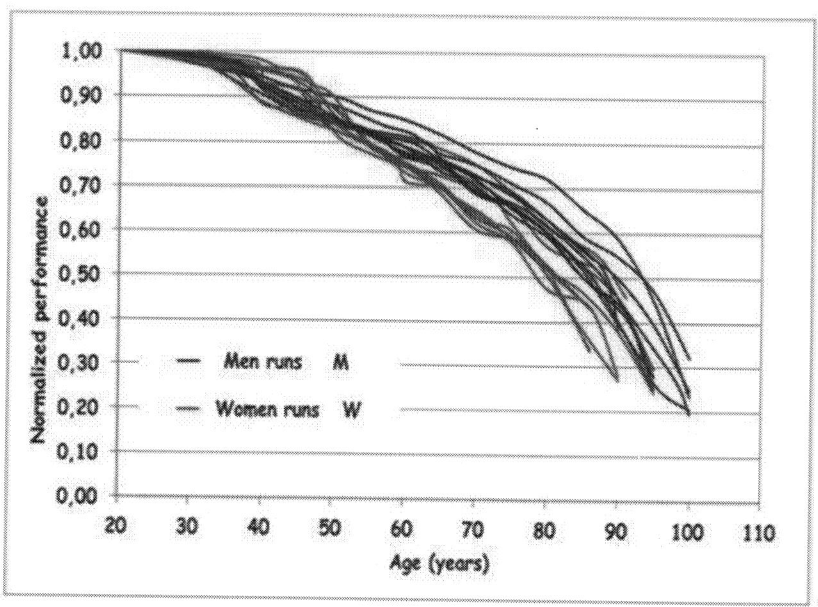

Comparison of normalized running parameters of male and female master athletes.

The analysis of World Records of Master athletes point to a similar "rate of aging decline" of females and males. (Gava, Giuriati, & Ravara, 2020)

<u>Endurance exercise performance in Masters athletes: age-associated changes and underlying physiological mechanisms</u>

The peak exercise performance of master athletes continues to increase each year.

Comparison of 1896 Olympic winning times in running events and current Master records that surpass those winning times (from ESPN and World Masters Records)

Running events	**1896 Olympic winning time (from the first Olympic games in Athens)**	**Current age-group records that surpass 1896 Olympic times and age at which these records were achieved**
100 m (s)	12.0	11.7 **(61 years)**
200 m (s)	22.2	22.1 **(46 years)**
400 m (s)	54.2	53.9 **(63 years)**
800 m	2:11.0	2:10.4 **(60 years)**
1500 m	4:33:2	4:27:7 **(60 years)**
Marathon	2:58:50	2:54:5 **(73 years)**

- Peak endurance running performance is maintained until about 35 years of age, followed by modest decreases until 50-60 years of age, with progressively steeper reductions thereafter.
- The pattern appears to be similar for both non-elite and elite endurance athletes.

Chapter 23: Aging Performance

- In general, the magnitude of decline in endurance running performance with age is greater in women than in men.

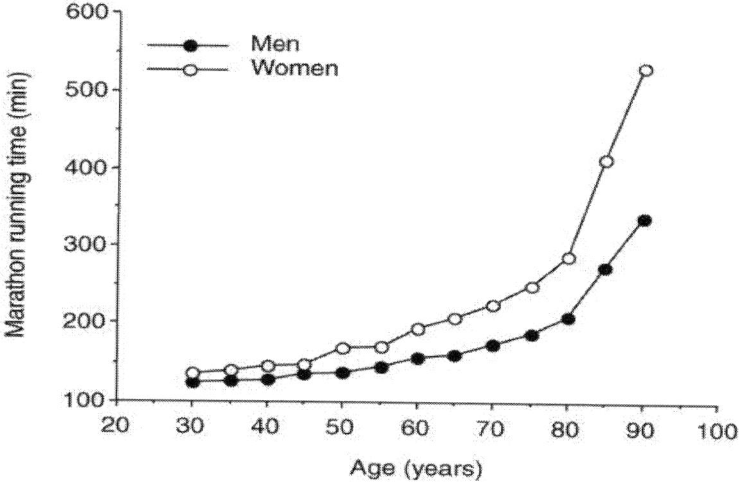

Changes in men's and women's marathon running times with advancing age (from USA Track & Field and World Masters Athletics)

- Studies suggest that V02max can be fairly well maintained in middle age, lasting up to 10 years in men and women who continue to train vigorously.
- The large elastic arteries stiffen with advancing age, thereby impeding the ejection of blood (Tanaka & Seals, 2008)

Several articles discuss running economy and how it does not change with age. Exercise economy is confusing to me. Perhaps I am confusing economy with efficiency or biomechanics.

When I see an older person run, I see a stiff-legged person with short, choppy strides with facial grimacing. A young runner looks like a well-choreographed dance. To me, that shows two vastly different economies. I will use a car analogy.

A Lamborghini probably has the same fuel economy as a rusted-out truck going from Place A to Place B. Although they look and act differently, the economy concept states that they burn the same amount of gas for a certain distance, which probably is true. To go from A to B requires the same energy expenditure and physics.

Understanding this concept reminds me of the movie "My Cousin Vinny." Attorney Joe Pesci harasses a witness about time and asks him about grits. The witness states he takes pride in his grits and that any self-respecting Southerner makes his own grits. The witness says it takes 5 minutes for him to make grits; Pesci responds that the whole-grit eating world takes about 20 minutes to make grits. "Are we to believe that boiling water soaks into your grits faster in your kitchen than anywhere else on the face of this earth or that the laws of physics cease to exist on your stove? Were these magic grits?" It's probably one of the few times Pesci goes on a rant and does not whack a guy.

<u>Pacing During and Physiological Response After a 12-Hour Ultra-Marathon in a 95-Year-Old Male Runner</u>

In a recent case report, a 94-year-old runner engaged in a six-hour ultra-marathon. In the present case report, we investigate the same runner one year later at the age of 95 years in a 12-hour run.

The Runner and the Race

- Our runner started running after his retirement at age 65.
- At the age of 90, he successfully completed his first marathon. He is the current European record holder in the half-marathon and marathon in males 90 and older. In preparation for this race, he trained five days a week with a break during the weekend. The daily training varied from 5 to 10 km. (2.3 to 5.4 miles).

- His medical problems are hypertension and osteopenia.
- On May 12, 2018, the athlete started in the 12-hour run at midnight.
- The 95-year-old man was able to run for 12 hours, achieving a total distance of nearly 53 km (24 miles). Lab abnormalities returned to pre-race values within five days.
- It is normal that labs of skeletal muscle, liver, and kidney damage increase during and after a marathon or ultra-marathon and return to normal several days later. (Knechtle, Jastrzebski, Rosemann, & Nikolaidis, 2019)

After reviewing this story more than once, I realized a few things. The runner really did not do an ultramarathon; an ultramarathon is a race longer than a marathon (26.2 miles), and he did only 24 miles. His pace is about 30 minutes per mile or 2 mph. The normal walking pace for a person is about 3 mph. I'm not sure I would call that running.

As a doctor who has seen older people for the past 30 years, I will put my petty criticisms into perspective. Walking 100 feet without an assistive device such as a cane or a walker is an achievement at 95 years old. The healthiest older person in my practice is 98 years old and looks 80. He uses a cane and can walk only one block. Anyone exerting himself for 12 hours is an achievement at any age.

I have done Pike's Peak Marathon several times, and my pace above the tree-line for the last 2-3 miles is about 30 minutes per mile. The tree-line is where trees disappear due to low oxygen levels and starts at about 10,000 feet. I suspect his running pace and my pace the last 2-3 miles is more like a death march, and I'm more than 30 years younger than he is. He's the tough guy and I'm the weakling.

I'm also amazed that he started running at 65 years of age and continued this for the next 30 years. It is hard to believe his body and joints tolerated the pounding.

Although this warrior is a badass, the top person on my list is probably Boston Marathoner Johnny Kelley. He was born on Sept. 6, 1907, the son of a letter carrier and the oldest of 10 children. The first two Boston Marathons he was not able to finish (his first one had only 285 runners). His last finished marathon was in 1992 at the age of 84 (9,629 men and women entered).

He won the Boston Marathon twice, in 1935 and 1945, finished second a record seven times and finished in the top 10 in 19 others. He went to the Berlin Olympics in 1936 and the London Olympics in 1948 at age 40.

The most amazing feat is that he started 61 Boston Marathons and completed 58. There are many great athletic records in the world but I cannot fathom someone breaking this one. He completed his last marathon in less than 6 hours, an awesome achievement.

A 7-foot bronze statue of Johnny Kelley was unveiled in 1993 about a mile from the base of Heartbreak Hill on the Marathon course. The statue is actually two likenesses of Kelley: one of him as a 27-year-old winning the Marathon in 1935, the other of him as an 84-year-old finishing his sixty-first and last marathon. They hold hands as they break the tape crossing the finish line. Johnny Kelley died at the age of 97.

Performance in 100-km Ultramarathoners-At Which Age, It Reaches Its Peak?

Study to analyze the age at which female and male runners achieve their peak performance. We reviewed 370,051 athletes (44,601 women and 325,450 men) who finished a 100-km ultramarathon (45.45 miles) between 1959 and 2016.

- **The age of peak performance was 41 years in women and 45 years in men,** 39 years in women and 41 years in men averaging the top 10 finishers.

Compared with previous studies, we observed the peak performance at an age older by ~10 years. (Nikolaidis & Knechtle, 2020)

Linear Decrease in Athletic Performance During the Human Life Span

The study included a total of 27,088 athletes between 11 and 89 years of age (17,372 males and 9,716 females). The performance in all disciplines showed a linear decline up to age 70. This is identical to the linear decline in VO_2max (exercise capacity) and power in master endurance and power lifting athletes. (Ganse, Ganse, Dahl, & Degens, 2018)

Chapter 24: Life Expectancy of Elite Athletes

The definition of an elite athlete is not always easy. An elite athlete can be a paid professional or an amateur. An easy definition is an athlete that competes at the national, international or professional level. Another is a person that competes at the highest level of competition which is the one I like. A definition that expresses a sad aspect of elite athletes is a 2002 definition; an athlete with potential for competing in the Olympics or as a professional. Elite athletes are at increased risk for injuries, given the amount of training, psychological abuse by coaches and parents, and self-abuse. This definition must be thinking of female gymnasts.

Health Consequences of an Elite Sporting Career: Long-Term Detriment or Long-Term Gain? A Meta-Analysis of 165,000 Former Athletes

Compare the mortality of former elite athletes to their non-elite counterparts. The total number of athletes in the 24 studies was 165,033 with 84.4% males and 15.6% females. Of the male sample, 47.3% were endurance athletes, 47.7% were team sport athletes,1.9% were power sport athletes, and 3.1% were Olympians/world champions.

Discussion

- Male and female athletes had a 31% and 49% lower risk of all-cause mortality than the general population. The female survival advantage (females are expected to live 6-8 years longer than males at birth) persists, even after a career in elite sports.
- Clarke et al. in 2012 reported an average 2.8 years survival advantage in 15,174 Olympic athletes from nine countries, with a 2018 study of 2,814 French Olympians gaining an average of 6.5 years.
- Elite athletes usually have healthier lifestyles post-retirement and more physical activity, both of which predict improved all-cause mortality.
- Sarna et al. in 1993 and Kettunen et al. in 2015 used a control group formed of military fit personnel. The statistics were not significantly different relative to elite athletes, implying physical fitness is the key variable.

Sport-Specific Mortality

- Male endurance athletes lived significantly longer than the general population.
- Clarke et al. reported a 13% longer survival for medalists in endurance sports; marathon runners (+ 4.3 years), Tour de France cyclists (+ 8 years) and Olympic endurance sports (+ 6.3 years).
- The difference is unlikely to be explained by genetic factors as endurance athletes are still predisposed to similar levels of disease and cancer as the general population.
- American football linemen, who share a lot of characteristics with power sport athletes, had a two to threefold increase in cardiovascular disease mortality compared to other positions.
- Endurance athletes' cancer mortality was not significantly different from the general population. Since endurance athletes live longer, they have more

years to potentially develop cancer. (Runacres, Mackintosh, & McNarry, 2021)

Mortality of Japanese Olympic athletes in 1964 Tokyo Olympic Games

355 (295 men, 60 women) athletes with follow-up for 53 years.

- Japanese athletes lived longer than the Japanese population. The same trend was observed in Olympic athletes in other countries.
- Body mass index of 25 or greater was associated with higher mortality, whereas smoking history and handgrip strength were not associated with mortality. (Takeuchi, et al., 2021)

All-cause and disease-specific mortality among male, former elite athletes: an average 50-year follow-up

This study is an analysis of cause-specific deaths of former Finnish male athletes (N=2,363) and controls (N=1,657). The median follow-up time was 50 years.

- Median life expectancy was higher in the endurance athletes at 79.1 years and team athletes at 78.8 years than in controls 72.9 years.
- For dementia mortality, the power sports athletes, particularly boxers, had 4.2 times increased risk.

Elite athletes have five to six years of additional life expectancy compared to men who were healthy as young adults. (Kettunen, et al., 2015)

Increased life expectancy of world class male athletes

Elite Finnish athletes during 1920-65 were included (N=2,613 men). The control group, 1,712 healthy men, were selected from the Finnish Defense Forces conscription register matched on age and area of residence.

- Mean life expectancy (reference group 69.9 years).

1. long distance running and cross-country skiing, 75.6 years.
2. team games (soccer, ice hockey, basketball, track events), 73.9 years.
3. power sports (boxing, wrestling, weight lifting, field events), 71.5 years.

The increased mean life expectancies were mainly explained by decreased cardiovascular mortality. (Sarna, Sahi, Koskenvuo, & Kaprio, 1993)

Mortality and health-related habits in 900 Finnish former elite athletes and their brothers

The mortality of male Finnish elite athletes, who represented Finland between 1920 and 1965 (n=900) and their age-matched brothers (n=900), were followed from the time the athlete started an elite career until Dec. 31, 2015.

Median age at death was;

- 79.9 years for endurance athletes (brothers 77.5).
- 75.9 years for mixed sports (brothers 73.7).
- 72.2 years for power sports athletes (brothers 72.2).

Former elite athletes live longer than their brothers. No difference was noted in power sport athletes and their brothers. (Kontro, Sarna, Kaprio, & Kujala, 2018)

Do Elite Athletes Live Longer? A Systematic Review of Mortality and Longevity in Elite Athletes

- A 2014 meta-analysis by Garatachea et al. indicated that elite athletes live longer than the general population and have a lower risk of cardiovascular disease and cancer.
- A 2009 meta-analysis performed by Löllgen et al. examined 38 studies and reported an overall significant relationship between exercise and lower all-cause mortality.

Chapter 24: Life Expectancy of Elite Athletes

The present review included a total of 465,575 athletes with 5,610 (1.2 %) females.

- Greater longevity for elite athletes relative to the general population.
- Studies by international researchers from 12 different countries reflect an increased survival rate for a diverse group of athletes.
- Elite cyclists, such as French, Italian, and Belgian Tour de France participants, had greater lifespans compared to their countries' general population.
- Norwegian divers, skiers, and Italian track and field athletes had greater lifespans.
- Elite Finnish powerlifters displayed lower life spans compared to the Finnish general population.
- The largest gains were in endurance and mixed-sport athletes.
- The greatest longevity advantages were found in European cyclists.
- Some evidence of increased premature mortality in power sport athletes from suicide is suspected from prior anabolic steroid use.

Weight is a very important predictor of mortality risk for athletes and non-athletes especially after retirement. (Lemez & Baker, 2015)

Chapter 25: Rate Limiting Systems

The rate limiting systems that decrease performance in endurance events are the heart and lungs. Our muscle mass decreases with age but the declines in our heart and lung function are the key factors.

J.B. Wolffe memorial lecture. Is the lung built for exercise?

The design of the pulmonary system is clearly intended for the exercising state. The system shows remarkable capability for true adaptation. At the same time, there are limits to the system's capabilities. The healthy pulmonary system may become a so-called "*limiting factor*" at least during short-term maximum exercise in the highly trained. No organ system has limitless functional capacity. (Dempsey, 1986)

Relationship between ventilatory function and age in master athletes and a sedentary reference population

During aging, there is a progressive decline in respiratory function

1. loss of respiratory muscle strength
2. increased stiffness of the chest wall

3. reduced elastic recoil of the lung
4. reduced diffusion capacity (how well oxygen and carbon dioxide transfer from blood to lungs).

The aim of the present study was to compare respiratory function in track and field master athletes and sedentary control people.

- We recruited 71 female and 84 male master elite athletes and sedentary control participants.
- Weekly training hours were negatively related to age, indicating a decrease of 3/4 hour training per week per decade.
- FEV1 (Forced Expiratory Volume-maximum air expired in one second) decreased 34 mL/year in all groups, irrespective of being an athlete or not.
- FVC (Forced Vital Capacity-maximum air expired in one breath) decreased with age by 36 mL/year.
- Other breathing measures were negatively associated with age.
- **The results support a decrease in ventilatory function may become a more important limiting factor of aerobic capacity with increasing age.**
  (Degens, et al., 2016)

Training can lower the physiological age of your lungs, but loss of lung function is inevitable in everyone.

This seems to be the exact issue that I am frustrated with. In 10 years, a person will lose about a 12-ounce soda-can (355 cc) of breathing ability or essentially one breath per minute.

<u>Exercise, aging and the lung</u>

- The age-associated decline in pulmonary function is not recovered by training. Thus, loss in pulmonary function may lead to breathing issues in exercise in the active elderly.

- VO2max declines with a rate ~0.5% per year after the age of 30 years, while studies suggest that VO2max decline may accelerate after ages 40-50 years.

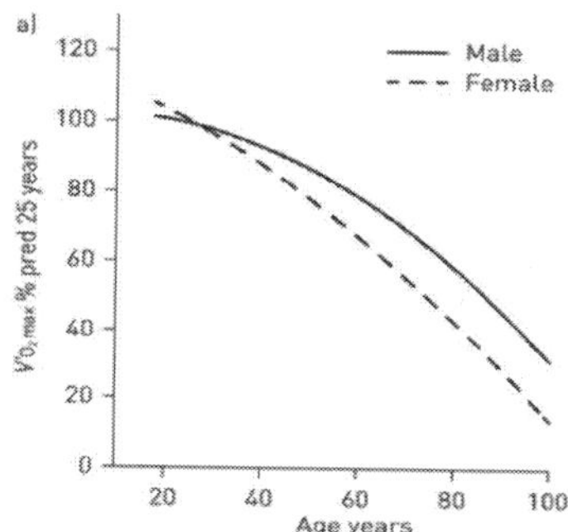

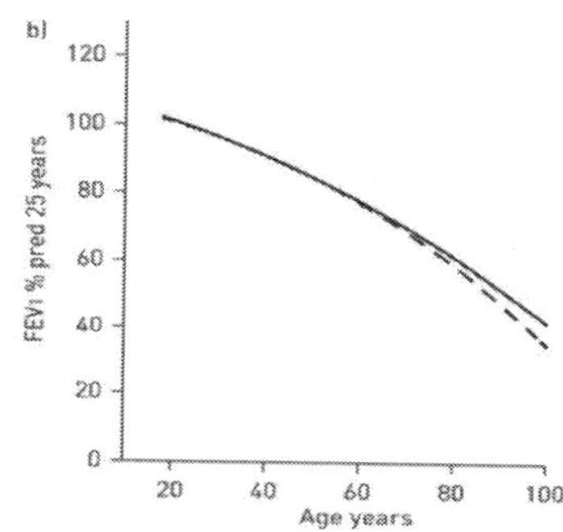

FIGURE 1

a) Decline in maximal oxygen uptake (VO2max) with age. VO2max is compared to predicted value [10] for a 25-year-old individual.

b) Decline in forced expiratory volume in 1 s (FEV1) with age. FEV1 is compared to predicted value [11] for a 25-year-old individual.

- The lactate threshold declines with age. Our bodies are not able to push ourselves as hard as we get older.
- Muscle fibrosis and reduced elasticity reduce biomechanics more, thus increasing energy cost with exertion.
- Peak cardiac output falls ~25% with age. Reduced maximum heart rate. The exercise cardiac response from aging is like that of a young person on beta blockers. (i.e. beta blockers decrease heart rate).
- Decreased efficacy in adding oxygen to blood occurs with aging.
- Ventilation to lower distal lung areas is decreased (more basilar atelectasis). More wasted airspace occurs with aging.
- Pulmonary function begins to decline at about age 25.

- Mean bronchial diameter decreases with age, increasing airway resistance (i.e. asthma).
- Respiratory muscle strength decreases with age. Diaphragm strength in the elderly was 13-25% less than in a younger group. (Roman, Rossiter, & Casaburi, 2016)

Exercise-training-induced changes in metabolic capacity with age: the role of central cardiovascular plasticity

Maximal oxygen consumption (V02max) falls steadily from 35 to 40 years of age at a rate of ~10 % per decade.
The aim of this study was to examine if young and old subjects would gain similar benefits following high-intensity aerobic training.

- A total of 30 (15 young, 24 ± 2 years and 15 old, 60 ± 3 years) healthy, non-obese (BMI < 30) and non-smoking males were matched for V02max, of a similar height and weight.
- All performed supervised high-intensity aerobic training three times a week for eight weeks, with both heart rate and power output monitored to ensure the same relative intensity for all participants.

As the eight-week training program progressed, the young improved significantly more than the old.

- V02max improved significantly in both the young (13 %) and the old (6 %).
- The young increased maximal power output by 20%; the old 10%.
- Maximum heart rate remained unchanged in the old, but was significantly decreased in the young.

The benefits in the young group were about twice as large as the older group. (Wang, et al., 2014)

Chapter 25: Rate Limiting Systems

Working out as we get older is similar to the catchphrase "Two steps forward, one step back". Strangely, Vladimir Lenin coined the phrase "One Step Forward, Two Steps Back" as a title of a 1904 revolutionary pamphlet.

Chapter 26: Extreme Exercise Hypothesis

Caffeine improves our rate of perceived exertion, giving the impression that exercise may be easier and allowing one to train harder. There comes a point at which dedication becomes non-productive and overtraining or burnout occurs. Moderation is a good generalization when discussing almost everything, including exercise. Performing activities to extreme levels can cause hardship or great success. Exercise has a continuum, and at some level it becomes counterproductive. "*Peanuts*" cartoonist Charles M. Schultz said "*Exercise is a dirty word... Every time I hear it, I wash my mouth out with chocolate.*"

The "Extreme Exercise Hypothesis": Recent Findings and Cardiovascular Health Implications

In 2017, The World Health Organization recommends that adults aged 18-64 engage in at least 150 minutes a week of moderate-intensity aerobic activities. Muscle-strengthening activities should be done on two or more days a week.

- **The WHO recommends that more exercise is better, and it is estimated that maximal health benefits require up to ~ three to four times the current exercise recommendations.**

- Some epidemiological studies in 2015 reported an increased risk of disease and/or mortality at the highest exercise volumes, suggesting that health benefits may plateau or even decline in extreme exercisers. Hence, the "Extreme Exercise Hypothesis."

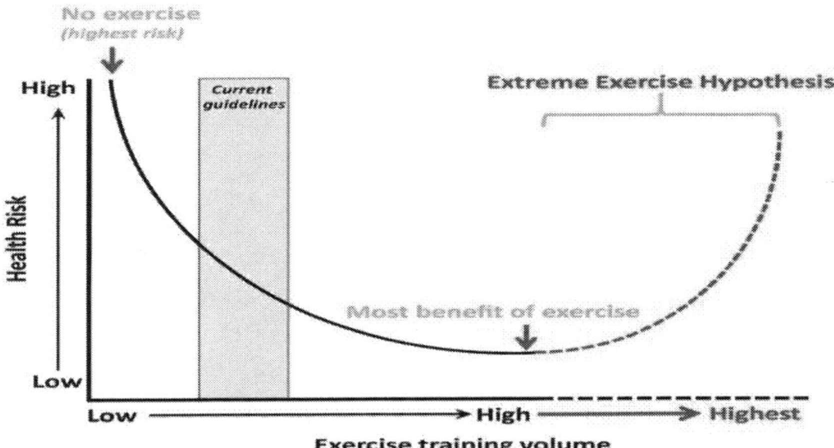

Fig.1: Conceptual overview of the "Extreme Exercise Hypothesis." Increasing volumes of exercise lead to a curvilinear decrease in health risks, but these health benefits may be partially lost once an individual performs exercise training beyond the optimal exercise dose.

- Arem et al. (2015) combined data with a study population of 661,137 individuals. **Maximal risk reduction for all-cause mortality occurred at an exercise volume of three to five times current exercise recommendations**.
- Lear et al. analyzed a cohort of 130,843 individuals from 17 countries. Individuals in the high physical activity group had a 35% decreased risk for all-cause mortality and 25% reduced risk for major cardiovascular disease compared to the low physical activity group.

Exercise and atrial fibrillation

The association between habitual physical activity and atrial fibrillation is complex. Some studies show increased risk;

some show decreased risk. The best summary opinion is that light-to-moderate amounts of exercise decrease, but larger volumes of exercise potentially increase the risk of atrial fibrillation.

- Two recent studies (2015, 2016) reported that higher physical fitness was associated with a graded reduction in the risk of atrial fibrillation.

Sudden cardiac death

- High-intensity exercise can acutely, albeit transiently, increase the risk for sudden cardiac arrest or sudden cardiac death in individuals with underlying cardiac disease. The cause of death is usually different for young (40 or younger) versus older athletes. Inherited or congenital cardiac conditions predominate as the cause in young athletes, and atherosclerotic coronary artery disease is the primary cause of death in older athletes.
- A 2017 New England Journal of Medicine Canadian study of athletic participants aged 12–45 years old found 74 cases with sudden cardiac arrest over the course of 18.5 million person-years of observation, yielding an incidence of 0.76 cases per 100,000 athletes per year.

Conclusions

- There is no clear threshold for an upper limit of exercise-induced health benefit.
- There is limited evidence that supports the "extreme exercise hypothesis," the most compelling data relating to the increased risk of atrial fibrillation at high volumes of exercise.
- Cardiac anomalies may be present in a small proportion of the most active veteran athletes.
- The combination of high-intensity physical activity in the presence of known or occult cardiovascular disease

seems to be the major cause of exercise-related fatalities. (Eijsvogels, Thompson, & Franklin, 2018)

Training for Longevity: The Reverse J-Curve for Exercise

The most physically active group in middle age has a predicted life expectancy eight years longer than a sedentary group.

- Paffenbarger (1986) reported a reverse J-shaped association between exercise and all-cause mortality. That prospective study followed 16,936 male Harvard alumni for 16 years and found that death rates declined as physical activity increased from fewer than 500 to 3,500 kcal/week._However, the 18% of men exercising at a level of more than 3,500 kcal/week had a 38% rather than a 54% mortality reduction compared to those doing 3,000 to 3,500 kcal/week.
- In 1998, Karajalainen et al. examined 300 veteran endurance athletes and reported a fivefold greater incidence of atrial fibrillation compared to a sedentary control group.
- 2013 study, atrial fibrillation was associated with higher-intensity exercise regimens, faster competitive finishing times and total number of endurance races completed.
- Long-term endurance exercise - 2,000 or more hours and/or 20 or more years of training -- displays a strong correlation with atrial fibrillation even in individuals without cardiovascular risk factors (2014, 2016 studies).
- A 2009 study showed chronic endurance sports can increase risk of atrial fibrillation anywhere between two- and ten-fold.
- Above 10 hours of vigorous exercise/week, the risk of developing atrial fibrillation begins to exceed that of a sedentary group in a 2018 study.

Chapter 26: Extreme Exercise Hypothesis

- Up to 90% of all exercise-related sudden cardiac deaths occur in recreational athletes rather than competitive athletes. This points away from "*extreme exercise hypothesis.*"
- In athletes older than 35, more than 80% of the sudden cardiac deaths are caused by coronary artery disease; whereas among younger athletes, congenital abnormalities of the heart muscle, coronaries and conduction system are the most common cause of sudden cardiac deaths.

Current studies suggest that 2.5 to 5 hours a week of moderate or vigorous physical activity confers maximal benefits; more than 10 hours a week may reduce these health benefits. (O'Keefe, Torres-Acosta, O'Keefe, & Lavie, 2020)

Heart of the World's Top Ultramarathon Runner—Not Necessarily Much Different from Normal

We tested a 36-year-old athlete (one of the most titled ultramarathon runners in the world) before and after a 24-hour ultramarathon. We hypothesized that many years of intensive training may have adverse effects on his heart.

- He has been running for 20 years and about 62,000 miles. He ran in nearly 50 ultramarathons, the longest of which was a 48-hour run. He is a two-time Polish champion in the 24-hour ultramarathon. ECG, echocardiogram, MRI, nuclear medicine MRI, and blood tests were performed three times.

Multiple years of extreme aerobic training did not cause any permanent abnormal cardiac issues as assessed by extensive cardiac testing. (Gajda, Klisiewicz, Matsibora, Piotrowska-Kownacka, & Biernacka, 2020)

Ten-year follow-up of cardiac function and neural regulation in a group of amateur half-marathon runners

Evaluate the cardiovascular function of a group of amateur half-marathon runners over a 10 years period.

Regular moderate–vigorous physical training over many years was beneficial in a group of middle-aged amateur half-marathon runners. They had normal echocardiographic findings. They did not damage their hearts with all the training. (De Maria, et al., 2021)

Chapter 27: Hypoxic Training, etc.

The goal of training is to improve performance. No one disagrees that hard work is necessary. If someone can achieve the same results in less time or effort, that is an important advantage. Supplementing with coffee/caffeine is one idea.

Another idea is to add some variable that makes exercise more difficult. A simple example would be to run 2 miles instead of 1 mile since 2 miles is better training then one mile. Now, add ankle weights. After that, let's run uphill for 2 miles with ankle weights. After that, let's wear a mask that makes you feel like you're breathing through a straw. Essentially, you figure out the limit one can "up the ante" until it becomes non-productive.

Training at higher altitude or simulating high altitude is one approach. It causes our body to compensate for the lower oxygen level by making more red blood cells that can carry more oxygen. If we can carry more oxygen to our lungs and muscles, we can do more work. Elite cyclists such as Lance Armstrong have used certain drugs or simulations for years to obtain this advantage. The main Olympic training center in Colorado Springs, Colorado, is at an altitude of about 6,000 feet above sea level. This is not a coincidence.

Unfortunately, not all athletes like or respond to high altitude training.

Effects of caffeine on neuromuscular fatigue and performance during high-intensity cycling exercise in moderate hypoxia

Investigate the effects of caffeine during high-intensity cycling exercise in moderate hypoxia.

- Seven males underwent an incremental exercise test on a cycle ergometer in conditions of acute hypoxia (oxygen level decreased to 15%; normal is 21%) to establish baseline data. In the following two visits, subjects performed a time to exhaustion test in the same hypoxic conditions (15%) after caffeine ingestion (4 mg/kg) and one after placebo ingestion in a double-blind, randomized, counterbalanced crossover design.
- **Caffeine significantly improved time to exhaustion by 12%.**
- **A significant decrease in subjective fatigue was found after caffeine consumption. Perception of effort was lower despite heart rate higher in the caffeinated condition.**

Background/Discussion

- Little is known about caffeine in conditions of hypoxia (low oxygen). The Tour de France is staged at high altitude. Physical endurance is also required of mountaineers and soldiers operating at high altitude.
- Berglund and Hemmingsson (1982) found that caffeine (6 mg/kg) significantly improves performance in 14 well-trained cross country skiers competing in a 21-km time trial at 2,900 meters (9,514 feet) above sea level.
- Stadheim et al. (2015) tested 13 well-trained cross-country skiers at a simulated altitude of 2,000 meters (6,562 ft) and found that caffeine (4.5 mg/kg) significantly improved time to exhaustion by 20%.

- Fulco et al. (1994) found a 54% improvement in cycling after caffeine ingestion (4 mg/kg) at an altitude of 4,300 meters (14,108 feet).

The most likely explanation for enhanced endurance performance in hypoxic conditions is the reduction in perception of effort induced by caffeine. (Smirmaul, de Moraes, Angius, & Marcora, 2017)

An Updated Panorama of "Living Low-Training High" Altitude/Hypoxic Methods

The altitude training model of "living low-training high" is becoming an important intervention for modern sports. Athletes are exposed to hypoxia that typically lasts less than 2 hours at rest or while training two to five times per week. Its effects on the human body have been studied as early as the 1940s. During World War II, the Soviet Union used hypobaric chambers to condition their pilots to fly open-cockpit airplanes at altitudes higher than 7,000 meters (23,000 feet). (For comparison, Mount Everest is 29,032 feet.)

Intermittent hypoxic exposure at rest

- Intermittent hypoxic exposure refers to the use of "brief" periods (3-6 minutes) of relatively severe levels of hypoxia (oxygen levels of 9% to 15% are equal to 9,186-18,049 feet altitude) interspersed with normal oxygen episodes of similar duration (normal oxygen 21%).
- Hypoxic exposure lasting 30 minutes to five hours have also been introduced for high-altitude expedition pre-acclimatization protocols, and performance at altitude.
- An International Olympic Committee expert group concluded that "*the use of intermittent hypoxic exposure does not increase sea-level performance and is not recommended. Further research in this area with respect to improving endurance performance does not seem warranted*".

- Repeated sprints in hypoxia is a recent training method. This is the repetition of short (less than 30 seconds) "all-out" sprints with incomplete recoveries (less than 60 seconds) in hypoxia, also including fewer rest periods to increase difficulty. The general consensus is that repeated sprints in hypoxia leads to superior (1–5%) ability in normal conditions. Encouraging results have been reported in professional rugby players and swimmers.
- Short and intense workouts in hypoxia promote several beneficial adaptations.

Despite evidence of "*living low-training high*" safety and efficacy, some uncertainty remains:

- Hypoxia is a stressor that may do more harm than good if it is too intense. It cannot be assumed that "more is better" regarding the "*living low-training high*" dosage. Consequently, if the total training load (i.e., exercise-to-rest ratio, recovery times) is not adjusted accordingly, the amplified training can swiftly lead to overreaching or overtraining.
- The desire for hypoxic conditions has led to development of portable mask-system hypoxicator machines or masks. (Girard, Brocherie, Goods, & Millet, 2020)

One idea is to use hypoxia in people who have difficulty exercising as a result of arthritis or difficulty moving. Although theoretically it sounds feasible, my clinical impression is that this would be too stressful for a patient to do. Being short of breath is very stressful to everyone and discourages exercise tremendously. The only people really trained well to deal with hypoxia are probably Navy SEALs.

Using hypoxic environments potentially promotes larger gains by starting out in a heightened stress environment from the beginning. It promotes mental toughness, but I'm not sure it's worth the stress.

Chapter 27: Hypoxic Training, etc.

Training at higher altitude is not easy and athletes do not always respond favorably.

Combining hypoxic methods for peak performance

Altitude training was developed in Scandinavia and the USA in the early 1990s.

At present, several forms of hypoxic training and/or altitude exposure exist:

1. Traditional live high-train high
2. Contemporary live high-train low
3. Intermittent hypoxic exposure during rest
4. Intermittent hypoxic exposure during continuous session

All have the same goal: improve performance at sea level.

- Live high-train low was shown to be an efficient method. The optimal altitude for living high has been defined as being 2,200-2,500 meters (7,218-8,202 feet) to provide an optimal erythropoietic (blood-making) effect.
- The optimal duration at altitude appears to be four weeks for inducing accelerated erythropoiesis; less than three weeks (i.e., 18 days) is long enough for beneficial changes in acclimation.
- One critical point is the daily dose of altitude. A natural altitude of 2,500 meters (8,202 feet) for 20-22 hours/day appears sufficient to increase erythropoiesis and improve sea-level performance. "*Longer is better,*" since additional benefits have been shown as hypoxic exposure increases beyond 16 hours/day.
- The minimum daily dose for stimulating erythropoiesis seems to be 12 hours/day.

There is clear evidence that intense exercise at high altitude stimulates muscle adaptation better then sea-level work. (Millet, Roels, Schmitt, Woorons, & Richalet, 2010)

Comparison of Tibial Shock during Treadmill and Real-World Running

Does treadmill running compare to outdoor running in regards to stress endured on the legs?

- This study compares tibial shock (shin pain/stress) between treadmill and road marathon conditions.
- A total of 192 runners (men/women, 105/87; age, 44.9 years) wore a tibial-mounted measuring unit on a treadmill several days before completing a marathon race. Participants ran at 90% of their projected race speed and 30 seconds of tibial shock data were collected. Participants then wore the sensors during the race with tibial shock averaged over the 12th, 23rd, and 40th kilometers.
- A significant difference was found for tibial shock between outdoors and treadmill. At the 12th kilometer of the race, only 40% to 42% of the variance in outdoor tibial shock was expressed on the treadmill.
- Running on a treadmill takes a lot of the stress away from running outdoors. (Johnson, et al., 2020)

One of the times I ran the Boston Marathon, I had trained only on a treadmill and would run 16.2 miles four times per week, thinking I could "suck it up" for the last 10 miles. I stopped at about 16 miles in disappointment. I still completed the marathon at a decent time of about 3 hours, 40 minutes, but realized that the pounding from running outside is important. I stopped that training method. I probably watched the movie "Armageddon" more than 50 times on VHS including the same previews, while on the treadmill in front of a dumpy small TV in my basement.

A Comparison of the Energetic Cost of Running in Marathon Racing Shoes

Chapter 27: Hypoxic Training, etc.

Reducing the energetic cost of running seems the most feasible path to a sub-2-hour marathon. Eighteen high-caliber athletes ran six five-minute trials with two established marathon shoes along with a prototype running shoe.

- Compared with the established racing shoes, the new shoes reduced the energetic cost of running in all 18 subjects tested.

The prototype shoes lowered the energetic cost of running by 4% on average. (Hoogkamer W, 2018)

Improving 4% is a big deal. I'd pay an extra $50 for that benefit.

Effects of 4-Week Inspiratory Muscle Training on Sport Performance in College 800-Meter Track Runners

- The diaphragm, one of the respiratory muscles, is essential for respiratory movement.
- Previous studies have indicated that inspiratory muscle training significantly reduces fatigue and improves athletic performance.

Johnson and colleagues used the threshold inspiratory muscle training intervention (PowerBreath®®) for six weeks on cyclists. Results indicated improved performance, which was supported in multiple other studies. (Chang, et al., 2021)

Effects of 120 g/h of Carbohydrates Intake during a Mountain Marathon on Exercise-Induced Muscle Damage in Elite Runners

High-intensity efforts induce exercise-induced muscle damage.

Muscle damage markers show a rise in blood after exercise, increase further after 24-72 hours, with a total time of several days to return to baseline values.

- The present study analyzed the effects of 120 g/hour of carbohydrate supplementation on exercise-induced muscle damage markers (CK, LDH, SGOT, urea and creatinine).
- This carbohydrate intake was compared to international recommendations for events of longer than three hours (90 g/h), and regular athletes' carbohydrate intake during ultra-endurance races (60 g/h).

Thirty-one elite male athletes (including two world champions) were recruited.

- The main findings revealed that higher carbohydrate intake (120g/h) significantly limits the increase in exercise-induced muscle damage markers.
- Current recommendations of 90 g/h carbohydrates for exercise lasting more than 2.5 hours might not be enough to limit metabolic responses.

The effects of this higher carbohydrate intake (120 g/h) compared to the recommended 90 g/h or 60 g/h amount might lead to a new and more suitable strategy to limit inflammation in demanding endurance exercises. (Viribay, et al, 2020)

1 gram of carbohydrates equals 4 calories, that's 480 calories per hour.

<u>The Role of Environmental Conditions on Marathon Running Performance in Men Competing in Boston Marathon from 1897 to 2018</u>

- The ranges of temperature 40-59° F or 50-54° F have been recommended as the most advantageous for performance.

- Performances were fastest, on average, in the top 100 and top 10 finisher groups when the temperature was lower than 46° F.
- Wind speed of 7 mph was the most favorable.
- Increasing temperature by 1 °C (1.8 F) significantly worsened performance by almost 2 minutes for all finishers.
- The direct relationship of race times with temperature, i.e., the hotter the temperature, the slower the race time, was in agreement with previous observations in marathon races. (Nikolaidis, et al., 2019)

The temperature is ideal when you're cold at the start of the race and it takes a few miles to warm up. It should be "nippy" at the start. Spectators should be wearing winter jackets or sweatshirts.

Crawling to the finish line: Why do endurance runners collapse? Implications for understanding of mechanisms underlying pacing and fatigue.

Effective regulation of pace enables the majority of runners to complete endurance events without mishap. However, some runners experience exercise-induced collapse. Some runners persist in attempting to reach the finish line, and this often results in changes in posture and gait. The initial stage involves an unstable gait that further degrades into a shuffle. If the condition worsens, the runner will fall to the ground, crawling forward on knees and elbows. The runner may collapse and remain prone until recovering either with or without assistance or medical treatment. Continuing to reach the finish line is perhaps indicative of a high psychological drive or unrealistic situational appraisal. (St Clair Gibson, et al., 2013)

This is what I call uncomfortable poetry in motion. No one ever wants a DNF (did not finish). This happens more in Ironman competitions and is painful to watch.

Chapter 28: Obesity

More than 60 diseases and 12 cancers are associated with obesity. Over 60% of obese Americans attempt weight loss each year. On June 21, 2013, the American Medical Association declared obesity a disease. Weight loss of 5-10% is clinically significant to reduce disease risk. Coffee/Caffeine decreases "*perceived exertion*" and may encourage people to exercise more and therefore help decrease the epidemic of obesity. In 1900, Dr Lister noted "More people die of overfeeding than over-fasting"

<u>Association of midlife obesity and cardiovascular risk with old age frailty: a 26-year follow-up of initially healthy men</u>

Investigate whether old age frailty is predicted by midlife weight issues.

- 1,815 initially healthy men (mean age 47 years) had their weight status, cardiovascular disease risk factors assessed in 1974.
- After a 26-year follow-up in 2000, the frailty status was assessed using the RAND-36 (well-established 36 question health survey).
- Compared with normal weight, the development of frailty was more than twice (odds ratio 2.06) as likely among men who were overweight and more than five

times (odds ratio 5.41) more likely in obese men in midlife. (Strandberg, et al., 2012)

Preventing old-age frailty should be recognized as an important goal of treating obesity in midlife.

Regular Coffee Consumption Is Associated with Lower Regional Adiposity Measured by DXA among US Women

- Coffee consumption has been associated with a reduction in adiposity. DXA (bone density) is a means to assess body fat and fat distribution.
- Participants were 20-69 years-old.
- Women aged 20–44 y who drank 2–3 cups of coffee per day and women aged 45–69 y who drank >4 cups of coffee per day had the lowest levels of adiposity.

Higher coffee consumption was associated with significantly lower total body fat percentage and trunk body fat percentage in a dose-response manner among women but not men. (Cao, et al., 2020)

Body Mass Index Versus Body Fat Percentage in Prospective National Football League Athletes: Overestimation of Obesity Rate in Athletes at the National Football League Scouting Combine

Obesity is a major issue in the National Football League with a reported obesity rate of 56% (body mass index≥30.0). However, BMI does not take into account muscle mass, and may overestimate the prevalence of obesity.

A total of 1,958 NFL Combine participants from 2010 to 2016 completed body composition testing. Based on BMI (≥30.0), the obesity rate was 53.4% versus an 8.9% obesity rate using body composition.

- Drafted players demonstrated a significantly lower body fat percentage than undrafted players, with the exception of quarterbacks and running backs.
- All positions of play, with the exception of defensive linemen, demonstrated a decrease in body fat percentage between 2010 and 2017.
- Body fat percentage was more valid than BMI for determining an NFL candidate's true body composition. (Provencher, et al., 2018)

Obesity, based on BMI, is sometimes overestimated in young people due to abundant muscle mass and underestimated in elderly people due to lack of muscle mass.
Professional athletes are getting bigger, stronger, faster and leaner over time. Unfortunately, I probably reached my athletic peak at 12 years old and 75 pounds.

Chapter 29: Crazy Sports

What does ice swimming and sauna competitions have to do with coffee and caffeine? Absolutely nothing. We know caffeine has been shown to consistently improve performance. Inspirational stories help motivate people to exercise. These stories are fascinating outliers. Competition is important to our species both from a social and survival point of view.

Cold Water Swimming-Benefits and Risks: A Narrative Review

Cold-water swimming is a general umbrella term for swimming in water with a temperature of less than 15°C (59°F).

- In countries such as Finland, Poland, Russia, Norway, Sweden, Denmark, Estonia, Lithuania, the Czech Republic and Latvia, cold-water swimming is practiced regularly and is mostly recreational.
- Ice swimming is an official competition at water temperatures of less than 5°C (41°F).
- Ice swimming is specifically practiced by extreme athletes. American Lynne Cox and Briton Lewis Gordon Pugh are among the world's best known and most extreme ice swimmers.

- In 2002, Cox swam in the ice-cold waters of the Antarctic for around 25 min, reaching around 1.7 km (1 mile).
- Pugh made the first attempt in July 2007 to swim as close as possible to the geographical North Pole. He managed to swim a distance of 1 km for 18:50 min in −1.7°C (35°F) water at an open point in the ice. He suffered frostbite in his fingers and took four months to recover.
- Sports scientist Timothy David Noakes has shown that Pugh's ability to raise his body temperature by 2°C enabled him to survive the cold water. His term for this, "*anticipatory thermo-genesis*," is a process never registered with any other person. Recently, this increase in core body temperature when immersed in ice-cold water was confirmed several times by German ice swimmer Bruno *"Orca"* Dobelmann. In both swimmers, body core temperature was measured in the rectum. "*Anticipatory thermo-genesis*" should, therefore, be a normal physiological reaction in a trained ice swimmer when immersed in ice-cold water.

Ice Swimming as a Competition

- The International Ice Swimming Association was founded on July 1, 2009.
- **Official ice swimmers do not swim with wetsuits or other thermal protection, only standard swimwear.**
- The question arises whether this sport is healthy or harmful?
- Swimming in ice-cold water has a positive mental effect as well as improving lipid profile, blood pressure, and depression. Standard exercise in a normal environment will have the same effect and would be much easier.
- The study of hypothermia was accelerated by the sinking of the Titanic and observations made during the maritime conflicts of World War II.

- **Even in the most experienced ice swimmers, cold-water immersion carries a risk of death.**
- **The initial shock and loss of breathing control is where the swimmer is at greatest risk of drowning and death.**

Symptoms of cold-water immersion according to core body temperature.

36 °C (96.8F)	Spontaneous shivering, rapid heart rate, rapid breathing rate
35 °C (95F)	Confusion, disorientation, decreased muscle coordination
34 °C (93.2)	Amnesia
33 °C (91.4F)	Cardiac arrhythmias, poor perfusion of the skin
33–30 °C (86-91.4F)	Clouding of consciousness, spontaneous shivering stops, rigid muscle tone
30 °C (86F)	Stupor or unconsciousness, diminished respirations, poor muscle tone, hypotension
28 °C (82.4)	Ventricular fibrillation, near-absent respiration, vital signs near absent
25 °C (77F)	Cardiac arrest, death

- Acclimatization to cold improves over the course of about 10 days.
- **The most significant risk of cold-water swimming is hypothermia.**
- **According to various estimates, a person can survive in water at 0.3°C (32.5 F) for 45 minutes. However, exhaustion or loss of consciousness is expected to occur within 15 minutes.**
- Exercise might also have an effect on the decline in body core temperature during swimming in cold water. A study investigating men while immersed in water of 3.6°C (38 F) showed that periods of work gave better chances of survival than continuous heat production by shivering in a well-insulated suit.

- Chlorine added to the water in swimming pools and the salt in sea water enables the water to remain liquid at sub-zero temperatures. Swimming in such waters is much more challenging and dangerous.
- A large proportion of cold-water immersion deaths can be attributed to arrhythmias.
- **After a person is immersed in cold water, a cold shock reaction occurs that causes uncontrollable heavy breathing and hyperventilation. With prolonged exposure, the respiratory rate is high and leads to progressive respiratory muscle fatigue. Although it is possible to improve the initial cold shock response, drowning may still occur. Uncontrollable hyperventilation leads to a reduction in cerebral blood flow with disorientation and loss of consciousness.**
- So far, two deaths have been reported in official ice swimming competitions.
- A systematic review showed a connection between water temperature and swimming-induced pulmonary edema.

(Knechtle, Waśkiewicz, Sousa, Hill, & Nikolaidis, 2020)

I enjoy exercise and the endorphins that are released after exercise, but I do not need the adrenaline rush resulting from knowing whether I will survive every time I participate in ice swimming. From a medical point of view, this is crazy. This is the ultimate stress test. This is a great example of how bodies can tolerate and adapt to toxic environments if conditioned enough. This is not an extreme environment, like the desert, but more like Mount Everest and "dead zone" stuff. My hat's off (better yet, my coat is off) to show these extreme athletes the respect they have earned. The great baseball announcer Harry Caray, God rest his soul, would say "Holy Cow" to this sport while opening an ice-cold Budweiser.

Clinical Effects of Regular Dry Sauna Bathing: A Systematic Review

Many health benefits are claimed by sauna bathing. The medical evidence is not well established.

- Literature search from 2000 onward.
- Only one small study reported an adverse health outcome of disrupted male spermatogenesis, demonstrated to be reversible after ceasing sauna activity.

Tragic Death in World Sauna Championship

The latest Sauna World Championships ended in tragedy on Aug. 7, 2010. Vladimir Ladyzhenskiy, in his 60s, and Timo Kaukonen collapsed with severe burns after about six minutes into the event.

Ladyzhenskiy died late the same day. Ossi Arvela, a competition organizer, said the competition would never be held again.

The Sauna World Championships took place every August in Heinola, Finland. Thousands of spectators flocked to the sauna competition while 50+ took part in the event.

What sauna temperatures are reached?

The sauna is pre-heated to 110°C (water boils at 100°C), that's 230° Fahrenheit (the average temperature in recreational saunas is 150-195°F).

Every 30 seconds, half a liter of water is thrown onto the hot sauna. Contestants have to sit with their buttocks and thighs on a bench, with their elbows on their knees, their arms raised, with good posture. The contestants have to stay in this position; if they touch their skin, they are disqualified. If they can't make it out of the sauna by themselves, they are disqualified.

> Males and females do not compete against each other. The winners tend to be from Finland.
> The 2003 champion and world record holder, Timo Kaukonen, stayed in the sauna for a whopping 16 minutes,15 seconds. Some competitors don't even last two minutes, and some of the most seasoned sauna users only manage to last five or six minutes. Many contestants experience first-degree burns and have red or pink blotchy skin after experiencing such heat for this short amount of time.
> (Hussain & Cohen, 2018)

The cliché "*it's a dry heat*" clearly does not apply here. If I had to choose between being cooked alive in essentially an oven or freezing to death in ice water, I would take ice water every time. When JFK stated that he wanted the USA to go to the moon because *"it is hard,"* I can guarantee he was not thinking of ice swimming or sauna competitions.

Definitions

The book contains many scientific terms that are not familiar to many people. I had to look up many words to understand the meanings and explanations myself. Statistical terms are confusing and throughout the book I tried to choose the term that may be the easiest to grasp.

Ergogenic: Intended to enhance physical performance, stamina, or recovery.

Cost-benefit ratio: Process used to measure the benefits of a decision versus the costs associated with taking that action.

Linear-dose relationship: the effect of a substance increases or decreases in a similar pattern to dose. A consistent increase in biologic response occurs as an increased amount of a test substance is administered. For example, doubling the dose of a medicine causes it be twice as effective.

Nonlinear relationship: the effect of one variable is not proportional to another and the relationship does not fit a simple line on a graph. The benefits of a blood pressure medicine may double by doubling the dose but then not be any more effective at a higher dose.

Case-control study: Compares the odds of having an experience with the outcome to the odds of having an experience without the outcome, such as not wearing seatbelts and fatal injuries.

Cohort study (prospective observational study): A study of a group of similar people to see whether there is a link between something and an outcome, such as men over 50 years and prostate cancer.

Crossover studies: Studies comparing two or more treatments or interventions in which the subjects or patients, upon completion of the course of one treatment, are switched to another. For example, effects on cholesterol levels of replacing butter with margarine with patients randomized to a six-week butter diet followed by a six-week margarine diet, or the reverse sequence.

Cross-sectional study: The observation of a defined population at a single point in time or time interval. Exposure and outcome are determined simultaneously, such as with smoking habits and lung cancer.

Double-blind method: studying a drug or procedure in which both the subjects and investigators are kept unaware of who is actually getting which specific treatment.

Longitudinal study: Study in which variables relating to an individual or group of individuals are assessed over a period of time, such as studying all identical twins born in 1970 over a 30-year time frame for diabetes.

Matched-pair analysis: A type of analysis in which subjects in a study group and a comparison group are made comparable with respect to extraneous factors by individually pairing subjects. For example, 60-year-old males with diabetes are compared with 60-year-old males without diabetes.

Definitions

Meta-analysis: A way of combining data from many different research studies.

Nested case-control study: Looks at a particular aspect of a larger study that may have had a different focus. For example, a large study looking at the incidence of smoking and cancer may have a nested cohort study looking at the incidence of diabetes in the subjects who had cancer.

Numbers needed to treat: Number of patients who need to be treated to prevent one additional bad outcome. For example, if a drug has a number needed to treat of 10, it means you have to treat 10 people with the drug to prevent one additional bad outcome.

Prospective study: Observation of a population for a sufficient number of subjects over a sufficient number of years to generate incidence or mortality rates subsequent to the selection of the study group. For example, 100 people with diabetes are followed for 20 years to see how many suffer a heart attack.

Randomized controlled trial: A clinical trial that randomly (by chance) assigns participants to one of two or more groups.

Retrospective study: A study in which some of the people under study have the outcome of interest; their characteristics are compared with those of others unaffected. For example, 100 people with diabetes are asked how much they exercised in the past.

RR (relative risk, risk ratio): Gives a number that tells whether the exposure to something makes the outcome more likely or less likely.
RR=1 means that exposure does not affect the outcome. For example, wearing black socks does not increase lung cancer.
RR<1 means that the risk of the outcome is decreased by the exposure, which can be called a "protective factor." For example, exercise decreases obesity.
RR>1 means that the risk of the outcome is increased by the exposure. For example, cigarette smoking increases lung cancer.
A risk ratio of 0.28 indicates that the risk is only 28% compared to a different outcome. Risk ratio=6.1 indicates the outcome is 6.1 times more likely.
Remember, a 50% higher risk does not mean that the bad outcome occurs in every other person but that the risk may increase from 10% to 15%.

Single-blind method: A method in which either the observer(s) or the subject(s) is kept ignorant of the group to which the subjects are assigned. For example, only the researcher doing the study knows which treatment the participant is receiving until the trial is over.

Statistical significance: The claim that a result is not likely to occur randomly or by chance but is instead likely to be attributable to a specific cause. A p-value (probability value) of 5% or lower is often considered to be statistically significant.

Systematic review: A summary of the clinical literature, or a critical assessment and evaluation of all research studies that address a particular clinical issue.

Definitions

Umbrella review: A synthesis of existing reviews, only including the highest level of evidence such as systematic reviews and meta-analyses.

VO_2 max (maximum oxygen uptake): Reflects the maximal ability of a person to take in, transport, and use oxygen -- that person's functional aerobic capacity. VO_2 max has become the "gold standard" laboratory measure of cardiorespiratory fitness and is the most important parameter measured during functional exercise testing. In layman's terms, it measures "how in shape someone is".

Wingate Test: Well-accepted reproducible test to assess a person's fitness level. Typical description involves a warm-up on a bicycle with two or three 15-second "sprints" to make sure the subject is used to the fast movement before the test begins. On completing the warmup, the subject rests for one minute, after which the test begins. The subject gets a five-second countdown to the beginning of the test, during which time they pedal as fast as they can. At the start of the test, the workload drops instantly (making it hard to pedal) and the subject continues to pedal quickly for 30 seconds.

Prediabetes: A condition in which a person has a fasting blood glucose level between 100 and 125 mg/dl and/or two-hour blood glucose between 140 and 199 mg/dl during an oral glucose tolerance test.

Metabolic syndrome (syndrome X): A cluster of conditions that increase the risk of heart disease, stroke, and diabetes. Metabolic syndrome includes high blood pressure, high blood sugar, excess body fat around the waist, and abnormal cholesterol levels

Half-life: The time it takes a substance such as a drug to lose half its activity. For example, the half-life of caffeine is about five hours, meaning half its effect is gone in that time.

Hypoxia: A low oxygen level. An oxygen saturation level lower than 90% is usually defined as hypoxia.

Lactic acid: A chemical that builds up when there's not enough oxygen in the muscles to break down glucose and glycogen. This is called anaerobic metabolism; fatigue sets in rapidly at this level.

Antioxidants: Molecules that fight free radicals in your body. Your body has its own antioxidant defenses to keep free radicals in check. Antioxidants neutralize free radicals by giving up some of their own electrons. In making this sacrifice, they act as a natural "off" switch for free radicals.

Free radicals: Oxygen-containing molecules with an uneven number of electrons. The uneven number allows them to react easily with other molecules. Free radicals can cause large-chain chemical reactions in the body because they react so easily with other molecules. These free radicals are unstable atoms that can damage cells, causing illness and aging.

Nonalcoholic fatty liver disease (NAFLD): A disease in females and males who drink less than 10 and 20 grams of alcohol/day, respectively (one alcoholic drink is 14 grams alcohol). The progressive disease is first apparent by benign fatty liver (steatosis), which can evolve to non-alcoholic steatohepatitis, which adds inflammation to steatosis. Later progression leads to steatosis with inflammation and mild to advanced fibrosis, to steatosis with fibrosis alone, to cirrhosis and finally to end-stage liver disease. Serious outcomes include cirrhosis, hepatocellular carcinoma, coronary heart disease, and diabetes. NAFLD is recognized as the leading cause of chronic liver disease in adults and children.

References

Abalo, R. (2021, Sep). Coffee and Caffeine Consumption for Human Health. *Nutrients, 13*(9), 2918. doi:https://doi.org/10.3390/nu13092918

Acciai, F., & Firebaugh, G. (2017, Oct). Why did life expectancy decline in the United States in 2015? A gender-specific analysis. *Soc Sci Med, 190*, 174-180. doi:https://doi.org/10.1016/j.socscimed.2017.08.004

Agritelley, M., & Goldberger, J. (2021, Jul). Caffeine supplementation in the hospital: Potential role for the treatment of caffeine withdrawal. *Food Chem Toxicol*, 112228. doi:https://doi.org/10.1016/j.fct.2021.112228

Ahmadyar, B., Rosemann, T., Rüst, C., & Knechtle, B. (2016, Jun 30). Improved Race Times in Marathoners Older than 75 Years in the Last 25 Years in the World's Largest Marathons. *Chin J Physiol, 59*(3), 139-47. doi:https://doi.org/10.4077/cjp.2016.bae382

Ailshire, J., Beltrán-Sánchez, H., & Crimmins, E. (2015, Feb). Becoming Centenarians: Disease and Functioning Trajectories of Older U.S. Adults as They Survive to 100. *J Gerontol A Biol Sci Med Sci, 70*(2), 193-201. doi:https://doi.org/10.1093/gerona/glu124

Archimandritis, A., Sipsas, N., Tryphonos, M., Tsirantonaki, M., & Tjivras, M. (1995). Significance of various factors in patients with functional dyspepsia and peptic ulcer disease in Greece. A comparative prospective study. *Ann Med Interne, 146*(5), 299-303.

Athletics and Motherhood: An American View. (1912, Nov 30). *53*(1378), 253-254. Retrieved from https://www.ncbi.nlm.nih.gov/pmc/articles/PMC5213583/?page=1

Bachmann, J., DeFina, L., Franzini, L., Gao, A., Leonard, D., Cooper, K., . . . Willis, B. (2015, Oct 27). Cardiorespiratory Fitness in Middle Age and Health Care Costs in Later Life. *J Am Coll Cardiol, 66*(17), 1876-85. doi:https://doi.org/10.1016/j.jacc.2015.08.030

Bakuradze, T., Lang, R., Hofmann, T., Eisenbrand, G., Schipp, D., Galan, J., & Richling, E. (2015, Feb). Consumption of a dark roast coffee decreases the level of spontaneous DNA strand breaks: a randomized controlled trial. *Eur J Nutr, 54*(1), 149-56. doi:https://doi.org/10.1007/s00394-014-0696-x

Baladia, E., Basulto, J., Manera, M., Martínez, R., & Calbet, D. (2014, Mar 1). Effect of green tea or green tea extract consumption on body weight and body composition; systematic review and meta-analysis. *Nutricion Hospitalaria, 29*(3), 479-90. doi:https://doi.org/10.3305/nh.2014.29.3.7118

Basu, A., Du, M., Sanchez, K., Leyva, M., Betts, N., Blevins, S., . . . Lyons, T. (2011, Feb). Green tea minimally affects biomarkers of inflammation in obese subjects with metabolic syndrome. *Nutrition, 27*(2), 206-13. doi:https://doi.org/10.1016/j.nut.2010.01.015

Bauer, P., & Sander, J. (2019). The Use of Caffeine by People with Epilepsy: The Myths and the Evidence. *Curr Neurol Neurosci Rep, 19*(6), 32. doi:https://doi.org/10.1007/s11910-019-0948-5

Baur, D., Lange, D., Elmenhorst, E., Elmenhorst, D., Bauer, A., Aeschbach, D., & Landolt, H. (2021, Jul 13). Coffee effectively attenuates impaired attention in ADORA2A C/C-allele carriers during chronic sleep restriction. *Prog Neuropsychopharmacol Biol Psychiatry, 109*, 110232. doi:https://doi.org/10.1016/j.pnpbp.2020.110232

Beaumont, R., Cordery, P., Funnell, M., Mears, S., James, L., & Watson, P. (2017, Oct). Chronic ingestion of a low dose of caffeine induces tolerance to the performance benefits of caffeine. *J Sports Sci, 35*(19), 1920-7. doi:https://doi.org/10.1080/02640414.2016.1241421

Belayneh, A., & Molla, F. (2020). The Effect of Coffee on Pharmacokinetic Properties of Drugs: Review. *BioMed Research International.* doi: https://doi.org/10.1155/2020/7909703

Blanchard, J., & Sawers, S. (1983). The absolute bioavailability of caffeine in man. *Eur J Clin Pharmacol, 24*(1), 93-8. doi:https://doi.org/10.1007/bf00613933

Bodar, V., Chen, J., Sesso, H., Gaziano, J., & Djoussé, L. (2020, Dec). Coffee consumption and risk of heart failure in the Physicians' Health Study. *Clin Nutr ESPEN, 40*, 133-137. doi:https://doi.org/10.1016/j.clnesp.2020.09.216

Booth, F., Roberts, C., & Laye, M. (2012, Apr). Lack of exercise is a major cause of chronic diseases. *Compr Physiol, 2*(2), 1143-1211. doi:https://doi.org/10.1002/cphy.c110025

Bozkurt Koseoglu, S., Korkmaz Toker, M., Gokbel, I., Celikkol, O., & Gungorduk, K. (2020). Can coffee consumption be used to accelerate the recovery of bowel function after cesarean section? Randomized prospective trial. *Ginekol Pol, 91*(2), 85-90. doi:https://doi.org/10.5603/gp.2020.0014

Bright, M., Raman, V., & Laupland, K. (2021). Use of therapeutic caffeine in acute care postoperative and critical care settings: a scoping review. *BMC*

Anesthesiology, 21(1), 100. doi:https://doi.org/10.1186/s12871-021-01320-x

Buijsse, B., Weikert, C., Drogan, D., Bergmann, M., & Boeing, H. (2010, Jul). Chocolate consumption in relation to blood pressure and risk of cardiovascular disease in German adults. *Eur Heart J, 31*(13), 1616-23. doi:https://doi.org/10.1093/eurheartj/ehq068

Cao, C., Liu, Q., Abufaraj, M., Han, Y., Xu, T., Waldhoer, T., . . . Smith, L. (2020, Jul). Regular Coffee Consumption Is Associated with Lower Regional Adiposity Measured by DXA among US Women. *J Nutr, 150*(7), 1909-1915. doi:https://doi.org/10.1093/jn/nxaa121

Carswell, A., Howland, K., Martinez-Gonzalez, B., Baron, P., & Davison, G. (2020). The effect of caffeine on cognitive performance is influenced by CYP1A2 but not ADORA2A genotype, yet neither genotype affects exercise performance in healthy adults. *Eur J Appl Physiol, 120*(7), 1495-1508. doi:https://doi.org/10.1007/s00421-020-04384-8

Caruso, C., & Puca, A. (2021, Feb). Special Issue "Centenarians—A Model to Study the Molecular Basis of Lifespan and Health-span". *Int J Mol Sci, 22*(4), 2044. doi:https://doi.org/10.3390/ijms22042044

Chan, L., Hong, C., & Bai, C. (2021, Oct 2). Coffee consumption and the risk of cerebrovascular disease: a meta-analysis of prospective cohort studies. *BMC Neurol, 21*(1), 380. doi:https://doi.org/10.1186/s12883-021-02411-5

Chang, Y., Chang, H., Ho, C., Lee, P., Chou, Y., Tsai, M., & Chou, L. (2021, Jan). Effects of 4-Week Inspiratory Muscle Training on Sport Performance in College 800-Meter Track Runners. *Medicina (Kaunas), 57*(1), 72. doi:https://doi.org/10.3390/medicina57010072

Chaput, J., Dutil, C., & Sampasa-Kanyinga, H. (2018). Sleeping hours: what is the ideal number and how does age impact this? *Nat Sci Sleep, 10*, 421-430. doi:https://doi.org/10.2147/nss.s163071

Chen, J., Scheltens, P., Groot, C., & Ossenkoppele, R. (2020). Associations Between Caffeine Consumption, Cognitive Decline, and Dementia: A Systematic Review. *J Alzheimers Dis, 78*(4), 1519-1546. doi:https://doi.org/10.3233/jad-201069

Chen, S., Wang, Z., Ma, Y., Zhang, W., Lu, J., Liang, Y., & Zheng, X. (2018, Mar). Neuroprotective Effects and Mechanisms of Tea Bioactive Components in Neurodegenerative Diseases. *Molecules, 23*(3), 512. doi:https://doi.org/10.3390/molecules23030512

Choi, H., Koo, S., & Park, H. (2020, Feb 21). Maternal coffee intake and the risk of bleeding in early pregnancy: a cross-sectional analysis. *BMC Pregnancy Childbirth, 20*(1), 121. doi:https://doi.org/10.1186/s12884-020-2798-1

Chou, T., & Benowitz, N. (1994, Oct). Caffeine and coffee: effects on health and cardiovascular disease. *Comp Biochem Physiol C Pharmacol Toxicol Endocrinol, 109*(2), 173-89.

Chrysant, S. (2015, Sep 1). Coffee Consumption and Cardiovascular Health. *Am J Cardiol, 116*(5), 818-821. doi:https://doi.org/10.1016/j.amjcard.2015.05.057

Cipollone, G., Gehrman, P., Manni, C., Pallucchini, A., Maremmani, A., Palagini, L., . . . Maremmani, I. (2020, Nov). Exploring the Role of Caffeine Use in Adult-ADHD Symptom Severity of US Army Soldiers. *J Clin Med, 9*(11), 3788. doi:https://doi.org/10.3390/jcm9113788

Clarke, N., & Duncan, M. (2016, Jan). Effect of Carbohydrate and Caffeine Ingestion on Badminton Performance. *Int J Sports Physiol Perform, 11*(1), 108-15. doi:https://doi.org/10.1123/ijspp.2014-0426

Clarke, N., Kirwan, N., & Richardson, D. (2019, October 25). Coffee Ingestion Improves 5 km Cycling Performance in Men and Women by a Similar Magnitude. *Nutrients, 11*(11), 2575. doi:https://doi.org/10.3390/nu11112575

Clarke, N., Richardson, D., Thie, J., & Taylor, R. (2018, July 1). Coffee Ingestion Enhances 1-Mile Running Race Performance. *Int J Sports Physiol Perform, 13*(6), 789-794. doi:https://doi.org/10.1123/ijspp.2017-0456

Clauson, K., Shields, K., McQueen, C., & Persad, N. (2008, May). Safety issues associated with commercially available energy drinks. *J Am Pharm Assoc, 48*(3), 55-63. doi:https://doi.org/10.1331/japha.2008.07055

Coffee Inebriety. (1890, Jun 20). *Science, 15*(385), 374. doi:https://doi.org/10.1126/science.ns-15.385.374-b

Cohen, A. (2014). Nascher's Geriatrics at 100. *J Am Geriatr Soc, 62*(12), 2428-2429. doi:https://doi.org/10.1111%2Fjgs.13155

Competitive Athletics. (1912, Mar 30). *Hospital (London 1886), 51*(1342), 644. Retrieved from https://www.ncbi.nlm.nih.gov/pmc/articles/PMC5224326/

Cornelis, M., El-Sohemy, A., Kabagambe, E., & Campos, H. (2006, Mar 8). Coffee, CYP1A2 genotype, and risk of myocardial infarction. *JAMA, 295*(10), 1135-41. doi:https://doi.org/10.1001/jama.295.10.1135

Čulić, V., AlTurki, A., & Proietti, R. (2021, May). Public health impact of daily life triggers of sudden cardiac death: A systematic review and comparative risk assessment. *Resucitation, 162*, 154-162. doi:https://doi.org/10.1016/j.resuscitation.2021.02.036

Da Silva, V., Messias, F., Zanchi, N., Gerlinger-Romero, F., Duncan, M., & Guimarães-Ferreira, L. (2015). Effects of acute caffeine ingestion on resistance training performance and perceptual responses during repeated sets to failure. *J Sports Med Phys Fitness, 55*(5), 383-9. Retrieved from https://pubmed.ncbi.nlm.nih.gov/26068323/#:~:text

=Conclusion%3A%20Acute%20caffeine%20ingestion%20can,RTIME%20in%20resistance%2Dtrained%20men.

Daneschvar, H., Smetana, G., Brindamour, L., Bain, P., & Mukamal, K. (2021, May). Impact of Coffee Consumption on Physiological Markers of Cardiovascular Risk: A Systematic Review. *Am JJ Med, 134*(5), 626-636. doi:https://doi.org/10.1016/j.amjmed.2020.09.036

Dangers of Middle-Class Restaurants, Coffee Stalls and some Public Houses. (1919, May 31). *Hospital (Lond 1886), 66*(1721), 208. Retrieved from https://www.ncbi.nlm.nih.gov/pmc/articles/PMC5252178/

De Maria, B., de Oliveira Gois, M., Catai, A., Marra, C., Lucini, D., Porta, A., . . . Dalla Vecchia, L. (2021). Ten-year follow-up of cardiac function and neural regulation in a group of amateur half-marathon runners. *Open Heart, 8*(1), e001561. doi:https://doi.org/10.1136/openhrt-2020-001561

Degens, H., Maden-Wilkinson, T., Ireland, A., Korhonen, M., Suominen, H., Heinonen, A., . . . Rittweger, J. (2016, Jun). Relationship between ventilatory function and age in master athletes and a sedentary reference population. *Age (Dordr), 35*(3), 1007-1015. doi:https://doi.org/10.1007/s11357-012-9409-7

Del Coso, J., Lara, B., Ruiz-Moreno, C., & Salinero, J. (2019, March 29). Challenging the Myth of Non-Response to the Ergogenic Effects of Caffeine Ingestion on Exercise Performance. *Nutrients, 11*(4), 732. doi:https://doi.org/10.3390/nu11040732

Del Giorno, R., Scanzio, S., De Napoli, E., Stefanelli, K., Gabutti, S., Troiani, C., & Gabutti, L. (2022, Feb). Habitual coffee and caffeinated beverages consumption is inversely associated with arterial stiffness and central and peripheral blood pressure. *Int J Food Sci Nutr, 73*(1), 106-115. doi:https://doi.org/10.1080/09637486.2021.1926935

Dempsey, J. (1986, Apr). J.B. Wolffe memorial lecture. Is the lung built for exercise? *Med Sci Sports Exerc, 18*(2), 143-55. Retrieved from https://pubmed.ncbi.nlm.nih.gov/3517547/

Desbrow, B., Biddulph, C., Devlin, B., Grant, G., Anoopkumar-Dukie, S., & Leveritt, M. (2012). The effects of different doses of caffeine on endurance cycling time trial performance. *Journal of Sports Sciences, 30*(2), 115-120. doi:https://doi.org/10.1080/02640414.2011.632431

Di Maso, M., Boffetta, P., Negri, E., La Vecchia, C., & Bravi, F. (2021, Jul 30). Caffeinated Coffee Consumption and Health Outcomes in the US Population: A Dose-Response Meta-Analysis and Estimation of Disease Cases and Deaths Avoided. *Adv Nutr, 12*(4), 1160-76. doi:https://doi.org/10.1093/advances/nmaa177

Ding, M., Bhupathiraju, S., Chen, M., van Dam, R., & Hu, F. (2014, Feb). Caffeinated and decaffeinated coffee consumption and risk of type 2 diabetes: a systematic review and a dose-response meta-analysis. *Diabetes Care, 37*(2), 569-86. doi:https://doi.org/10.2337/dc13-1203

Ding, M., Satija, A., Bhupathiraju, S., Hu, Y., Sun, Q., Han, J., . . . Hu, F. (2015, Dec 15). Association of Coffee Consumption with Total and Cause-Specific Mortality in Three Large Prospective Cohorts. *Circulation, 132*(24), 2305-15. doi:https://doi.org/10.1161/circulationaha.115.017341

Djoussé, L., Hopkins, P., Arnett, D., Pankow, J., Borecki, I., North, K., & Curtis Ellison, R. (2011, Feb). Chocolate Consumption is Inversely Associated with Calcified Atherosclerotic Plaque in the Coronary Arteries: The

NHLBI Family Heart Study. *Clin Nutr, 30*(1), 38-43. doi:https://doi.org/10.1016/j.clnu.2010.06.011

Domínguez, R., Veiga-Herreros, P., Sánchez-Oliver, A., Montoya, J., Ramos-Álvarez, J., Miguel-Tobal, F., . . . Jodra, P. (2021). Acute Effects of Caffeine Intake on Psychological Responses and High-Intensity Exercise Performance. *International Journal of Environmental Research and Public Health., 18*(2), 584. doi: https://doi.org/10.3390/ijerph18020584

Dong, X., Li, S., Sun, J., Li, Y., & Zhang, D. (2020, Mar 20). Association of Coffee, Decaffeinated Coffee and Caffeine Intake from Coffee with Cognitive Performance in Older Adults: National Health and Nutrition Examination Survey (NHANES) 2011-2014. *Nutrients, 12*(3), 840. doi:https://doi.org/10.3390/nu12030840

Drake, C., Roehrs, T., Shambroom, J., & Roth, T. (2015, Nov 15). Caffeine Effects on Sleep Taken 0, 3, or 6 Hours before Going to Bed. *J Clin Sleep Med, 9*(11), 1195-1200. doi:https://doi.org/10.5664/jcsm.3170

Driscoll, I., Shumaker, S., Snively, B., Margolis, K., Manson, J., Vitolins, M., . . . Espeland, M. (2016, Dec). Relationships Between Caffeine Intake and Risk for Probable Dementia or Global Cognitive Impairment: The Women's Health Initiative Memory Study. *J Gerontol A Biol Sci Med Sci, 71*(12), 1596-1602. doi:https://doi.org/10.1093/gerona/glw078

Du, Y., Lv, Y., Zha, W., Hong, X., & Luo, Q. (2020, Nov 27). Effect of coffee consumption on dyslipidemia: A meta-analysis of randomized controlled trials. *Nutr Metab Cardiovasc Dis, 30*(12), 2159-70. doi:https://doi.org/10.1016/j.numecd.2020.08.017

Duncan, M., Clarke, N., Tallis, J., Guimarães-Ferreira, L., & Leddington Wright, S. (2014, Dec). The effect of caffeine ingestion on functional performance in older adults. *J Nutr Health Aging, 18*(10), 883-887. doi:https://doi.org/10.1007/s12603-014-0474-8

Durkalec-Michalski, K., Nowaczyk, P., Główka, N., & Grygiel, A. (2019, September 5). Dose-dependent effect of caffeine supplementation on judo-specific performance and training activity: a randomized placebo-controlled crossover trial. *J Int Soc Sports Nutr, 16*(1), 38. doi:https://doi.org/10.1186/s12970-019-0305-8

Eijsvogels, T., Thompson, P., & Franklin, B. (2018, Aug 28). The "Extreme Exercise Hypothesis": Recent Findings and Cardiovascular Health Implications. *Curr Treat Options Cardiovasc Med, 20*(10), 84. doi:https://doi.org/10.1007/s11936-018-0674-3

Eskelinen, M., & Kivipelto, M. (2010). Caffeine as a protective factor in dementia and Alzheimer's disease. *J Alzheimer's Dis, 20*(S1), S167-74. doi:https://doi.org/10.3233/jad-2010-1404

Eskelinen, M., Ngandu, T., Tuomilehto, J., Soininen, H., & Kivipelto, M. (2009). Midlife coffee and tea drinking and the risk of late-life dementia: a population-based CAIDE study. *J Alzheimers Dis, 16*(1), 85-91. doi:https://doi.org/10.3233/jad-2009-0920

Evans, J., Richards, A., & Battisti. (2021). *Caffeine.* Treasure Island, FL: StatPearls Publishing.

Farewell Chocolate Soldier. (1942, Jun). *Can Med Assoc J, 46*(6), 620. Retrieved from https://www.ncbi.nlm.nih.gov/pmc/articles/PMC1827319/

Farvid, M., Spence, N., Rosner, B., Willett, W., Eliassen, A., & Holmes, M. (2021, May). Post-diagnostic coffee and tea consumption and breast cancer survival. *Br J Cancer, 124*(11), 1873-1881. doi:https://doi.org/10.1038/s41416-021-01277-1

Ferreira, R., Pacheco, R., de Oliveira Cruz Latorraca, C., Riera, R., Eid, R., & Martimbianco, A. (2021, Jul). Effects of

Caffeine Supplementation on Physical Performance of Soccer Players: Systematic Review and Meta-Analysis. *Sports Health, 13*(4), 347-358. doi:https://doi.org/10.1177/1941738121998712

Filip-Stachnik, A., Wilk, M., Krzysztofik, M., Lulińska, E., Tufano, J., Zajac, A., . . . Del Coso, J. (2021, Maqrch 30). The effects of different doses of caffeine on maximal strength and strength-endurance in women habituated to caffeine. *Journal of the International Society of Sports Nutrition, 18*(1), 25. doi:https://doi.org/10.1186/s12970-021-00421-9

Finlay, J., Esposito, M., Kim, M., Gomez-Lopez, I., & Clarke, P. (2019, Nov). Closure of 'Third Places'? Exploring Potential Consequences for Collective Health and Wellbeing. *Health Place, 60*, 102225. doi:https://doi.org/10.1016/j.healthplace.2019.102225

Gajda, R., Klisiewicz, A., Matsibora, V., Piotrowska-Kownacka, D., & Biernacka, E. (2020, Feb). Heart of the World's Top Ultramarathon Runner—Not Necessarily Much Different from Normal. *Diagnostics, 10*(2), 73. doi:https://doi.org/10.3390/diagnostics10020073

Gajendragadkar, P., Moualed, D., Nicolson, P., Adjei, F., Cakebread, H., Duehmke, R., & Martin, C. (2013, Dec). The survival time of chocolates on hospital wards: covert observational study. *BMJ, 347*. doi:https://doi.org/10.1136/bmj.f7198

Ganio, M., Klau, J., Casa, D., Armstrong, L., & Maresh, C. (2009, January). Effect of caffeine on sport-specific endurance performance: a systematic review. *J Strength Cond Res, 23*(1), 315-24. doi:https://doi.org/10.1519/jsc.0b013e31818b979a

Ganse, B., Ganse, U., Dahl, J., & Degens, H. (2018, Aug 21). Linear Decrease in Athletic Performance During the Human Life Span. *Front Physiol, 9*, 1100. doi:https://doi.org/10.3389/fphys.2018.01100

Garatachea, N., Pareja-Galeano, H., Sanchis-Gomar, F., Santos-Lozano, A., Fiuza-Luces, C., Morán, M., . . . Lucia, A. (2015, Feb 1). Exercise Attenuates the Major Hallmarks of Aging. *Rejuvenation Res, 18*(1), 57-89. doi:https://doi.org/10.1089/rej.2014.1623

Gava, P., Giuriati, W., & Ravara, B. (2020, Apr 7). Gender difference of aging performance decay rate in normalized Masters World Records of Athletics: much less than expected. *Eur J Transl Myol, 30*(1), 8869. doi:https://doi.org/10.4081/ejtm.2019.8869

Gavrilov, L., & Gavrilova, N. (2015). New Developments in Biodemography of Aging and Longevity. *Gerentology, 61*(4), 364-371. doi:https://doi.org/10.1159/000369011

Gavrilova, N., & Gavrilov, L. (2020, May 22). Are We Approaching a Biological Limit to Human Longevity? *J Gerentol A Biol Sci Med Sci, 75*(6), 1061-67. doi:https://doi.org/10.1093/gerona/glz164

Girard, O., Brocherie, F., Goods, P., & Millet, G. (2020). An Updated Panorama of "Living Low-Training High" Altitude/Hypoxic Methods. *Front Sports Act Living, 2*, 26. doi:https://doi.org/10.3389/fspor.2020.00026

Glaister, M., Chopra, K., Pereira De Sena, A., Sternbach, C., Morina, L., & Mavrommatis, Y. (2021, Jun). Caffeine, exercise physiology, and time-trial performance: no effect of ADORA2A or CYP1A2 genotypes. *Appl Physiol Nutr Metab, 46*(6), 541-51. doi:https://doi.org/10.1139/apnm-2020-0551

Gleason, J., Tekola-Ayele, F., Sundaram, R., Hinkle, S., Vafai, Y., Buck Louis, G., . . . Grantz, K. (2021, Mar 1). Association Between Maternal Caffeine Consumption and Metabolism and Neonatal Anthropometry: A Secondary Analysis of the NICHD Fetal Growth Studies-Singletons. *JAMA Netw Open, 4*(3), e213238. doi:https://doi.org/10.1001/jamanetworkopen.2021.3238

References

Goldstein, E., Ziegenfuss, T., Kalman, D., Kreider, R., Campbell, B., Wilborn, C., . . . Wildman, R. (2010, December). International society of sports nutrition position stand: caffeine and performance. *Journal of the International Society of Sports Nutrition, 7*(1), 1-5. doi:doi: 10.1186/1550-2783-7-5.

Gonçalves, L., Painelli, V., Yamaguchi, G., Oliveira, L., Saunders, B., da Silva, R., . . . Gualano, B. (2017, July 1). Dispelling the myth that habitual caffeine consumption influences the performance response to acute caffeine supplementation. *Journal of Applied Physiology, 123*(1), 213-220. doi:10.1152/japplphysiol.00260.2017.

Graham, T. (2001, September). Caffeine and exercise: metabolism, endurance and performance. *Sports Medicine, 31*, 785-807. doi:https://doi.org/10.2165/00007256-200131110-00002

Grgic, J. (2022, May). Exploring the minimum ergogenic dose of caffeine on resistance exercise performance: A meta-analytic approach. *Nutrition, 97*, 111604. doi:10.1016/j.nut.2022.111604.

Grgic, J., Grgic, I., Pickering, C., Schoenfeld, B., Bishop, D., & Pedisic, Z. (2020, June). Wake up and smell the coffee: caffeine supplementation and exercise performance-an umbrella review of 21 published meta-analyses. *British Journal of Sports medicine, 54*(11), 681-688. doi:https://doi.org/10.1136/bjsports-2018-100278

Grobbee, D., Rimm, E., Giovannucci, E., Colditz, G., Stampfer, M., & Willett, W. (1990, Oct 11). Coffee, caffeine, and cardiovascular disease in men. *N Engl J Med, 323*(15), 1026-32. doi:https://doi.org/10.1056/nejm199010113231504

Grosso, G., Micek, A., Castellano, S., Pajak, A., & Galvano, F. (2016, Jan). Coffee, tea, caffeine and risk of depression: A systematic review and dose-response meta-analysis of observational studies. *Mol Nutr Food Res, 60*(1), 223-34. doi:https://doi.org/10.1002/mnfr.201500620

Guest, N. (2021). International society of sports nutrition position stand: caffeine and exercise performance. *Journal of the International Society of Sports Nutrition, 18*, 1. doi:https://doi.org/10.1186/s12970-020-00383-4

Guest, N., Corey, P., Vescovi, J., & El-Sohemy, A. (2018, Aug). Caffeine, CYP1A2 Genotype, and Endurance Performance in Athletes. *Med Sci Sports Exerc, 50*(8), 1570-1578. doi:https://doi.org/10.1249/mss.0000000000001596

Gutiérrez-Hellín, J., Ruiz-Moreno, C., Aguilar-Navarro, M., Muñoz, A., Varillas-Delgado, D., Amaro-Gahete, F., . . . Del Coso, J. (2021, March). Placebo Effect of Caffeine on Substrate Oxidation During Exercise. *Nutrients, 13*(3), 782.

Hart, M. (1892, Nov 19). RESTORATIVES. COFFEE-COCOA-CHOCOLATE. *Hospital (Lond 1886), 13*(321), 116-117. Retrieved from https://www.ncbi.nlm.nih.gov/pmc/articles/PMC5251715/?page=2

Hayat, U., Siddiqui, A., Okut, H., Afroz, S., Tasleem, S., & Haris, A. (2021, Jan-Feb). The effect of coffee consumption on the non-alcoholic fatty liver disease and liver fibrosis: A meta-analysis of 11 epidemiological studies. *Ann Hepatol, 20*, 100254. doi:https://doi.org/10.1016/j.aohep.2020.08.071

Heart-Strain and School Athletics. (1905, Apr 8). *Hospital (London 1886), 38*(967), 28-29.

Higgins, J., Babu, K., Deuster, P., & Shearer, J. (2018, Feb). Energy Drinks: A Contemporary Issues Paper. *Curr Sports Med Rep, 17*(2), 65-72. doi:https://doi.org/10.1249/jsr.0000000000000454

Higgins, S., Straight, C., & Lewis, R. (2016, June). The Effects of Pre-exercise Caffeinated Coffee Ingestion on

Endurance Performance: An Evidence-Based Review. *nt J Sport Nutr Exerc Metab, 26*(3), 221-39. doi:https://doi.org/10.1123/ijsnem.2015-0147

Hinkle, S., Gleason, J., Yisahak, S., Zhao, S., Mumford, S., Sundaram, R., . . . Zhang, C. (2021, Nov 1). Assessment of Caffeine Consumption and Maternal Cardiometabolic Pregnancy Complications. *AMA Netw Open, 4*(11), e2133401. doi:https://doi.org/10.1001/jamanetworkopen.2021.33401

Hodgson, A., Randell, R., & Jeukendrup, A. (2013). The metabolic and performance effects of caffeine compared to coffee during endurance exercise. *PloS One, 8*(4), e59561. doi:https://doi.org/10.1371/journal.pone.0059561

Hoogkamer W, K. S. (2018, Apr). A Comparison of the Energetic Cost of Running in Marathon Racing Shoes. *Sports Med, 48*(8), 1009-1019. doi:https://doi.org/10.1007/s40279-017-0811-2

Hsu, C., Tsai, T., Kao, Y., Hwang, K., Tseng, T., & Chou, P. (2008, Jun). Effect of green tea extract on obese women: a randomized, double-blind, placebo-controlled clinical trial. *Clin Nutr, 27*(3), 363-70. doi:https://doi.org/10.1016/j.clnu.2008.03.007

Huang, Q., Braffett, B., Simmens, S., Young, H., & Ogden, C. (2020, Nov). Dietary Polyphenol Intake in US Adults and 10-Year Trends: 2007-2016. *Journal of the Academy of Nutrition and Dietetics, 120*(11), 1821-1833. doi:https://doi.org/10.1016/j.jand.2020.06.016

Hussain, J., & Cohen, M. (2018, Apr). Clinical Effects of Regular Dry Sauna Bathing: A Systematic Review. *Evid Based Complement Alternat Med*, 1857413. doi:https://doi.org/10.1155/2018/1857413

Igho-Osagie, E., Cara, K., Wang, D., Yao, Q., Penkert, L., Cassidy, A., . . . Wallace, T. (2020, Dec 10). Short-Term

Tea Consumption Is Not Associated with a Reduction in Blood Lipids or Pressure: A Systematic Review and Meta-Analysis of Randomized Controlled Trials. *J Nutr, 150*(12), 3269-79. doi:https://doi.org/10.1093/jn/nxaa295

Irwin, C., Desbrow, B., Ellis, A., O'Keeffe, B., Grant, G., & Leveritt, M. (2011, March). Caffeine withdrawal and high-intensity endurance cycling performance. *Journal of Sports Sciences, 29*(5), 509-515. doi:https://doi.org/10.1080/02640414.2010.541480

Jagim, A., Harty, P., Fischer, K., Kerksick, C., & Erickson, J. (2020, Aug). Adverse Events Reported to the United States Food and Drug Administration Related to Caffeine-Containing Products. *Mayo Clin Proc, 95*(8), 1594-1603. doi:https://doi.org/10.1016/j.mayocp.2020.02.033

Jee, H., Lee, S., Bormate, K., & Jung, Y. (2020, Oct). Effect of Caffeine Consumption on the Risk for Neurological and Psychiatric Disorders: Sex Differences in Human. *Nutrients, 12*(10), 3080. doi:https://doi.org/10.3390/nu12103080

Jiménez, S., Díaz-Lara, J., Pareja-Galeano, H., & Del Coso, J. (2021, September). Caffeinated drinks and physical performance in sport: a systematic Review. *Nutrients, 13*(9), 2944. doi:https://doi.org/10.3390/nu13092944

Jodra, P., Lago-Rodríguez, A., Sánchez-Oliver, A., López-Samanes, A., Pérez-López, A., Veiga-Herreros, P., . . . Domínguez, R. (2020, January 3). Effects of caffeine supplementation on physical performance and mood dimensions in elite and trained-recreational athletes. *Journal of the International Society of Sports Nutrition, 17*(1), 2. doi:https://doi.org/10.1186/s12970-019-0332-5

Johnson, C., Outerleys, J., Jamison, S., Tenforde, A., Ruder, M., & Davis, I. (2020, Jul). Comparison of Tibial Shock during Treadmill and Real-World Running. *Med Sci*

Sports Exerc, 52(7), 1557-62. doi:https://doi.org/10.1249/mss.0000000000002288

Jyväkorpi, S., Urtamo, A., Kivimäki, M., & Strandberg, T. (2021, May). Associations of coffee drinking with physical performance in the oldest-old community-dwelling men The Helsinki Businessmen Study (HBS. *Aging Clin Exp Res, 33*(5), 1371-5. doi:https://doi.org/10.1007/s40520-020-01645-6

Kanbay, M., Siriopol, D., Copur, S., Tapoi, L., Benchea, L., Kuwabara, M., . . . Afsar, B. (2021, Jan). Effect of Coffee Consumption on Renal Outcome: A Systematic Review and Meta-Analysis of Clinical Studies. *J Ren Nutr, 31*(1), 5-20. doi:https://doi.org/10.1053/j.jrn.2020.08.004

Karayigit, R., Naderi, A., Akca, F., Cruz, C., Sarshin, A., Yasli, B., . . . Kaviani, M. (2021, December 22). Effects of Different Doses of Caffeinated Coffee on Muscular Endurance, Cognitive Performance, and Cardiac Autonomic Modulation in Caffeine Naive Female Athletes. *Nutrients, 13*(1), 2. doi:https://doi.org/10.3390/nu13010002

Kaufman, L., Setiono, T., Doros, G., Andersen, S., Silliman, R., Friedman, P., & Perls, T. (2014, Jun). An oral health study of centenarians and children of centenarians. *J Am Geriatr Soc, 62*(6), 1168-73. doi:https://doi.org/10.1111/jgs.12842

Kawachi, I., Willett, W., Colditz, G., Stampfer, M., & Speizer, F. (1996, March 11). A prospective study of coffee drinking and suicide in women. *Arch Intern Med, 156*(5), 521-5. Retrieved from https://pubmed.ncbi.nlm.nih.gov/8604958/

Keast, R., Swinburn, B., Sayompark, D., Whitelock, S., & Riddell, L. (2015, Jan 28). Caffeine increases sugar-sweetened beverage consumption in a free-living population: a randomized controlled trial. *Br J Nutr,*

113(2), 366-70. doi:https://doi.org/10.1017/s000711451400378x

Keller, A., & Wallace, T. (2021, Dec). Tea intake and cardiovascular disease: an umbrella review. *Ann Med, 53*(1), 929-44. doi:https://doi.org/10.1080/07853890.2021.1933164

Kennedy, O., Roderick, P., Buchanan, R., Fallowfield, J., Hayes, P., & Parkes, J. (2017, May 9). Coffee, including caffeinated and decaffeinated coffee, and the risk of hepatocellular carcinoma: a systematic review and dose-response meta-analysis. *BMJ, 7*(5), e013739. doi:https://doi.org/10.1136/bmjopen-2016-013739

Kettunen, J., Kujala, U., Kaprio, J., Bäckmand, H., Peltonen, M., Eriksson, J., & Sarna, S. (2015, Jul). All-cause and disease-specific mortality among male, former elite athletes: an average 50-year follow-up. *Br J Sports Med, 49*(13), 893-7. doi:https://doi.org/10.1136/bjsports-2013-093347

Killgore, W., & Kamimori, G. (2020). Multiple caffeine doses maintain vigilance, attention, complex motor sequence expression, and manual dexterity during 77 hours of total sleep deprivation. *Neurobiol Sleep Circadian Rhythms*, Nov. doi:https://doi.org/10.1016/j.nbscr.2020.100051

Kim, S., Tan, L., & Shin, S. (2021, Nov). Coffee Consumption and the Risk of All-Cause and Cause-Specific Mortality in the Korean Population. *J Acad Nutr Diet, 121*(11), 2221-2223. doi:https://doi.org/10.1016/j.jand.2021.03.014

Kim, Y., Je, Y., & Giovannucci, E. (2019, Aug). Coffee consumption and all-cause and cause-specific mortality: a meta-analysis by potential modifiers. *Eur J Epidemiol, 34*(8), 731-52. doi:https://doi.org/10.1007/s10654-019-00524-3

Knechtle, B., Di Gangi, S., Rüst, C., & Nikolaidis, P. (2020, Feb). Performance Differences Between the Sexes in the Boston Marathon from 1972 to 2017. *J Strength Cond Rs, 34*(2), 566-576. doi:https://doi.org/10.1519/jsc.0000000000002760

Knechtle, B., Jastrzebski, Z., Rosemann, T., & Nikolaidis, P. (2019, Jan 4). Pacing During and Physiological Response After a 12-Hour Ultra-Marathon in a 95-Year-Old Male Runner. *Front Physiol, 9*, 1875. doi:https://doi.org/10.3389/fphys.2018.01875

Knechtle, B., Waśkiewicz, Z., Sousa, C., Hill, L., & Nikolaidis, P. (2020, Dec 2). Cold Water Swimming-Benefits and Risks: A Narrative Review. *Int J Environ Res Public Health, 17*(23), 8984. doi:https://doi.org/10.3390/ijerph17238984

Kochman, J., Jakubczyk, K., Antoniewicz, J., Mruk, H., & Janda, K. (2021, Jan). Health Benefits and Chemical Composition of Matcha Green Tea: A Review. *Molecules, 26*(1), 85. doi:https://doi.org/10.3390/molecules26010085

Kolb H, K. K. (2020). Health Effects of Coffee: Mechanism Unraveled? *Nutrients, 12*(6), 1842. doi:https://doi.org/10.3390/nu12061842

Kolb, H., Kempf, K., & Martin, S. (2020, Jun). Health Effects of Coffee: Mechanism Unraveled? *Nutrients, 12*(6), 1842. doi:https://doi.org/10.3390/nu12061842

Kolb, H., Martin, S., & Kempf, K. (2021, Mar 31). Coffee and Lower Risk of Type 2 Diabetes: Arguments for a Causal Relationship. *Nutrients, 13*(4), 1144. doi:https://doi.org/10.3390/nu13041144

Komorita, Y., Iwase, M., Fujii, H., Ohkuma, T., Ide, H., Jodai-Kitamura, T., . . . Kitazono, T. (2020, Oct). Additive effects of green tea and coffee on all-cause mortality in patients with type 2 diabetes mellitus: the Fukuoka Diabetes Registry. *BMJ Open Diabetes Res Care, 8*(1), e001252. doi:https://doi.org/10.1136/bmjdrc-2020-001252

Kondo, K., Suzuki, K., Washio, M., Ohfuji, S., Adachi, S., Kan, S., . . . Hirota, Y. (2021, Mar 10). Association between coffee and green tea intake and pneumonia among the Japanese elderly: a case-control study. *Sci Rep, 11*(1), 5570. doi:https://doi.org/10.1038/s41598-021-84348-w

Kontro, T., Sarna, S., Kaprio, J., & Kujala, U. (2018, Jan). Mortality and health-related habits in 900 Finnish former elite athletes and their brothers. *Br J Sports Med, 52*(2), 89-95. doi:https://doi.org/10.1136/bjsports-2017-098206

Kudwongsa, W., Promthet, S., Suwanrungruang, K., Phunmanee, A., & Vatanasapt, P. (2020, Aug 1). Coffee Consumption and Lung Cancer Risk: A Prospective Cohort Study in Khon Kaen Thailand. *Asian Pac J Cancer Prev, 21*(8), 2367-2371. doi:https://doi.org/10.31557/apjcp.2020.21.8.2367

Kujawska, A., Kujawski, S., Hajec, W., Skierkowska, N., Kwiatkowska, M., Husejko, J., . . . Kędziora-Kornatowska, K. (2021, Sep 25). Coffee Consumption and Blood Pressure: Results of the Second Wave of the Cognition of Older People, Education, Recreational Activities, Nutrition, Comorbidities, and Functional Capacity Studies (COPERNICUS). *Nuitrients, 13*(10), 3372. doi:https://doi.org/10.3390/nu13103372

Kusnik, A., Hunter, N., Rasbach, E., Miethke, T., Reissfelder, C., Ebert, M., & Teufel, A. (2021). Co-Medication and Nutrition in Hepatocellular Carcinoma: Potentially Preventative Strategies in Hepatocellular Carcinoma. *Dig Dis, 39*(5), 526-33. doi:https://doi.org/10.1159/000514277

Kwok, C., Boekholdt, S., Lentjes, M., Loke, Y., Luben, R., Yeong, J., . . . Khaw, K. (2015, Aug). Habitual chocolate consumption and risk of cardiovascular disease among healthy men and women. *Heart, 101*(16),

1279-1287. doi:https://doi.org/10.1136/heartjnl-2014-307050

Landry, T., Saunders, M., Akers, J., & Womack, C. (2019, September). Caffeine added to coffee does not alter the acute testosterone response to exercise in resistance trained males. *Journal of SPorts Medicine and Physical Fitness, 59*(9), 1435-1441. doi:https://doi.org/10.23736/s0022-4707.19.09183-7

Lazarus, N., & Harridge, S. (2017, May 1). Declining performance of master athletes: silhouettes of the trajectory of healthy human aging? *J Physiol, 595*(9), 2941-8. doi:https://doi.org/10.1113/jp272443

Lee, D., Lee, J., Rota, M., Lee, J., Ahn, H., Park, S., & Shin, D. (2014, Jun). Coffee consumption and risk of fractures: a systematic review and dose-response meta-analysis. *Bone, 63*, 20-28. doi:https://doi.org/10.1016/j.bone.2014.02.007

Lemez, S., & Baker, J. (2015, Dec). Do Elite Athletes Live Longer? A Systematic Review of Mortality and Longevity in Elite Athletes. *Sports Med Open, 1*(1), 16. doi:https://doi.org/10.1186/s40798-015-0024-x

Lepers, R., & Stapley, P. (2016, Dec). Master Athletes Are Extending the Limits of Human Endurance. *Front Physiol, 7*, 613. doi:https://doi.org/10.3389/fphys.2016.00613

Leszynsky, W. (1891, Feb). Coffee Poisoning. *JAMA*.

Lister, T. (1900, Jun 23). The abuse of exercise. *Hospital (Lond 1886), 28*(717), 201. Retrieved from https://www.ncbi.nlm.nih.gov/pmc/articles/PMC5272764/?page=1

Liu, H., Hu, G., Wang, X., Huang, T., Xu, L., Lai, P., . . . Xu, Y. (2015). Coffee consumption and prostate cancer risk: a meta-analysis of cohort studies. *Nutr Cancer, 67*(3), 392-400. doi:https://doi.org/10.1080/01635581.2015.1004727

Loftfield, E., Freedman, N., Graubard, B., Guertin, K., Black, A., Huang, W., . . . Sinha, R. (2015, Dec 15). Association of Coffee Consumption with Overall and Cause-Specific Mortality in a Large US Prospective Cohort Study. *Am J Epidemiol, 182*(12), 1010-1022. doi:https://doi.org/10.1093/aje/kwv146

Lopez-Garcia, E., van Dam, R., Li, T., Rodriguez-Artalejo, F., & Hu, F. (2008, Jun 17). The relationship of coffee consumption with mortality. *Ann Intern Med, 148*(12), 904-14. doi:https://doi.org/10.7326/0003-4819-148-12-200806170-00003

Loureiro, L., Dos Santos Neto, E., Molina, G., Amato, A., Arruda, S., Reis, C., & da Costa, T. (2021, Oct). Coffee Increases Post-Exercise Muscle Glycogen Recovery in Endurance Athletes: A Randomized Clinical Trial. *Nutrients, 13*(10), 3335. doi:https://doi.org/10.3390/nu13103335

Love, I. (1891, Apr). Coffee. *Dent Regist, 45*(4), 193. Retrieved from https://www.ncbi.nlm.nih.gov/pmc/articles/PMC6951626/?page=1

Lucas, M., O'Reilly, E., Pan, A., Mirzaei, F., Willett, W., Okereke, O., & Ascherio, A. (2014, Jul). Coffee, caffeine, and risk of completed suicide: results from three prospective cohorts of American adults. *World J Biol Psychiatry, 15*(5), 377-86. doi:https://doi.org/10.3109/15622975.2013.795243

Machado-Fragua, M., Struijk, E., Ballesteros, J., Ortolá, R., Rodriguez-Artalejo, F., & Lopez-Garcia, E. (2019, May 1). Habitual coffee consumption and risk of falls in 2 European cohorts of older adults. *Am J Clin Nutr, 109*(5), 1431-1438. doi:https://doi.org/10.1093/ajcn/nqy369

Machado-Fragua, M., Struijk, E., Yévenes-Briones, H., Caballero, F., Rodríguez-Artalejo, F., & Lopez-Garcia,

E. (2021, May). Coffee consumption and risk of hearing impairment in men and women. *Clin Nutr, 40*(5), 3429-3435. doi:https://doi.org/10.1016/j.clnu.2020.11.022

Maleki, V., Taheri, E., Varshosaz, P., Tabrizi, F., Moludi, J., Jafari-Vayghan, H., . . . Alizadeh, M. (2021). A comprehensive insight into effects of green tea extract in polycystic ovary syndrome: a systematic review. *Reprod Biol Endocrinol, 19*(1), 147. doi:https://doi.org/10.1186/s12958-021-00831-z

Malerba, S., Turati, F., Galeone, C., Pelucchi, C., Verga, F., La Vecchia, C., & Tavani, A. (2013, Jul). A meta-analysis of prospective studies of coffee consumption and mortality for all causes, cancers and cardiovascular diseases. *Eur J Epidemiol, 28*(7), 527-39. doi:https://doi.org/10.1007/s10654-013-9834-7

Martins, G., Guilherme, J., Ferreira, L., de Souza-Junior, T., & Lancha, A. J. (2020). Caffeine and Exercise Performance: Possible Directions for Definitive Findings. *Front Sports Act Living*, e574854. doi:https://doi.org/10.3389/fspor.2020.574854

Maskarinec G, J. S. (2019, May). Intake of cocoa products and risk of type-2 diabetes: the multiethnic cohort. *Eur J Clin Nutr, 73*(5), 671-678. doi:https://doi.org/10.1038/s41430-018-0188-9

Matsushita, N., Nakanishi, Y., Watanabe, Y., Kitamura, K., Kabasawa, K., Takahashi, A., . . . Nakamura, K. (2021, Dec). Association of coffee, green tea, and caffeine with the risk of dementia in older Japanese people. *J Am Geriatr Soc, 69*(12), 3529-44. doi:https://doi.org/10.1111/jgs.17407

McCusker, R., Fuehrlein, B., Goldberger, B., Gold, M., & Cone, E. (2006). Caffeine content of decaffeinated coffee. *Journal of Analytical Toxicology, 30*(8), 611–613. doi:https://doi.org/10.1093/jat/30.8.611

McCusker, R., Goldberger, B., & Cone, E. (2003, Oct). Caffeine content of specialty coffees. *Journal of Analytical Toxicology, 27*(7), 520-522. doi:https://doi.org/10.1093/jat/27.7.520

McKetin, R., & Coen, A. (2014, Aug). The effect of energy drinks on the urge to drink alcohol in young adults. *Alcohol Clin Exp Res, 38*(8), 2279-85. doi:https://doi.org/10.1111/acer.12498

Medical Degrees for Women. (1877, Mar). *Am J Dent Sci, 10*(11), 521. Retrieved from https://pubmed.ncbi.nlm.nih.gov/30752829/

Mensah, G., Wei, G., Sorlie, P., Fine, L., Rosenberg, Y., Kaufmann, P., . . . Gordon, D. (2017, Jan 20). Decline in Cardiovascular Mortality: Possible Causes and Implications. *Circ Res, 120*(2), 366-380. doi:https://doi.org/10.1161/circresaha.116.309115

Mentis, A., Dardiotis, E., Efthymiou, V., & Chrousos, G. (2021, Jan 13). Non-genetic risk and protective factors and biomarkers for neurological disorders: a meta-umbrella systematic review of umbrella reviews. *BMC Med, 19*(1), 6. doi:https://doi.org/10.1186/s12916-020-01873-7

Mesas, A., Leon-Muñoz, L., Rodriguez-Artalejo, F., & Lopez-Garcia, E. (2011, Oct). The effect of coffee on blood pressure and cardiovascular disease in hypertensive individuals: a systematic review and meta-analysis. *Am J Clin Nutr, 94*(4), 1113-26. doi:https://doi.org/10.3945/ajcn.111.016667

Micek, A., Godos, J., Lafranconi, A., Marranzano, M., & Pajak, A. (2018, Jun). Caffeinated and decaffeinated coffee consumption and melanoma risk: a dose-response meta-analysis of prospective cohort studies. *Int J Food Sci Nutr, 69*(4), 417-426. doi:https://doi.org/10.1080/09637486.2017.1373752

References

Miller, P., Zhao, D., Frazier-Wood, A., Michos, E., Averill, M., Sandfort, V., . . . Martin, S. (2017, Feb). Associations of Coffee, Tea, and Caffeine Intake with Coronary Artery Calcification and Cardiovascular Events. *Am J Med, 130*(2), 188-197. doi:https://doi.org/10.1016/j.amjmed.2016.08.038

Millet, G., Roels, B., Schmitt, L., Woorons, X., & Richalet, J. (2010, Jan 1). Combining hypoxic methods for peak performance. *Sports Med, 40*(1), 1-25. doi:https://doi.org/10.2165/11317920-000000000-00000

Miranda, A., Goulart, A., Benseñor, I., Lotufo, P., & Marchioni, D. (2021, Feb). Coffee consumption and risk of hypertension: A prospective analysis in the cohort study. *Clin Nutr, 40*(2), 542-549. doi:https://doi.org/10.1016/j.clnu.2020.05.052

Miranda, A., Goulart, A., Benseñor, I., Lotufo, P., & Marchioni, D. (2021, Sep). Moderate coffee consumption is associated with lower risk of mortality in prior Acute Coronary Syndrome patients: a prospective analysis in the ERICO cohort. *Int J Food Sci Nutr, 72*(6), 794-804. doi:https://doi.org/10.1080/09637486.2020.1862069

Montella, M., Tramacere, I., Tavani, A., Gallus, S., Crispo, A., Talamini, R., . . . La Vecchia, C. (2009). Coffee, decaffeinated coffee, tea intake, and risk of renal cell cancer. *Nutr Cancer, 61*(1), 76-80. doi:https://doi.org/10.1080/01635580802670754

Morvaridi, M., Rayyani, E., Jaafari, M., Khiabani, A., & Rahimlou, M. (2020, May 15). The effect of green coffee extract supplementation on cardio metabolic risk factors: a systematic review and meta-analysis of randomized controlled trials. *J Diabetes Metab Disord, 19*(1), 645-660. doi:https://doi.org/10.1007/s40200-020-00536-x

Mostofsky, E., Rice, M., Levitan, E., & Mittleman, M. (2012, Jul 1). Habitual coffee consumption and risk of heart failure: a dose-response meta-analysis. *Circ Heart Fail, 5*(4), 401-5. doi:https://doi.org/10.1161/circheartfailure.112.967299

Mumford, P., Tribby, A., Poole, C., Dalbo, V., Scanlan, A., Moon, J., . . . Young, K. (2016, Jan). Effect of Caffeine on Golf Performance and Fatigue during a Competitive Tournament. *Med Sci Sports Exerc, 48*(1), 132-8. doi:https://doi.org/10.1249/mss.0000000000000753

Nehlig, A. (2022, Jan). Effects of Coffee on the Gastro-Intestinal Tract: A Narrative Review and Literature Update. *Nutrients, 14*(2), 399. doi:https://doi.org/10.3390/nu14020399

Nehlig, A., Daval, J., & Debry, G. (1992, May-Aug). Caffeine and the central nervous system: mechanisms of action, biochemical, metabolic and psychostimulant effects. *Brain Res Brain Res Rev, 17*(2), 139-70. doi:https://doi.org/10.1016/0165-0173(92)90012-b

New Drugs and Preparations- Carreine. (1894, Mar 24). *Hospital (Lond 1886), 15*(391), 465. Retrieved from https://www.ncbi.nlm.nih.gov/pmc/articles/PMC5250388/?page=1

Nicks, C., & Martin, E. (2020, Jul). Effects of caffeine on inspiratory muscle function. *Eur J Sport Sci, 20*(6), 813-8. doi:https://doi.org/10.1080/17461391.2019.1675767

Nie, J., Yu, C., Guo, Y., Pei, P., Chen, L., Pang, Y., . . . Li, L. (2021, Jul 1). Tea consumption and long-term risk of type 2 diabetes and diabetic complications: a cohort study of 0.5 million Chinese adults. *Am J Clin Nutr, 114*(1), 194-202. doi:https://doi.org/10.1093/ajcn/nqab006

Nigra, A., Teodoro, A., & Gil, G. (2021, Sep 15). A Decade of Research on Coffee as an Anticarcinogenic Beverage.

Oxid Med Cell Longev. doi:https://doi.org/10.1155/2021/4420479

Nikolaidis, P., & Knechtle, B. (2020, May). Performance in 100-km Ultramarathoners-At Which Age, It Reaches Its Peak? *J Strength Cond Res, 34*(5), 1409-1415. doi:https://doi.org/10.1519/jsc.0000000000002539

Nikolaidis, P., Di Gangi, S., Chtourou, H., Rüst, C., Rosemann, T., & Knechtle, B. (2019, Feb). The Role of Environmental Conditions on Marathon Running Performance in Men Competing in Boston Marathon from 1897 to 2018. *Int J Environ Res Public Health, 16*(4), 614. doi:https://doi.org/10.3390/ijerph16040614

Nordestgaard, A., & Nordestgaard, B. (2016, Dec 1). Coffee intake, cardiovascular disease and all-cause mortality: observational and Mendelian randomization analyses in 95,000 to 230,000 individuals. *Int J Epidemiol, 45*(6), 1938-1952. doi:https://doi.org/10.1093/ije/dyw325

Nurminen, M., Niittynen, L., Korpela, R., & Vapaatalo, H. (1999, Nov). Coffee, caffeine and blood pressure: a critical review. *Eur J Clin Nutr, 53*(11), 831-9. doi:https://doi.org/10.1038/sj.ejcn.1600899

Nwabuo, C., Betoko, A., Reis, J., Moreira, H., Vasconcellos, H., Guallar, E., . . . Lima, J. (2020, Aug). Coffee and tea consumption in the early adult lifespan and left ventricular function in middle age: the CARDIA study. *ESC Heart Fail, 7*(4), 1510-1519. doi:https://doi.org/10.1002/ehf2.12684

Odegaard, A., Koh, W., Yuan, J., & Pereira, M. (2015, Mar). Beverage habits and mortality in Chinese adults. *J Nutr, 145*(3), 595-604. doi:https://doi.org/10.3945/jn.114.200253

O'Keefe, E., Torres-Acosta, N., O'Keefe, J., & Lavie, C. (2020, Jul). Training for Longevity: The Reverse J-Curve for Exercise. *Mo Med, 117*(4), 355-361. Retrieved from https://pubmed.ncbi.nlm.nih.gov/32848273/

O'Keefe, J. H., DiNicolantonio, J. J., & Lavie, C. J. (2018). Coffee for Cardioprotection and Longevity. *Progress in Cardiovascular Diseases, 61*(1), 38-42. doi:https://doi.org/10.1016/j.pcad.2018.02.002.

O'Keefe, J., Vogel, R., Lavie, C., & Cordain, L. (2010, Dec). Achieving Hunter-gatherer Fitness in the 21(st) Century: Back to the Future. *Am J Med, 123*(12), 1082-6. doi:10.1016/j.amjmed.2010.04.026.

O'Neill, A. (2021, Feb 3). *statista.com*. Retrieved from Life expectancy in the United States, 1860-2020: https://www.statista.com/statistics/1040079/life-expectancy-united-states-all-time/#:~:text=Life%20expectancy%20in%20the%20United%20States%2C%201860%2D2020&text=Over%20the%20past%20160%20years,to%2078.9%20years%20in%202020.

Orr, L. (1920, May 15). Weight, Height, and longevity. *Br Med J, 1*(3098), 678-679. Retrieved from https://www.ncbi.nlm.nih.gov/pmc/articles/PMC2337636/

Pachimsawat, P., Tangprasert, K., & Jantaratnotai, N. (2021, Jan 14). The calming effect of roasted coffee aroma in patients undergoing dental procedures. *Sci Rep, 11*(1), 1384. doi:https://doi.org/10.1038/s41598-020-80910-0

Parra-Lara, L., Mendoza-Urbano, D., Bravo, J., Salamanca, C., & Zambrano, Á. (2020, Oct 2). Coffee Consumption and Its Inverse Relationship with Gastric Cancer: An Ecological Study. *Nutrients, 12*(10), 3028. doi:https://doi.org/10.3390/nu12103028

Patel, R., Brouner, J., & Spendiff, O. (2015). Dark chocolate supplementation reduces the oxygen cost of moderate intensity cycling. *J Int Soc Sports Nutr, 12*, 47. doi:https://doi.org/10.1186/s12970-015-0106-7

Pauwels, E., & Volterrani, D. (2021, Mar 24). Coffee Consumption and Cancer Risk; An Assessment of the

Health Implications Based on Recent Knowledge. *Med Princ Pract, 30*(5), 401-11. doi:https://doi.org/10.1159/000516067

Paz-Graniel, I., Babio, N., Becerra-Tomás, N., Toledo, E., Camacho-Barcia, L., & Corella, D. (2021, Aug). Association between coffee consumption and total dietary caffeine intake with cognitive functioning: cross-sectional assessment in an elderly Mediterranean population. *Eur J Nutr, 60*(5), 2381-2396. doi:https://doi.org/10.1007/s00394-020-02415-w

Petrone, A., Gaziano, J., & Djoussé, L. (2014, Dec). Chocolate consumption and risk of heart failure in the Physicians' Health Study. *Eur J Heart Fail, 16*(12), 1372-6. doi:https://doi.org/10.1002/ejhf.180

Pickering, C., & Grgic, J. (2019, July). Caffeine and Exercise: What Next? *Sports Medicine, 49*(7), 1007-1030. doi:10.1007/s40279-019-01101-0.

Poole, R., Kennedy, O., Roderick, P., Fallowfield, J., Hayes, P., & Parkes, J. (2017, NOV 22). Coffee consumption and health: umbrella review of meta-analyses of multiple health outcomes. *BMJ*, 359. doi:doi:10.1136/bmj.j5024

Provencher, M., Chahla, J., Sanchez, G., Cinque, M., Kennedy, N., Whalen, J., . . . LaPrade, R. (2018, Apr). Body Mass Index Versus Body Fat Percentage in Prospective National Football League Athletes: Overestimation of Obesity Rate in Athletes at the National Football League Scouting Combine. *J Strength Cond Res, 32*(4), 1013-1019. doi:https://doi.org/10.1519/jsc.0000000000002449

Qi, H., & Li, S. (2014, Apr). Dose-response meta-analysis on coffee, tea and caffeine consumption with risk of Parkinson's disease. *Geriatr Gerontol Int, 14*(2), 430-9. doi:https://doi.org/10.1111/ggi.12123

Ran, L., Liu, W., Fang, Y., Xu, S., Li, J., Luo, X., . . . Wang, W. (2021, Feb). Alcohol, coffee and tea intake and the risk of cognitive deficits: a dose–response meta-analysis. *Epidemiol Psychiatr Sci, 30*, e13. doi:https://doi.org/10.1017/s2045796020001183

Ren, Y., Liu, Y., Sun, X., Wang, B., Zhao, Y., Liu, D., . . . Hu, D. (2019, Jan). Chocolate consumption and risk of cardiovascular diseases: a meta-analysis of prospective studies. *Depress Anxiety, 105*(1), 49-55. doi:https://doi.org/10.1136/heartjnl-2018-313131

Rhee, J., Loftfield, E., Freedman, N., Liao, L., Sinha, R., & Purdue, M. (2021, Nov 10). Coffee consumption and risk of renal cell carcinoma in the NIH-AARP Diet and Health Study. *Int J Epidemiol, 50*(5), 1473-1481. doi:https://doi.org/10.1093/ije/dyab011

Ribeiro, E., Alves, M., Costa, J., Ferreira, J., Pinto, F., & Caldeira, D. (2020, Nov 27). Safety of coffee consumption after myocardial infarction: A systematic review and meta-analysis. *Nutr Metab Cardiovasc Dis, 30*(12), 2146-58. doi:https://doi.org/10.1016/j.numecd.2020.07.016

Ritchie, K., Carrière, I., de Mendonca, A., Portet, F., JF, D., Rouaud, O., . . . Ancelin, M. (2007, Sug 7). The neuroprotective effects of caffeine: a prospective population study (the Three City Study). *Neurology, 69*(6), 536-45. doi:https://doi.org/10.1212/01.wnl.0000266670.35219.0c

Rodak, K., Kokot, I., & Kratz, E. (2021). Caffeine as a Factor Influencing the Functioning of the Human Body—Friend or Foe. *Nutrients, 13*(9), 3088. doi:https://doi.org/10.3390/nu13093088

Rodríguez-Artalejo, F., & López-García, E. (2018, May 30). Coffee Consumption and Cardiovascular Disease: A Condensed Review of Epidemiological Evidence and Mechanisms. *J Agric Food Chem, 66*(21), 5257-5263. doi:https://doi.org/10.1021/acs.jafc.7b04506

References

Roman, M., Rossiter, H., & Casaburi, R. (2016, Nov). Exercise, aging and the lung. *Eur Respir J, 48*(5), 1471-1486. doi:https://doi.org/10.1183/13993003.00347-2016

Rosales Soto, G., Monsálves Álvarez, M., Yáñez Sepúlveda, R., & Durán Agüero, S. (2015, October 1). Caffeine intake and its effect on the maximal aerobic speed corridors 800 -meter athletes. *Nutricion Hospitalaria, 32*(4), 1703-7. doi:https://doi.org/10.3305/nh.2015.32.4.9200

Rosato, V., Guercio, V., Bosetti, C., Gracia-Lavedan, E., Villanueva, C., Polesel, J., . . . Tavani, A. (2021, May 1). Coffee consumption and colorectal cancer risk: a multicentre case-control study from Italy and Spain. *Eur J Cancer Prev, 30*(3), 204-210. doi:https://doi.org/10.1097/cej.0000000000000593

Rosenfeld, L. S., Mihalov, J. J., Carleson, S. J., & Mattia, A. (2014, October). Regulatory status of caffeine in the United States. *Nutrition Reviews, 72*(1), 23-33. doi:https://doi.org/10.1111/nure.12136

Rudelle, S., Ferruzzi, M., Cristiani, I., Moulin, J., Macé, K., Acheson, K., & Tappy, L. (2007, Feb). Effect of a thermogenic beverage on 24-hour energy metabolism in humans. *Obesity (Silver Spring), 15*(2), 349-55. doi:https://doi.org/10.1038/oby.2007.529

Runacres, A., Mackintosh, K., & McNarry, M. (2021). Health Consequences of an Elite Sporting Career: Long-Term Detriment or Long-Term Gain? A Meta-Analysis of 165,000 Former Athletes. *Sports Med, 51*(2), 289-301. doi:https://doi.org/10.1007/s40279-020-01379-5

Saadat, S., Ahmadi, K., & Panahi, Y. (2015). The effect of on-demand caffeine consumption on treating patients with premature ejaculation: a double-blind randomized clinical trial. *Curr Pharm Biotechnol, 16*(3), 281-7. doi:https://doi.org/10.2174/13892010166661501181 3 3045

Sajja, K., El-Serag, H., & Thrift, A. (2016, May). Coffee or Tea, Hot or Cold, are not Associated with Risk of Barrett's Esophagus. *Clin Gastroenterol Hepatol, 14*(5), 769-72. doi:https://doi.org/10.1016/j.cgh.2015.12.007

Sakamaki, T., Kayaba, K., Kotani, K., Namekawa, M., Hamaguchi, T., Nakaya, N., & Ishikawa, S. (2021, Feb). Coffee consumption and mortality in Japan with 18 years of follow-up: the Jichi Medical School Cohort Study. *Public Health, 191*, 23-30. doi:https://pubmed.ncbi.nlm.nih.gov/?term=Hamaguchi+T&cauthor_id=33476939

Salari-Moghaddam, A., Milajerdi, A., Surkan, P., Larijani, B., & Esmaillzadeh, A. (2019, Nov 1). Caffeine, Type of Coffee, and Risk of Ovarian Cancer: A Dose-Response Meta-Analysis of Prospective Studies. *J Clin Endocrinol Metab, 104*(11), 5349-5359. doi:https://doi.org/10.1210/jc.2019-00637

Salatto, R., Arevalo, J., Brown, L., Wiersma, L., & Coburn, J. (2020, Jun). Caffeine's Effects on an Upper-Body Resistance Exercise Workout. *J Strength Cond Res, 34*(16), 1643-1648.

Samoggia, A., & Riedel, B. (2019, March). Consumers' Perceptions of Coffee Health Benefits and Motives for Coffee Consumption and Purchasing. *Nutrients, 11*(3), 653. doi:https://doi.org/10.3390%2Fnu11030653

Santos-Mariano, A., Tomazini, F., Rodacki, C., Bertuzzi, R., De-Oliveira, F., & Lima-Silva, A. (2021, Mar). Effects of Caffeine on Performance During High- and Long-Jump Competitions. *Int J Sports Physiol Perform, 16*(10), 1516-21. doi:https://doi.org/10.1123/ijspp.2020-0755

Sarna, S., Sahi, T., Koskenvuo, M., & Kaprio, J. (1993, Feb). Increased life expectancy of world class male athletes. *Med Sci Sports Exerc, 25*(2), 237-44. Retrieved from https://pubmed.ncbi.nlm.nih.gov/8450727/

References

Sarriá, B., Martínez-López, S., Sierra-Cinos, J., García-Diz, L., Mateos, R., & Bravo-Clemente, L. (2018, Feb). Regularly consuming a green/roasted coffee blend reduces the risk of metabolic syndrome. *Eur J Nutr, 57*(1), 269-278. doi:https://doi.org/10.1007/s00394-016-1316-8

Scheidemann, N. (1932). An Apparent Epidemic of Left-Handedness. *Psychol Clin, 21*(4), 277-278. Retrieved from https://www.ncbi.nlm.nih.gov/pmc/articles/PMC5144410/

School Athletics and Boys' Races. (1905, Sep 25). *Br Med J, 2*(2543), 890-891. doi:https://www.ncbi.nlm.nih.gov/pmc/articles/PMC2320708/

Schubert, M., Hall, S., Leveritt, M., Grant, G., Sabapathy, S., & Desbrow, B. (2014, October 1). Caffeine consumption around an exercise bout: effects on energy expenditure, energy intake, and exercise enjoyment. *Journal of Applied Physiology, 117*(7), 745-54. doi:https://doi.org/10.1152/japplphysiol.00570.2014

Seligson, F., Krummel, D., & Apgar, J. (1994, Dec). Patterns of chocolate consumption. *Am J Clin Nutr, 60*(6 Supp), 1060SA-1064S. doi:https://doi.org/10.1093/ajcn/60.6.1060s

Shimamoto, T., Yamamichi, N., Kodashima, S., Takahashi, Y., Fujishiro, M., Oka, M., . . . Koike, K. (2013, Jun 12). No Association of Coffee Consumption with Gastric Ulcer, Duodenal Ulcer, Reflux Esophagitis, and Non-Erosive Reflux Disease: A Cross-Sectional Study of 8,013 Healthy Subjects in Japan. *PLoS One, 8*(6), e65996. doi:https://doi.org/10.1371/journal.pone.0065996

Silveira, R., Andrade-Souza, V., Arcoverde, L., Tomazini, F., Sansonio, A., Bishop, D., . . . Lima-Silva, A. (2018,

January). Caffeine Increases Work Done Above Critical Power, but Not Anaerobic Work. *Medical Science in Sports and Excercise, 50*(1), 131-140. doi:https://doi.org/10.1249/mss.0000000000001408

Silverman, K., Evans, S., Strain, E., & Griffiths, R. (1992, Oct 15). Withdrawal syndrome after the double-blind cessation of caffeine consumption. *N Engl J Med, 327*(16), 1109-14. doi:https://doi.org/10.1056/nejm199210153271601

Simon J, F. K.-E., Kolossváry, M., Merkely, B., Munroe, P., Harvey, N., Piechnik, S., . . . Maurovich-Horvat, P. (2022, May 6). Light to moderate coffee consumption is associated with lower risk of death: a UK Biobank study. *Eur J Prev Cardiol, 29*(6), 982-991. doi:https://doi.org/10.1093/eurjpc/zwac008

Skinner, T., Desbrow, B., Arapova, J., Schaumberg, M., Osborne, J., Grant, G., . . . Leveritt, M. (2019, Jun). Women Experience the Same Ergogenic Response to Caffeine as Men. *51*(6), 1195-1202. doi:https://doi.org/10.1249/mss.0000000000001885

Smirmaul, B., de Moraes, A., Angius, L., & Marcora, S. (2017, Jan). Effects of caffeine on neuromuscular fatigue and performance during high-intensity cycling exercise in moderate hypoxia. *Eur J Appl Physiol, 117*(1), 27-38. doi:https://doi.org/10.1007/s00421-016-3496-6

Soares, R., Schneider, A., Valle, S., & Schenkel, P. (2018, Jul). The influence of CYP1A2 genotype in the blood pressure response to caffeine ingestion is affected by physical activity status and caffeine consumption level. *Vascul Pharmacol, 106*, 67-73. doi:https://doi.org/10.1016/j.vph.2018.03.002

Socała, K., Szopa, A., Serefko, A., Poleszak, E., & Wlaź, P. (2020, Dec 24). Neuroprotective Effects of Coffee Bioactive Compounds: A Review. *Int J Mol Sci, 22*(1), 107. doi:https://doi.org/10.3390/ijms22010107

References

Somers, K., & Svatikova, A. (2020, Feb). Cardiovascular and Autonomic Responses to Energy Drinks—Clinical Implications. *J Clin Med, 9*(2), 431. doi:https://doi.org/10.3390/jcm9020431

Son, H., Song, H., Seo, H., Lee, H., Choi, S., & Lee, S. (2020, Sep 4). The safety and effectiveness of self-administered coffee enema: A systematic review of case reports. *Medicine, 99*(36), e21998. doi:https://doi.org/10.1097/md.0000000000021998

Southward, K., Rutherfurd-Markwick, K., & Ali, A. (2018, Aug). The Effect of Acute Caffeine Ingestion on Endurance Performance: A Systematic Review and Meta-Analysis. *Sports Medicine, 48*(8), 1913-1928. doi:https://doi.org/10.1007/s40279-018-0939-8

Southward, K., Rutherfurd-Markwick, K., Badenhorst, C., & Ali, A. (2018, Oct). The Role of Genetics in Moderating the Inter-Individual Differences in the Ergogenicity of Caffeine. *Nutrients, 10*(10), 1352. doi:https://doi.org/10.3390/nu10101352

Srithongkul, T., & Ungprasert, P. (2020, Jul). Coffee Consumption is Associated with a Decreased Risk of Incident Chronic Kidney Disease: A Systematic Review and Meta-analysis of Cohort Studies. *Eur J Intern Med, 77*, 111-16. doi:https://doi.org/10.1016/j.ejim.2020.04.018

St Clair Gibson, A., De Koning, J., Thompson, K., Roberts, W., Micklewright, D., Raglin, J., & Foster, C. (2013, Jun). Crawling to the finish line: Why do endurance runners collapse? Implications for understanding of mechanisms underlying pacing and fatigue. *Sports Med, 43*(6), 413-24. doi:https://doi.org/10.1007/s40279-013-0044-y

Strandberg, T., Sirola, J., Pitkälä, K., Tilvis, R., Strandberg, A., & Stenholm, S. (2012, Sep). Association of midlife obesity and cardiovascular risk with old age frailty: a 26-

year follow-up of initially healthy men. *Int J Obes (Lond), 36*(9), 1153-7. doi:https://doi.org/10.1038/ijo.2012.83

Struppek, J., Walther, C., Bunte, K., Zyriax, B., Wenzel, J., Senftinger, J., . . . Aarabi, G. (2022, Mar). The association between coffee consumption and periodontitis: a cross-sectional study of a northern German population. *Clin Oral Investig, 26*(3), 2421-27. doi:https://doi.org/10.1007/s00784-021-04208-9

Surma, S., & Oparil, S. (2021, Aug 9). Coffee and Arterial Hypertension. *Curr Hypertens Rep, 23*(7), 38. doi:https://doi.org/10.1007/s11906-021-01156-3

Takeuchi, T., Kitamura, Y., Ishizuka, S., Yamada, S., Aono, H., Kawahara, T., & Sobue, T. (2021). Mortality of Japanese Olympic athletes in 1964 Tokyo Olympic Games. *BMJ Open Sport Exerc Med, 7*(1), e000896. doi:https://doi.org/10.1136/bmjsem-2020-000896

Tanaka, H., & Seals, D. (2008, Jan 1). Endurance exercise performance in Masters athletes: age-associated changes and underlying physiological mechanisms. *J Physiol, 586*(1), 55-63. doi:https://doi.org/10.1113/jphysiol.2007.141879

Tarnopolsky, M., Atkinson, S., MacDougall, J., Sale, D., & Sutton, J. (1989, Aug). Physiological responses to caffeine during endurance running in habitual caffeine users. *Med Sci Sports Exerc, 21*(4), 418-24.

Taylor, C. (1912, Apr 15). Effects of Coffee-Drinking Upon Children. *Psychol Clin, 6*(2), 56-58. Retrieved from https://www.ncbi.nlm.nih.gov/pmc/articles/PMC5143586/

Temple, J. L. (2017, May 26). The safety of ingested caffeine: a comprehensive review. *Frontiers in psychiatry, 8*, 80. doi:https://doi.org/10.3389/fpsyt.2017.00080

Temple, J., Bernard, C., Lipshultz, S., Czachor, J., Westphal, J., & & Mestre, M. (2017, May 26). The safety of ingested caffeine: a comprehensive review. *Frontiers in psychiatry, 8*, 80. doi:https://doi.org/10.3389/fpsyt.2017.00080

Teng, C., Lim, W., Chua, C., Teo, R., Lin, K., & Yeo, J. (2016). Does a single cup of caffeinated drink significantly increase blood pressure in young adults? A randomized controlled trial. *Aust Fam Physician, 45*(1), 65-8.

Teramoto, M., Muraki, I., Yamagishi, K., Tamakoshi, A., & Iso, H. (2021, Mar). Green Tea and Coffee Consumption and All-Cause Mortality Among Persons With and Without Stroke or Myocardial Infarction. *Stroke, 52*(3), 957-96. doi:https://doi.org/10.1161/strokeaha.120.032273

The Public Well-Being. Athletics for Girls. (1921, May 21). *Hospital (Lond 1886), 70*(1824), 131. Retrieved from https://www.ncbi.nlm.nih.gov/pmc/articles/PMC5248027/

Torres-Collado, L., Compañ-Gabucio, L., González-Palacios, S., Notario-Barandiaran, L., Oncina-Cánovas, A., Vioque, J., & García-de la Hera, M. (2021, Apr 9). Coffee Consumption and All-Cause, Cardiovascular, and Cancer Mortality in an Adult Mediterranean Population. *Nutrients, 13*(4), 1241. doi:https://doi.org/10.3390/nu13041241

Tozaki, T., Ohnuma, A., Kikuchi, M., Ishige, T., Kakoi, H., Hirota, K., . . . Nagata, S. (2021, Aug 6). Rare and common variant discovery by whole-genome sequencing of 101 Thoroughbred racehorses. *Sci Rep, 11*(1), 16057. doi:https://doi.org/10.1038/s41598-021-95669-1

Tsugane, S. (2021, Jun). Why has Japan become the world's most long-lived country: insights from a food and nutrition perspective. *Eur J Clin Nutr, 75*(6), 921-928. doi:https://doi.org/10.1038/s41430-020-0677-5

Um, C., McCullough, M., Guinter, M., Campbell, P., Jacobs, E., & Gapstur, S. (2020, Aug). Coffee consumption and risk of colorectal cancer in the Cancer Prevention Study-II Nutrition Cohort. *Cancer Epidemiol*, 67. doi:https://doi.org/10.1016/j.canep.2020.101730

Urtamo, A., Jyväkorpi, S., Kautiainen, H., Pitkälä, K., & Strandberg, T. (2020). Major cardiovascular disease (CVD) risk factors in midlife and extreme longevity. *Aging Clin Exp Res, 32*(2), 299-304. doi:https://doi.org/10.1007/s40520-019-01364-7

Utility of Coffee in Soldiers' Diet. (1862, Jul). *Dent Regist, 16*(7), 310.

van Dam, R., & Hu, F. (2005, Jul 6). Coffee consumption and risk of type 2 diabetes: a systematic review. *JAMA, 294*(1), 97-104. doi:https://doi.org/10.1001/jama.294.1.97

van Dongen, L., Mölenberg, F., Soedamah-Muthu, S., Kromhout, D., & Geleijnse, J. (2017, Oct). Coffee consumption after myocardial infarction and risk of cardiovascular mortality: a prospective analysis in the Alpha Omega Cohort. *Am J Clin Nutr, 106*(4), 1113-1120. doi:https://doi.org/10.3945/ajcn.117.153338

van Etten ES, K. K., Ekker, M., Rasing, I., Voigt, S., Schreuder, F., Cannegieter, S., . . . Wermer, M. (2022). Trigger Factors for Spontaneous Intracerebral Hemorrhage: A Case-Crossover Study. *Stroke, 53*(5), 1692-1699. doi:https://doi.org/10.1161/strokeaha.121.036233

Vest, A. (2021). Two Coffees a Day Keep the Heart Doctor Away? *Circ Heart Fail, 14*(2), e008297. doi:https://doi.org/10.1161/circheartfailure.121.008297

Viribay, A., Arribalzaga, S., J, M.-A., Castañeda-Babarro, A., Seco-Calvo, J., & Urdampilleta, A. (2020, May). Effects of 120 g/h of Carbohydrates Intake during a Mountain Marathon on Exercise-Induced Muscle Damage in Elite Runners. *Nutrients, 12*(5), 1367. doi:https://doi.org/10.3390/nu12051367

References

Voskoboinik, A., Kalman, J., & Kistler, P. (2018, Apr). Caffeine and Arrhythmias: Time to Grind the Data. *JACC Clin Electrophysiol, 4*(4), 425-432. doi:https://doi.org/10.1016/j.jacep.2018.01.012

Wang, E., Næss, M., Hoff, J., Albert, T., Pham, Q., Richardson, R., & Helgerud, J. (2014, Apr). Exercise-training-induced changes in metabolic capacity with age: the role of central cardiovascular plasticity. *Age (Dordr), 36*(2), 665-676. doi:https://doi.org/10.1007/s11357-013-9596-x

Wang, J., Li, X., & Zhang, D. (2016, Jun). Coffee consumption and the risk of cutaneous melanoma: a meta-analysis. *Eur J Nutr, 55*(4), 1317-29. doi:https://doi.org/10.1007/s00394-015-1139-z

Wang, L., Shen, X., Wu, Y., & Zhang, D. (2016, Mar). Coffee and caffeine consumption and depression: A meta-analysis of observational studies. *Aust N Z J Psychiatry, 50*(3), 228-42. doi:https://doi.org/10.1177/0004867415603131

Weibel, J., Lin, Y., Landolt, H., Kistler, J., Rehm, S., Rentsch, K., . . . Reichert, C. (2021, Feb 25). The impact of daily caffeine intake on nighttime sleep in young adult men. *Sci Rep, 11*(1), 4668. doi:https://doi.org/10.1038/s41598-021-84088-x

Weinzirl, J. (1922, Nov). THE CAUSE OF EXPLOSION IN CHOCOLATE CANDIES. *J Bacteriol, 7*(6), 599-604. Retrieved from https://www.ncbi.nlm.nih.gov/pmc/articles/PMC378995/

White, J. J., Padowski, J., Zhong, Y., Chen, G., Luo, S., Lazarus, P., . . . McPherson, S. (2016). Pharmacokinetic analysis and comparison of caffeine administered rapidly or slowly in coffee chilled or hot versus chilled energy drink in healthy young adults. *Clin Toxicol, 54*(4), 308-

12. doi:https://doi.org/10.3109/15563650.2016.1146740

Wikoff, D., Welsh, B., Henderson, R., Brorby, G., Britt, J., Myers, E., . . . Doepker, C. (2017). Systematic review of the potential adverse effects of caffeine consumption in healthy adults, pregnant women, adolescents, and children. *Food and Chemical Toxicology, 109*(1), 585-648. doi:https://doi.org/10.1016/j.fct.2017.04.002

Wilk, M., Krzysztofik, M., Filip, A., Zajac, A., & Del Coso, J. (2019, Aug 15). The Effects of High Doses of Caffeine on Maximal Strength and Muscular Endurance in Athletes Habituated to Caffeine. *Nutrients, 11*(8), 1912. doi:https://doi.org/10.3390/nu11081912

Wilmoth, J. (2000, Dec). Demography of longevity: past, present, and future trends. *Exp Gerentol, 35*(9-10), 1111-29. doi:https://doi.org/10.1016/S0531-5565(00)00194-7

Wu, T., Willett, W., Hankinson, S., & Giovannucci, E. (2005, Jun). Caffeinated coffee, decaffeinated coffee, and caffeine in relation to plasma C-peptide levels, a marker of insulin secretion, in U.S. women. *Diabetes Care., 28*(6), 1390-6. doi:https://doi.org/10.2337/diacare.28.6.1390

Xie, L., Tang, Q., Yao, D., Gu, Q., Zheng, H., Wang, X., . . . Shen, X. (2021, Oct). Effect of Decaffeinated Green Tea Polyphenols on Body Fat and Precocious Puberty in Obese Girls: A Randomized Controlled Trial. *Front Endocrinol (Lausanne), 12*, e736724. doi:https://doi.org/10.3389/fendo.2021.736724

Xie, Y., Huang, S., He, T., & Su, Y. (2016). Coffee consumption and risk of gastric cancer: an updated meta-analysis. *Asia Pac J Clin Nutr, 25*(3), 578-88. doi:https://doi.org/10.6133/apjcn.092015.07

Xie, Y., Qin, J., Nan, G., Huang, S., Wang, Z., & Su, Y. (2016, Feb). Coffee consumption and the risk of lung cancer:

an updated meta-analysis of epidemiological studies. *Eur J Clin Nutr, 70*(2), 199-206. doi:https://doi.org/10.1038/ejcn.2015.96

Yi, M., Wu, X., Zhuang, W., Xia, L., Chen, Y., Zhao, R., . . . Zhou, Y. (2019, Aug). Tea Consumption and Health Outcomes: Umbrella Review of Meta-Analyses of Observational Studies in Humans. *Mol Nutr Food Res, 63*(16), e1900389. doi:https://doi.org/10.1002/mnfr.201900389

Yu, E., Wesselius, A., van Osch, F., Stern, M., Jiang, X., Kellen, E., . . . Zeegers, M. (2019, Aug). Coffee consumption and risk of bladder cancer: a pooled analysis of 501,604 participants from 12 cohort studies in the BLadder Cancer Epidemiology and Nutritional Determinants (BLEND) international study. *Cancer Causes Control, 30*(8), 859-870. doi:https://doi.org/10.1007/s10552-019-01191-1

Yuan, S., & Larsson, S. (2019, Nov). No association between coffee consumption and risk of atrial fibrillation: A Mendelian randomization study. *Nutr Metab Cardiovasc Dis, 29*(11), 1185-1188. doi:https://doi.org/10.1016/j.numecd.2019.07.015

Zhang, Y., Coca, A., Casa, D., Antonio, J., Green, J., & Bishop, P. (2015, Sep). Caffeine and diuresis during rest and exercise: A meta-analysis. *J Sci Med Sport, 18*(5), 569-74. doi:https://doi.org/10.1016/j.jsams.2014.07.017

Zhang, Y., Yang, H., Li, S., Li, W., & Wang, Y. (2021, Nov 16). Consumption of coffee and tea and risk of developing stroke, dementia, and poststroke dementia: A cohort study in the UK Biobank. *PLoS Med, 18*(11), e1003830. doi:https://doi.org/10.1371/journal.pmed.1003830

Zhong, G., Hu, T., Yang, P., Peng, Y., Wu, J., Sun, W., . . . Wang, C. (2021, Jul 31). Chocolate consumption and all-cause and cause-specific mortality in a US population: a post hoc analysis of the PLCO cancer screening trial. *Aging (Albany NY), 13*(14), 18564-18585. doi:https://doi.org/10.18632/aging.203302

Zhou, A., & Hyppönen, E. (2021, Jun). Habitual coffee intake and plasma lipid profile: Evidence from UK Biobank. *Clin Nutr, 40*(6), 4404-13. doi:https://doi.org/10.1016/j.clnu.2020.12.042

Zhu, Q., Fu, S., Zhang, Q., Tian, J., Zhao, Y., & Yao, Y. (2021, Feb 3). Female Fertility Has a Negative Relationship With Longevity in Chinese Oldest-Old Population: A Cross-Sectional Study. *Front Endocrinol (Lausanne), 11*, 616207. doi:https://doi.org/10.3389/fendo.2020.616207

Zuchinali, P., Souza, G., Pimentel, M., Chemello, D., Zimerman, A., Giaretta, V., . . . Rohde, L. (2016, Dec 1). Short-term Effects of High-Dose Caffeine on Cardiac Arrhythmias in Patients with Heart Failure: A Randomized Clinical Trial. *JAMA Intern Med, 176*(12), 1752-1759. doi:https://doi.org/10.1001/jamainternmed.2016.6374